WORLD-SYSTEMS ANALYSIS AT A CRITICAL JUNCTURE

As we enter the third decade of the twenty-first century, the world faces extraordinary system-level challenges—from deep inequality and xenophobic nationalism to militarism and neofascism, from the refugee crisis and environmental degradation to upsurges of social unrest and escalating rivalries among powerful states. This book begins from the premise that world-systems analysis can be a powerful tool for the study of these problems, with the potential to overcome the methodological and theoretical limitations of other social science perspectives. The editors argue, moreover, that world-systems analysis can be strengthened by drawing on its holistic methodologies, returning to its Third World roots, and learning from other critical approaches. The authors in this volume not only make important contributions to comparative and historical social science but also bring a new vigor to the world-systems perspective. Facing critical junctures in both the "state of knowledge" and the "state of the world," this book demonstrates the continued utility of, and future possibilities for, world-systems analysis.

Corey R. Payne is a PhD candidate in the Department of Sociology and the Arrighi Center for Global Studies at Johns Hopkins University. His research focuses on the dynamics of historical capitalism, social conflict, and war-making.

Roberto Patricio Korzeniewicz, PhD, is Professor of Sociology and Associate Dean for Faculty Affairs in the College of Behavioral & Social Sciences at the University of Maryland, College Park. His book *Unveiling Inequality* (NY, 2009), co-written with Timothy P. Moran, won the 2010 Best Book Award of the Political Economy of the World-System section of the American Sociological Association. His current research focuses on global patterns of income inequality, social stratification, and mobility.

Beverly J. Silver, PhD, is Professor of Sociology and Director of the Arrighi Center for Global Studies at Johns Hopkins University.

Political Economy of the World-System Annuals
Immanuel Wallerstein, Series Editor

Mass Migration in the World-System
Past, Present, and Future
Edited by Terry-Ann Jones, Eric Mielants (2010)

Global Crises and the Challenges of the 21st Century
Edited by Thomas Reifer (2012)

Overcoming Global Inequalities
*Edited by Immanuel Wallerstein, Christopher Chase-Dunn,
Christian Suter (2014)*

Social Movements and World-System Transformation
*Edited by Jackie Smith, Michael Goodhart, Patrick Manning,
John Markoff (2016)*

The World-System as Unit of Analysis
Edited by Roberto Patricio Korzeniewicz (2017)

Global Inequalities in World-Systems Perspective
Edited by Manuela Boatcă, Andrea Komlosy, Hans-Heinrich (2017)

Economic Cycles and Socials Movements
Edited by Eric Mielants and Katsiaryna Salavei-Bardos (2020)

Migration, Racism and Labor Exploitation in the World-System
Edited by Denis O'Hearn and Paul S. Ciccantell (2021)

World-Systems Analysis at a Critical Juncture
*Edited by Corey R. Payne, Roberto Patricio Korzeniewicz,
and Beverly J. Silver (2023)*

WORLD-SYSTEMS ANALYSIS AT A CRITICAL JUNCTURE

*Edited by Corey R. Payne,
Roberto Patricio Korzeniewicz,
and Beverly J. Silver*

NEW YORK AND LONDON

Designed cover image: Unsplash.com

First published 2023
by Routledge
605 Third Avenue, New York, NY 10158

and by Routledge
4 Park Square, Milton Park, Abingdon, Oxon, OX14 4RN

Routledge is an imprint of the Taylor & Francis Group, an informa business

© 2023 selection and editorial matter, Corey R. Payne, Roberto Patricio Korzeniewicz, and Beverly J. Silver; individual chapters, the contributors

The right of Corey R. Payne, Roberto Patricio Korzeniewicz, and Beverly J. Silver to be identified as the authors of the editorial material, and of the authors for their individual chapters, has been asserted in accordance with sections 77 and 78 of the Copyright, Designs and Patents Act 1988.

All rights reserved. No part of this book may be reprinted or reproduced or utilised in any form or by any electronic, mechanical, or other means, now known or hereafter invented, including photocopying and recording, or in any information storage or retrieval system, without permission in writing from the publishers.

Trademark notice: Product or corporate names may be trademarks or registered trademarks, and are used only for identification and explanation without intent to infringe.

ISBN: 978-1-032-35061-5 (hbk)
ISBN: 978-1-032-35057-8 (pbk)
ISBN: 978-1-003-32510-9 (ebk)

DOI: 10.4324/9781003325109

Typeset in Bembo
by Apex CoVantage, LLC

CONTENTS

List of Figures	*viii*
List of Tables	*ix*
List of Contributors	*x*

1 World–Systems Analysis at a Critical Juncture 1
Corey R. Payne, Roberto Patricio Korzeniewicz,
and Beverly J. Silver

PART I
World-Systems Analyses, Concepts, and Methods 15

2 Avoiding the Security Trap: The Contributions
of Terence Hopkins and World–Systems as Methodology
for Critical Police Studies 17
Brendan McQuade and Stuart Schrader

3 Terence K. Hopkins and Concepts as Relational
Categories: Different Manifestations of the
Relationship Between Religion and Neoliberalism
in the Global South 28
Gamze Evcimen

4 Symbolic Power and Geoculture in the World–System:
Ottoman and Russian Perspectives 42
Juho Korhonen

vi Contents

5 Reconstructing Commodity Chain Analysis
as World-Systems Analysis 54
David A. Smith, Paul S. Ciccantell, and Elizabeth A. Sowers

PART II
Continuity and Transformation in World-System
Hierarchies 67

6 The Rise of the Global South and the Redefinition
of World-System Hierarchies 69
*Víctor Ramiro Fernández, Luciano Moretti, Joel Sidler,
and Emilia Ormaechea*

7 Marxism and World-Systems Analysis in the Transition
to the Long Twenty-first Century 81
Carlos Eduardo Martins

8 On the Lineages of World-Systems Analysis:
Sub-imperialism as a Conjunctural Approach 93
Antônio Brussi

9 The Dialectics of Time and Value Accumulation:
Alienation on a World-Scale Dimension 110
Ísis Campos Camarinha

PART III
Social Contradictions of Capitalism in the
Twenty-first Century 125

10 "Primitive" Accumulation Under Historical Capitalism
and the Unequal Social Regulation of the
Global Labor Force 127
Kelvin A. Santiago-Valles

11 "Primitive" Accumulation in Urban Semiperiphery:
Ethno-racial Elites, Rezoning, and Displacement
in Manhattan, New York City 138
Kai Wen Yang

Contents **vii**

12 Global Crisis and Militarized Migration Management:
A World–Historic Perspective 156
David B. Feldman

13 Dilemma of the Rising Giant: China's Food Import
Strategy and Its Constraints 168
Shaohua Zhan and Lingli Huang

References *179*
Index *204*

FIGURES

8.1	Crisis in Brazilian Industry—Participation of Industry in GDP	98
11.1	Chinatown and the Lower East Side Soft Site Map	141
11.2	External Cores and the Division of the Corridor Region	142
11.3	Chinatown and the Lower East Side Zoning Districts	143
11.4	Canal Street Connective Corridor	147
11.5	Rebuilding Chinatown Initiative's 2004 Upzoning Framework	149
11.6	Proposal for Chinatown Special District	150
11.7	Proposed Zoning in SoHo/NoHo Rezoning Plan	151
11.8	Proposed Zoning in East Village and the Lower East Side	152
11.9	Extell Tower and Proposed Towers at Two Bridges, Lower East Side	153
13.1	China's Grain Production, Net Grain Imports, and Grain Self-sufficiency Ratio: 1979–2017	171

TABLES

8.1	Brazil: Exports to Central and South America, the Caribbean, and Africa (1997–2019) (US$)	100
8.2	Brazil: Percentage of values of total exports (US$) according to product type (2001–2019)	101
8.3	Engineering Services BNDS—Main-financing destination 1998–2019—US$ millions	103
8.4	Values and countries that have received financing from BNDES 1998–2018 (US$ millions)	104
9.1	Accumulation by type of balance of payments account, organic zones, and working time, 1960–2019	118
9.2	Period covered by country and type of balance of payments account	121
12.1	International migrants, 1970–2019	162

CONTRIBUTORS

Antônio Brussi is a professor at the Institute of Political Science at the University of Brasilia.

Ísis Campos Camarinha received her PhD in International Political Economy from the Federal University of Rio de Janiero. She was also substitute professor of IPPUR/UFRJ in Economic and Juridical International Institutions. She works on political-economy international relations, and the capitalist world-system.

Paul S. Ciccantell is Professor of Sociology in the Department of Sociology at Western Michigan University, USA and a former Program Officer for the Sociology Program at the National Science Foundation. His research examines socioeconomic change over the long term, the evolution of global industries, and the socioeconomic and environmental impacts of global industries, focusing particularly on raw materials extraction and processing and transport industries. He has published books with Johns Hopkins University Press, JAI/Elsevier Press, Routledge, and Greenwood Press. He has published more than forty journal articles and book chapters.

Gamze Evcimen is a visiting assistant professor of anthropology and sociology at Kalamazoo College. Evcimen's research addresses global neoliberalism, social inequalities, and contentious politics with a particular focus on twenty-first century protests and contemporary rise of right-wing politics. Evcimen has published chapters on coalescence of religion and neoliberalism in Global South, fundamentalism and globalization, and political subjectivity of Turkey's anti-capitalist Muslims. In her current book project, Evcimen analyzes the ways in which neoliberal globalization simultaneously enabled and constrained oppositional politics with a particular focus on AKP hegemony and Gezi protests in Turkey.

David B. Feldman is a PhD candidate in Sociology at the University of California, Santa Barbara, USA.

Víctor Ramiro Fernández is Professor of Economic Geography and State Theory in the School of Humanities and Sciences at the Universidad Nacional del Litoral, Argentina. After receiving his PhD in Political Science in 1999 from the Universidad Autónoma de Madrid, Spain, he was appointed researcher in Argentina's National Technical and Scientific Research Council (CONICET).

Lingli Huang received her doctoral degree in sociology from the Johns Hopkins University in 2017 and has since been working as a postdoctoral fellow at the Nanyang Centre for Public Administration of Nanyang Technological University (Singapore). Her research focuses on water governance, food security, migration, race relations, social welfare policy, and local governance. Dr Huang has published in *Geoforum*, *Studies in Comparative International Development*, *Asia and Pacific Migration Journal*, among others, and contributed to *Encyclopaedia of Gerontology and Population Aging* (Springer). She is a co-editor of *Political, Economic and Social Dimensions of Labour Markets: A Global Insight* (World Scientific Publishing, 2022).

Juho Korhonen is a historical and political sociologist and has published on post-socialist politics, on imperial transformations in the twentieth century, and on the politics of memory related to those issues.

Roberto Patricio Korzeniewicz, PhD, is Professor of Sociology at the University of Maryland, College Park (USA). His book *Unveiling Inequality* (NY, 2009), co-written with Timothy P. Moran, won the 2010 Best Book Award of the Political Economy of the World-System section of the American Sociological Association. His current research focuses on global patterns of income inequality, social stratification, and mobility.

Carlos Eduardo Martins has a PhD in sociology from the University of São Paulo (2003) and is Associate Professor in the Institute of International Relations and Defense at the Federal University of Rio de Janeiro and permanent staff of the Postgraduate Programme in International Political Economy (PEPI/ UFRJ). He is the editor-in-chief of *Reoriente: Studies on Marxism, Dependency, and World-Systems*, the coordinator of the Laboratory for Studies on Hegemony and Counter-Hegemony (LEHC/UFRJ), a researcher at CLACSO in the working groups of Studies on the United States and China and the Map of xii Contributors

World Power, and a coordinator of the Regional Integration and Latin American Unity group of CLACSO between 2010 and 2016. He won the Premio Jabuti de obra de noficción 2007 for his co-authorship and coordination, with Emir Sader, Ivana Jinkings and Rodrigo Nobile, of *Latinoamericana: Enciclopédia Contemporânea de América Latina e Caribe*. He is the author of *Globalization, Dependence, and Neoliberalism in Latin America*, published by Boitempo in 2011, and in English, in 2020, by Brill and Haymarket. He recently published "The Longue Dureé of Marxist Theory of Dependency and the Twenty-First Century" in *Latin American Perspectives*, issue 242 (2022)

Brendan McQuade is assistant professor in the criminology department at the University of Southern Maine and the author of *Pacifying the Homeland: Intelligence Fusion and Mass Supervision*, published by the University of California Press in 2019.

Luciano Moretti is Lecturer of Globalization and Development and Political Economy at The School of Social and Juridical Sciences of the Universidad Nacional del Litoral and Doctoral Fellow of Universidad Nacional del Litoral. He is a PhD candidate in Social Studies at the Universidad Nacional del Litoral.

Emilia Ormaechea is Lecturer of Globalization and Development at The School of Social and Juridical Sciences and Latin American Development at the School of Humanities and Sciences of the Universidad Nacional del Litoral and Doctoral Fellow of Argentina's National Scientific and Technical Research Council (CONICET). She received her MSc in Social Science in 2018 from the Universidad Nacional del Litoral and is a PhD candidate in Economic Development at the Universidad Nacional de Quilmes.

Corey R. Payne is a PhD candidate in the Department of Sociology and the Arrighi Center for Global Studies at Johns Hopkins University, USA. His research focuses on the dynamics of historical capitalism, social conflict, and war-making.

Kelvin Santiago-Valles is Professor, Sociology Department at Binghamton University-SUNY, USA and is the author of *"Subject People" and Colonial Discourses: Economic Transformation and Social Disorder in Puerto Rico, 1898–1947* (SUNY Press, 1994). He is currently revising a book manuscript for publication tentatively titled *Rethinking "Race," Labor, and Empire: Global-Racial Regimes and "Primitive" Accumulation in the Historical Long-Term*. His research and publications focus on social regulation (penality, in particular) in the political economy of racialized labor formation on a world-scale, with an emphasis on the Caribbean. Recent book chapters of his have appeared, among others, in: *The World-System as Unit of Analysis: Past Contributions* *and Future Advances*, edited by Roberto Patricio Korzeniewicz (Routledge, 2017); *On Coerced Labor: Work and Compulsion after Chattel Slavery*, edited by Marcel van der Linden and Magaly Rodríguez García (Brill, 2016); *Endless Empire: Spain's Retreat, Europe's Eclipse, and America's Decline*, edited by Alfred McCoy, Josep Fradera, Stephen Jacobson (University of Wisconsin Press, 2012); *Debates sobre ciudadanía y política raciales en las Américas negras* (Universidad del Valle/Universidad Nacional de Colombia, 2011); and *La régulation sociale entre l'acteur et l'institution. Pour une problématique historique de l'interaction*, edited by Jean-Marie Fecteau and Janice Harvey (Presses de l'Université du Québec, 2005).

Stuart Schrader is Associate Research Professor in the Center for Africana Studies and the Associate Director of the Program in Racism, Immigration, and Citizenship at Johns Hopkins University. He is the author of *Badges Without Borders: How Global Counterinsurgency Transformed American Policing*, published by University of California Press in 2019.

Joel Sidler is Lecturer of Globalization and Development and Political Economy at The School of Social and Juridical Sciences of the Universidad Nacional del Litoral and Doctoral Fellow of Argentina's National Scientific and Technical Research Council (CONICET). He is a master's student in Development and Public Policies and PhD candidate in Social Studies at the Universidad Nacional del Litoral.

Beverly J. Silver, PhD, is Professor of Sociology and Director of the Arrighi Center for Global Studies at Johns Hopkins University, USA.

David A. Smith is Professor of Sociology at UC-Irvine. He's been a journal editor at two major academic firms and a past president of both the Society for the Study of Social Problems (SSSP) and the ASA Political Economy of the World-System (PEWS). The expertise in this chapter is on the global commodity chain dynamics.

Elizabeth A. Sowers is Associate Professor of Sociology at California State University Channel Islands, USA. Her research is in the areas of globalization, economic sociology, and work, focusing specifically on the logistics, or goods movement industry. She has published articles in *Labor & Society*, *Journal of World-Systems Research*, and *Poetics*, as well as a book with Polity Press.

Kai Wen Yang is a Sociology/Feminist Research Institute Postdoctoral Fellow at the University of California, Davis. His recent research focuses on capital accumulation, "primitive" accumulation, urban spaces, anti-displacement movements, and new forms of gentrification.

Shaohua Zhan is Associate Professor and Deputy Head of Sociology Programme at Nanyang Technological University in Singapore. His research interests include land politics, food security, and international migration, with a focus on China and other East Asian nations. He is the author of *China and Global Food Security* (Cambridge University Press, 2022) and *The Land Question in China: Agrarian Capitalism, Industrious Revolution, and East Asian Development* (Routledge, 2019).

1
WORLD-SYSTEMS ANALYSIS AT A CRITICAL JUNCTURE

Corey R. Payne, Roberto Patricio Korzeniewicz, and Beverly J. Silver

When we issued the call for papers for the 44th annual Political Economy of the World-System (PEWS) conference in the spring of 2019, we were struck by the extraordinary system-level problems facing the world—from deep inequality and xenophobic nationalism to militarism and resurgent fascism, from the refugee crisis and environmental degradation to upsurges of social unrest and escalating rivalries among powerful states. We were convinced that world-systems analysis could be immensely productive in the study of these problems, with the potential to overcome the methodological and theoretical limitations of other social science perspectives. At the same time, however, we noted that some of the most useful methodological and theoretical foundations of world-systems analysis had fallen by the wayside—and that opportunities to incorporate insights from other critical epistemological perspectives had not been fully explored. We were thus facing "critical junctures" in both "the state of the world" and "the state of knowledge" (to draw on McMichael's (1990) distinction).

The call for papers asked participants to grapple with both of these critical junctures. The conference was delayed by the COVID-19 pandemic—itself both a reflection of the pre-existing systemic crisis and a further step into deepening systemic chaos. Making lemonade out of lemons, in fall 2020, the PEWS conference was conducted in a virtual format spread out over twelve weeks that allowed for consistent participation and exchange from colleagues on five continents. What's more, the participants rose to the challenge we posed in our call for papers. This volume is the result of these discussions and exchanges.[1]

In this introductory chapter, we offer some summative comments on the "state of the world" in this moment of history and on how the current "state

DOI: 10.4324/9781003325109-1

2 Corey R. Payne et al.

of knowledge" in the field of world-systems analysis offers both limits and opportunities for understanding it. We argue that world-systems analysis can be strengthened by more actively drawing on its holistic and Third World roots, as well as by learning from other critical perspectives. It is our hope that this volume advances this project, demonstrating the utility of and potential for world-systems analysis.

The State of Our World

The past two decades have been characterized by countless indicators that we are living through a terminal decline of United States world hegemony—beginning with the bursting of the New Economy stock market bubble in 2000–2001, deepening with the blowback from the 2003 invasion of Iraq and the endless War on Terror, reaching new heights with the 2008 financial meltdown, and coming into stark relief with the upsurge in social unrest and political upheavals of the succeeding decade. In many places, this explosion of social conflict and the deepening crises of capitalism have been accompanied by authoritarian and militarized forms of rule on the streets, in communities, and across borders.

Insofar as hegemony refers to the additional power acquired through *leadership* over *consenting* subordinate partners, one might say that the erosion of world hegemony is giving way to disparate attempts to cling to power through *coercion* as a replacement for consent and legitimacy. Inequality and narrow elite self-interest spark waves of unrest that in turn intensify calls for policing as a means for reimposing "order" worldwide. Whether the current militarism is a continuation (or extension) of the type of authoritarian rule that has always been reserved for the capitalist peripheries and the marginalized and excluded within the core, or if instead there is a significant change in the nature of consent and coercion, is one of the key questions addressed here (see, e.g., Feldman, this volume; McQuade and Schrader, this volume).

In either case, coercion at the present juncture is intertwined with a profound transformation in the balance of interstate power. The West—which had for centuries amassed an overwhelming preponderance of economic and military power vis-à-vis the rest of the world—must adjust to the rise of "the Rest." With the increasing economic power of the non-West in the twenty-first century, especially but not limited to China, a stable Western-dominated world order is no longer possible (Arrighi 2007). Collective action by states in the Global South reflected in institutional innovations such as BRICS and ALBA, further signal this impossibility. This transformation of world-system hierarchies (economic and geopolitical) is the critical context through which a host of other system-level problems—from rising inequalities and worsening ecological degradation to escalating militarism and deepening social conflict—must be understood and (one hopes) resolved (Karatasli, Kumral, Pasciuti, and

Silver 2017; Silver and Payne 2020; see also Fernández, Moretti, Sidler, and Ormaechea, this volume).

Amidst this changing balance of power, escalating economic and geopolitical rivalry among states has yielded military conflicts, sparked trade wars, intensified sanction regimes, and eroded organizations of interstate governance. The peculiar situation of the persistence of U.S. dollar hegemony in the face of weakening U.S. leadership and legitimacy raises questions about limits and alternatives (anti-systemic and otherwise). One particularly promising line of recent research has involved focusing more intensely on the role of specific social actors in shaping the past and present dynamics, from state officials to social movements and elites. For example, a focus on elites and their role in deepening systemic chaos, inequality, and secondary exploitation raises important questions about the interaction between narrow elite self-interest and the system-level problems we face in the twenty-first century (e.g., Lachmann 2020).

While, from a world-systems perspective, we have clearly entered a period of systemic chaos—which historically have been the nebula in which a new world hegemony emerges and transforms the world-system—the specific character of the moment is up for interpretation. Are we witnessing a return of classical inter-imperial rivalry? Is the world in the midst of a mercantilist redux? Is capitalism bursting asunder? Or has the rise of the Global South redefined the organization of the world-system in such a way as to render such centuries-old categories more confusing than useful? As the contributions to this volume make clear, the debate about imperialism is far from over, and that for it to be useful it must incorporate work beyond the Western canon (see, e.g., Martins, this volume; Fernández, Moretti, Sidler, and Ormaechea, this volume).

The changing balance of power and the coercive turn is intertwined with the rise of right-wing populism and authoritarianism in recent decades, from the United States to Britain, from Brazil to India, from Turkey to Hungary, and across the European Union. In the West, a backlash against the rise of the non-West, combined with the deleterious effects of post-1970s world-economic restructuring on a wide range of groups and classes (including much of the industrial working class) has fed into a narrative of white victimhood. As the militarist response to disorder has begot more disorder, migration flows into the West and refugee flows from conflict zones have both increased, contributing to the already brewing xenophobic nationalism at the heart of right-wing movements. The authoritarianism of the post-9/11 Western security apparatuses reverberates back into these movements, both directly—as veterans from imperial ventures return home disaffected and easily recruitable—and indirectly—as state leaders invented racialized enemies that must be defeated by any means necessary (e.g., Ackerman 2021). Making sense of the causes and articulations of such movements is a pressing task (see, e.g., Evcimen, this volume).

Policing plays a central role in maintaining social exclusion, as right-wing movements and leaders provide cover for brutality and racist othering, and as police provide support to these right-wing movements—often directly, through their participation, and always indirectly, through their maintenance of an unequal social order. As the unfolding systemic chaos yields greater flows of migrants, drives forward dispossession, and creates a global population superfluous to the needs of capitalist accumulation, the role of policing, surveillance, and incarceration in propping up the unequal system has grown (e.g., Gilmore 2007; McQuade 2019; Feldman, this volume).

Thus, the relationship between coercive power and capitalist accumulation in the modern world-system is a key problem we face in the twenty-first century. To make sense of this relationship, it is useful to return to Marx's writings on "primitive accumulation" that emphasize the ongoing and intertwined nature of processes of capital accumulation and primitive accumulation, the latter steeped in overt coercion and violence. A world-systems perspective allows us to see that these processes are uneven across time and space, as well as racialized and gendered in their unfolding; they produce inequalities and resistance from below (which are both racialized, gendered, and differentiated along core–periphery lines). A critical challenge we face today is understanding how the patterned forms of resistance relate to the patterned processes of capital accumulation, primitive accumulation, and violence around the world (see Santiago, this volume; Yang, this volume).

To be more precise, we must recognize (a) the fruitfulness of the concept of internalization and externalization of the costs of social reproduction for thinking about the contradictions and limits of historical capitalism in the twenty-first century and (b) the ambiguities of the concept as bequeathed to us by Arrighi in the 2010 postscript to the second edition of *The Long Twentieth Century*. Most adherents to a world-systems perspective start from the premise that profits in historical capitalism historically have been (and continue to be) based in large part on the externalization of the costs of reproduction of labor and nature. Put differently, if all the world's workers were paid the full costs of the reproduction of their labor power, there would be no surplus left to generate profits or further capital accumulation (Wallerstein 1995b). Profitability has also historically depended on capital not paying the full costs for the reproduction of nature—if it were even possible to conceptualize the price/cost for nonrenewable natural resources. Moreover, a world-systems perspective guides us to look for unevenness: As some costs of reproduction are internalized—in some spaces—others are externalized in order for capital accumulation to remain profitable (see Zhan and Huang, this volume). We are thus left with the question: Is it conceivable to internalize costs of reproduction and still have a system we would refer to as capitalism?

Another open question is which actors are in a position to effectively confront and overcome the deepening systemic chaos. Some have suggested that social movements and left parties are key in confronting global inequalities and building internationalism (see, e.g., Karatasli 2019). Other scholars argue that the nation-state and national economic strategies play an important role in challenging inequalities across (and within) core–periphery bounds (e.g., Cardoso and Faletto, 1979). Traditionally, a world-systems perspective would lead us to expect that national strategies are doomed to failure and that peripheral or semiperipheral efforts at industrialization would generate countervailing responses from the core—a phenomenon that Arrighi called the "developmentalist illusion" whereby semiperipheral states found themselves "running fast to stay in the same [relative] place" (Arrighi 1990). However, major shifts in hierarchies of wealth and power in the twenty-first century have potentially changed this situation, leading to a renewed debate about the role of national economic strategies and industrialization in this volume's pages (Fernández, et al., this volume; Brussi, this volume; Camarinha, this volume).

The State of (World-Systems) Knowledge

Over five decades, scholarship in the world-systems tradition—that is, the development of a methodological approach, a range of conceptual–theoretical tools, and a large body of historical–empirical research—has bequeathed to us a rich inheritance that can be effectively deployed in our attempts to make sense of the "state of the world" at this critical juncture. But some of the most useful methodological and theoretical foundations of world-systems analysis have largely fallen by the wayside and opportunities to incorporate the insights from other critical epistemological perspectives have not been fully explored. Thus, a fundamental premise of this volume is that, in order for practitioners of world-systems analysis to be up to the task of analyzing the "state of the world," a three-pronged effort in developing our collective tool kit is needed. First, we need to bring back to the center of the analysis some key but underused methodological works in the world-systems tradition. Second, we need to return to the Third World roots of world-systems analysis—especially the Dar es Salam and dependency schools. Finally, we need to engage more productively with other critical perspectives, searching for synergies while recognizing the tensions.

The unifying feature of a world-systems perspective is the use of the "actually existing" capitalist system as the unit of analysis in studies of the social world. Such a system has always been transnational, consisting of *a* world that grew over time to incorporate *the* world. For scholars using the perspective, while units of *observation* may vary, this world-system is seen as the most appropriate unit of *analysis* for the study of long-term, large-scale social change. While this is the unifying principle of world-systems analysis, debates rage about the origins, scope, and character of the world-system. While scholars in this perspective agree that this transnational system of historical capitalism should be the unit of analysis, we often agree on little else.

In fact, the purpose of our debates is often to identify the most productive ways of conceiving of the modern world-system: After all, it is only by identifying the essential (*sine qua non*) processes of the system that we can ascertain its historical and geographical boundaries, the extent to which it has changed over time, and whether it might be reaching its limits. Given the breadth of possible works that start from the unifying principle of world-systems analysis—that the transnational system of historical capitalism should be the unit of analysis—it is perhaps not surprising that one of the major features of the perspective is that it provides room for a broad spectrum of concerns and interpretations, even when these interpretations are at odds with one another.

At risk of oversimplification, perhaps the key divide in world-systems analysis today is between what Baronov (2018) calls the "analytical" and "holistic" approaches. On a conceptual level, both approaches endorse the idea that the study of the world-system requires an understanding of the social relationships, processes, and activities that comprise it. However, the analytical approach tends to collapse such dynamics into often-static categories or labels. Despite occasionally—though certainly not universally—falling into path dependency and teleology, it has become widespread in part because it simplifies research tasks. The analytical approach lends itself to the classification of "cases" into relevant categories by drawing on easily available indicators—for example, shares of agriculture and industry in GNP or exports become easily available proxies for core or peripheral status (see Korzeniewicz and Payne 2020). This analytical approach is used by those aiming to construct a general theory of the modern world-system. Per Baronov (2018), theory-building generally "adheres to a deductive-nomological mode of investigation whereby the aspirational guiding principle is the verification/refutation of general laws, based on the study of individual parts (as discrete cases) to test theories about the system as a whole." Such studies examine a wide range of theoretical elements of interest to world-systems analysts—core and periphery, exploitation and wage labor, inclusion and exclusions, dependency, and imperialism. But by nature of constructing a theory of the *whole* through the testing of the *individual* parts—and by nature of the universalizing tendency of such a project—the analytical approach ultimately defines the system as an expression of general laws *persistent through time and space*.

The analytical world-systems scholarship utilizes a methodological approach that Tilly (1984, 83) has called an "encompassing comparison," which "places different instances at various locations within the same system, on the way to explaining their characteristics as a function of their varying relationships to the system as a whole." Such a methodology begins with "a mental map of the whole system and a theory of its operation" and uses such a map to guide the analysis of the parts (Tilly 1984, 125).

On the other side of the divide, the holistic approach challenges traditional theory-building, emphasizing a changing landscape of interrelated processes and relationships. At any point in time, a snapshot of the constellation of such relationships can be observed, but the "parts" that are observed are not assumed to contain within their individual boundaries a logic that derives from the system as a "whole." Baronov (2018, 9) summarizes that "one side speaks of theories, the other of perspectives. One side dabbles with models and cases, the other with configurations and instances." In advocating for a holistic approach—though not using that term—Giovanni Arrighi (1999, 125) argued that world-system analysts

> must be prepared to unthink what many . . . have come to regard as the quintessence of world-systems theory. This is the idea that, in spite of their extraordinary geographical expansion, the structures of the world capitalist system have remained more or less the same ever since they first came into existence in the 'long' sixteenth century . . . [This] hypothesis does not stand up to historico-empirical scrutiny, and even worse, it prevents us from getting at the heart of the capitalist dynamics, both past and present.

A holistic approach, however, does not lend itself to as straightforward investigative methods as does the analytical approach. Seeking to map a changing landscape, involving relational processes *and* the shifting patterns of interaction among them, requires a different methodological toolkit.

In an effort to highlight the differences between the analytical and holistic approaches within the world-systems school, McMichael (1990) articulated a contrast between "encompassing comparisons" and what he called "incorporating comparisons." While an encompassing comparison is "a strategy that *presumes* a 'whole' that governs its 'parts'," an incorporating comparison "progressively *constructs* a whole as a methodological procedure by giving context to historical phenomena. In effect, the 'whole' emerges via comparative analysis of 'parts' as moments in a self-forming whole" (McMichael 1990, 386). Totality is thus a conceptual procedure, as opposed to a premise. It is "imminent" rather than "prima facie" as "the whole is discovered through the analysis of the mutual conditioning of parts" (McMichael 1990, 391).

Thus, a first step toward improving the collective toolkit for world-systems analysis is further developing the holistic approach. One important path toward this end is a serious engagement with the early methodological insights of Terence K. Hopkins (see, e.g., McQuade and Schrader, this volume; Evcimen, this volume; Santiago, this volume). In many ways Hopkins' writings prefigured McMichael's incorporating comparison and Baronov's analytical–holistic distinction. For Hopkins, social concepts cannot be abstracted from their geographical and temporal dimensions as is done in the analytical approach:

> To focus on certain seemingly similar conditions in various places at various times; to abstract those conditions from their place-time settings; and

8 Corey R. Payne et al.

> to inquire, abstractly, into the causes or consequences of the conditions is to proceed precisely in the one way clearly ruled out of court by the world-system or world-historical perspective on social change . . . It is the *a priori* elimination of each case's distinctiveness that the [holistic] world-system's approach rules out, not the claim that there are comparabilities or similarities.
>
> *(Hopkins 1982b, 155–56)*

For Hopkins, units are not analytical points of departure, but rather they are points of *observation* of systemic processes. Bringing these units together as "abstract parts" allows one to move toward a "concrete whole": One must "keep moving out by successive determinations, bringing in successive parts—themselves abstract processes—in continuous juxtaposition and in this way form the whole which you need for interpreting and explaining the historical changes or conditions under examination" (Hopkins 1982b, 147). The use of abstract parts ("interrelated," "conceptual schemas") to construct the concrete whole ("the notion of the modern world system") itself becomes an abstract conceptual schema, thus "the relations among the concepts which we used to gain our new vantage point must then be reworked in the light of the increments to our understanding which our newly acquired angle of vision affords us" (Hopkins 1982a, 37). Hopkins' methodological directive, then, is in multiple parts: Constructing a concrete whole through the continuous juxtaposition of abstract parts, followed by a reworking of those parts in light of the newly acquired understanding of the whole. For Hopkins, classificatory methods (including the analytical approach to world-systems analysis) can be useful, but they should

> serve, not to govern the structure of design . . . but instead, in preliminary work, to help isolate subjects for detailed inquiry or, in summarizing work, to help collate the result of several detailed inquires.

But, crucially, for Hopkins, historical analysis (narrative) is necessary to grasp the unfolding of relational processes over time and space (Hopkins 1982a, 32).

Second, re-engaging with the early Third World foundations of world-systems analysis—especially its roots in the Dar es Salaam and dependency schools—is essential for harnessing the full potential of world-systems analysis. Many of the key figures in early world-systems analysis—Amin, Arrighi, Frank, and Wallerstein—spent formative years in Africa and Latin America studying processes of capitalist development while learning from (and contributing to) local movements in the 1960s and 1970s. Anti-colonialism and the project of national liberation were animating forces behind the development of the world-systems perspective, and the scholarship of thinkers such as Frantz

Fanon, Amilcar Cabral, and Walter Rodney was foundational to the project. Early contributions to world-systems analysis were thus efforts at developing a global and historical perspective on imperialism and anti-imperialism (e.g., Amin 1979; Arrighi 1978; Frank 1978). Revisiting these foundations is useful for making sense of the intertwined nature of capitalism, racism, and militarism in the twenty-first century.

Recent attempts to accomplish this task include Plys' (2021) reappraisal of imperialism and anti-imperialism, which she accomplishes by resituating Walter Rodney within the world-systems canon (see also Ciccantell, Sowers, and Smith, this volume).[2] Plys (2021, 309) notes that world-systems analysis can better serve "contemporary struggles across the globe" by "recovering [its] intellectual roots in Dar es Salaam and reviving the concept of capitalist imperialism." Similar efforts have been made to reassess the political potential of the perspective via a return to the work of Samir Amin. As part of a posthumous tribute, a symposium in the *Journal of World-Systems Research* on his final essay sparked a lively debate about the practical implications of world-systems analysis (e.g., Amin 2019). What's more, a rich engagement with the works of dependency theorists and Latin American scholars of global capitalism such as Andre Gunder Frank, José Carlos Mariátegui, Ruy Mauro Marini, and Theotônio dos Santos has been ongoing by world-systems analysts seeking to chart a course for development in the twenty-first century (e.g., Garcia, Martins, and Menezes 2021; Martins, this volume; Camarinha, this volume; Brussi, this volume).

Finally, alongside a return to the holistic and Global South foundations of world-systems analysis, weaving together insights from other critical perspectives is an important direction for new scholarship. Serious advances toward this end are already being made on many fronts. For example, Fenelon and his collaborators' work on capitalism and indigeneity has long demonstrated the productive potential of fusing world-systems analysis with other critical epistemologies and sources of knowledge (e.g., Fenelon 2016; Fenelon and Alford 2020). Moore's work on world-ecology has pushed the boundaries of world-systems analysis to incorporate an environmental history that has yielded insights on some of the twenty-first century's most pressing system-level problems (e.g., Moore 2015; Moore and Patel 2017). Chitty's pathbreaking fusion of queer theories of sexuality with world-systems analyses of historical capitalism has opened new lines of research (Chitty 2020). And others have successfully developed synergies between world-systems analysis and the Black radical tradition (e.g., Bush 2009; West, Martin, and Wilkins 2009) as well as between the world-systems and post-colonial schools (e.g., Grosfoguel 2006; Boatcă 2006; Komlosy, Boatcă, and Nolte 2016). These are far from the only examples of productive syntheses with world-systems analysis, and several chapters in this book contribute to this endeavor (McQuade and Schrader, this volume; Korhonen, this volume; Ciccantell, Sowers, and Smith, this volume).

10 Corey R. Payne et al.

The Scope of the Book

In a variety of ways, the chapters in this book deal with the issues facing the "state of the world" and the "state of (world-systems) knowledge" in this critical juncture. Using methodological tools on both sides of the analytical–holistic divide, they analyze one or more system-level problems and demonstrate the utility of world-systems analysis for understanding the present moment.

World-Systems Analysis, Concepts, and Methods

In the book's first section, each chapter takes a foundational, often decades-old concept or method from the world-systems canon and deploys it to understand a system-level problem. In each case, the authors synthesize world-systems analysis with other social science perspectives and often merge concepts or methods to bring new vigor to the world-systems perspective.

First, in Chapter 2, Brendan McQuade and Stuart Schrader draw from Terence Hopkins' world-systems methodological insights to demonstrate how to avoid the "security trap," in which good-faith attempts to critique the security apparatus result in conclusions that reinforce it. They argue that studies of security fail to offer an adequate critique if they begin from security as an analytic category. Instead, one must draw from world-systems analysis to recognize that "analyst and object of analysis are co-produced" and that a genuine "critique of security requires seeing security studies itself as a process-instance of security, which then demands historicizing its emergence." They offer a review of how to accomplish such a task via Terence Hopkins' directives, beginning with a small, single "security" program, and moving outward to construct the social relations that unfold around it—offering glimpses of the totality of historical capitalism and its constituent relations along the way.

In Chapter 3, Gamze Evcimen also draws from Terence Hopkins' methodological contributions to construct a relational perspective for studying distinct instances of interaction between religion and neoliberalism in the Global South. By understanding "concepts as constituted by relations between them," Evcimen is able to understand the interrelationship of seemingly disparate moments in the unfolding of systemic and anti-systemic tendencies in the manifestation of the assemblages between religion and neoliberalism. She examines Hindu nationalism in India, political Islam and Islamic Calvinists in Turkey, pious neoliberalism in Egypt, and neo-Pentecostalism in Latin America and Africa as instances of systemic tendencies and Liberation Theology in Latin America and anti-capitalist Muslims in Turkey as instances of anti-systemic tendencies.

Next, in Chapter 4, Juho Korhonen brings together the concepts of Immanuel Wallerstein and Pierre Bourdieu to explore how "symbolic power" shaped the "geoculture" of the world-system and the cultural hegemony of the capitalist core. He demonstrates how the geoculture of the world-system in the long nineteenth century was challenged and developed by contestations over the symbolic meanings of statehood, citizenship, and historical social science— what Wallerstein dubbed the "three crucial spheres" of geoculture in the long nineteenth century. To do so, Korhonen reviews how two empires on the edge of the core—Russian and Ottoman—interacted with each other and with the Atlantic empires, identifying both the importance of these interactions in shaping geoculture and the role of symbolic power in this process.

In Chapter 5, the final chapter of this section, Paul Ciccantell, Elizabeth Sowers, and David Smith aim to realign world-systems analysis and commodity chain analysis, which, despite having originated in world-systems scholarship in the 1970s, diverged from its world-systems' essence over time. Through what they call "raw materialist lengthened global commodity chains," they return commodity chain analysis to its world-systems roots, emphasizing class, spatiotemporal, and interstate relations in a long-term perspective. While rescuing the world-systems lineage of commodity chain analysis, they also endeavor to fuse it with recent advances in the literature on racism, development, contestation, and resistance in the "sinews" and at the "chokepoints" of the capitalist world-system.

Continuity and Transformation in World-Systems Hierarchies

The chapters in the second section of the book tussle with key debates among world-systems scholars about the roots of global inequality and core–periphery hierarchies within the modern world-system. Central debates in these chapters focus on the role of industrialization in development and underdevelopment, the effects of deindustrialization in the capitalist core, and how to interpret the relative rise of the Global South—most notably China—through the hierarchies of political and economic power in the interstate system.

In Chapter 6, Víctor Ramiro Fernández, Luciano Moretti, Joel Sidler, and Emilia Ormaechea examine the divergence in developmental paths between regions comprising the Global South, with an eye toward understanding whether the recent transformations in world-system hierarchies will ultimately perpetuate the logic of subordination that has always characterized capitalist development or whether these transformations present opportunities to promote a new developmental model. Focusing on the role of industrialization, the authors argue that East Asia's state-led industrialization allowed it to develop "a more inclusive socio-spatial pattern of capital accumulation" that, through the deployment of national and regional control over key functions in global commodity chains, yielded a structural power to resist the eventual subordinating projects of foreign financial capital. On the other hand, the absence of such industrial developments in Africa and Latin America explains their relative stagnation and increasing divergence from East Asia. In teasing out the inequalities between the Global North and Global South *and* within the Global

12 Corey R. Payne et al.

South itself, the chapter aims to illuminate potential paths forward for autonomous development in the twenty-first century.

Next, in Chapter 7, Carlos Eduardo Martins seeks to articulate and then bridge the divide between what he calls the Braudelian and Marxist strands of world-systems analysis, fusing the works of Immanuel Wallerstein and Giovanni Arrighi (as examples of the former) with the works of Samir Amin and Theotonio Dos Santos (as examples of the latter) to add greater understanding to the concept of systemic chaos in the twenty-first century. Martins argues that the modern world-system entered a period of systemic chaos only recently, as an expansive Kondratieff cycle initiated in the mid-1990s came to an end. He concludes that the present crises, most notably those associated with the COVID-19 pandemic, are striking at the heart of neoliberal globalization and highlight the vulnerability of its main pillars.

In Chapter 8, Antônio Brussi returns to the subject of industrialization and provides a critical evaluation of the work of Ruy Mauro Marini through an analysis of Brazilian development. Brussi argues that many concepts, such as "sub-imperialism," captured momentary phenomena that were intricately tied to the specific patterns of industrialization in the post-war era. He argues that, rather than being the expression of a clear alternative strategy of development, industrialization was the ad hoc outcome of efforts by state and economic elites in Brazil to (temporarily and only partially) overcome structural limitations to economic growth—such as severe social inequality. For Brussi, the persistence of such constraints into the twenty-first century raises serious doubts about the prospects for Brazil's future developmental success.

In Chapter 9, the final chapter of this section, Ísis Campos Camarinha picks up on a similar thread—Marini's concept of "super-exploitation"—to explore the asymmetric transfer of value from peripheries to the core through the international division of labor. Camarinha notes that, in a Marxian view, such a transfer—which has an historic sum and has reproduced itself over the *longue durée*—is not simply "a transfer of monetary value, it is also, essentially, a transfer of time worked—as the substance of value is labor time." She argues that by examining such a transfer with Marini's concepts of unequal exchange and super-exploitation alongside Wallerstein's concept of "timespace," one can begin to grasp a process of alienation on a world-scale.

Social Contradictions of Capitalism in the Twenty-first Century

The chapters in the final section of the book center around key social contradictions of capitalism in the twenty-first century. They analyze how contemporary capitalism—*via ongoing* primitive accumulation, dispossession, and concentration/centralization of capital—has led to an explosion in the size of the global surplus population; a surplus which is itself unevenly distributed across race, ethnic, gender, and citizenship lines. This contradiction of capitalism—the tendency to destroy established livelihoods faster than it creates new ones—is not only leading to a vicious circle of growing xenophobia, militarism, and the break-down of consent-based social compacts, but also to rising and widespread resistance from below. At the same time, one of the central processes through which the social contradictions of capitalism have been managed (and profitability maintained) over the longue durée—that is, via the externalization of the costs of reproduction of labor and nature—is also reaching its limits. By examining these contradictions and limits, the chapters in this section shine light on the social roots of systemic chaos in the twenty-first century.

First, in Chapter 10, Kelvin Santiago-Valles provides a reinterpretation of Marx's analysis of coercion within primitive accumulation using the work of Terence Hopkins (thus straddling the first and final sections of this book). He identifies shifting cycles of primitive accumulation that have been uneven across time and space, as well as racialized and gendered in their unfolding. The chapter demonstrates how rethinking the complex relationship between historical capitalism, highly coerced labor, and heterogeneous labor formations provides new insights into the specificities of "primitive" accumulation as a concept and as an historical process.

Kai Wen Yang continues the exploration of primitive accumulation in Chapter 11 by linking it together with the emergence of "ethno-racial enclaves" in urban centers in the capitalist core. Yang demonstrates how combining the concepts of primitive accumulation and the semiperiphery contribute to the urban studies literature. Using New York City as his case study, Yang shows how securitized capitalist enclaves (like Wall Street or Hudson Yard) and ethno-racial enclaves (like the Lower East Side or Chinatown) "are spatial units of a single unified process of 'primitive' accumulation." For Yang, these ethno-racial enclaves are semiperipheral spaces where core–peripheral relations are constituted and reproduced, in addition to being sites where the fracturing of the urban capitalist core can be observed in the present period of U.S. decline.

In Chapter 12, David Feldman intervenes on a related key social contradiction of our time: As "widespread dispossession and extreme wealth polarization have rendered large swathes of the world's population superfluous," elites have had to grapple with how to handle this excluded population. Feldman zeros in on how this situation has led to changes in the global governance of migration. He introduces the concept of "militarized migration management" to "describe a nascent world-historic project for controlling, supplying, and disciplining migrant populations." Situating this theoretical contribution in the world-systems and global capitalism literatures on migration and crisis, Feldman demonstrates how his construct operates in a middle ground of abstraction that is able to take into account both the specificity of political mechanisms and the transformation of structural regulatory systems over time.

In Chapter 13, the book's final chapter, Shaohua Zhan and Lingli Huang tackle another element of social reproduction that has long been of interest to

14 Corey R. Payne et al.

world-systems analysts: the inability of the capitalist world-economy to internalize the costs associated with the reproduction of labor and nature. Zhan and Huang engage this literature by examining the externalization of food costs—a key cost of labor reproduction—by China in recent decades. They contend that China's strategy to expand food imports to feed its population has both internal and external constraints, and that it represents a fundamental contradiction of China's rise. Such a contradiction, they note, sets China's recent ascent apart from historical world-hegemonic powers such as Great Britain and the United States, as the former had a vast colonial empire from which to extract food and the latter had substantial domestic agricultural resources. In examining the dilemmas that the Chinese state faces over the social reproduction of its labor force, Zhan and Huang demonstrate the important ways that China's rise differs from that of historical world-hegemonic powers.

Conclusion

The chapters in this volume thus bring world-systems analysis to bear on the extraordinary system-level problems facing humanity in the twenty-first century. It is only through an approach that identifies historical patterns and evolutions of these system-level problems that we can make sense of the global challenges we face. We have argued that world-systems analysis can be strengthened by a more active engagement with its holistic and Third World roots, and by learning from other critical perspectives as we move forward. This volume's chapters—individually and collectively—advance this project, taking steps not only toward mapping a changing landscape of social forces but also enhancing our navigating capacity. As we face a critical juncture in both the "state of knowledge" and the "state of the world," it is our hope that this book demonstrates the continued utility of, and future possibilities for, world-systems analysis.

Notes

1. The 44th annual Political Economy of the World-System conference was co-sponsored by the Department of Sociology at the University of Maryland, College Park, and the Arrighi Center for Global Studies at Johns Hopkins University.
2. The Arrighi Center for Global Studies has also engaged with Rodney's contributions to world-systems analysis, for example, through a 2020 workshop on "Global Groundings: Evaluating Walter Rodney's Legacies" (see: https://krieger.jhu.edu/arrighi/2020/01/30/global-groundings-evaluating-walter-rodneys-legacies/), as well as through collaborations with the Walter Rodney Foundation.

PART I
World-Systems Analyses, Concepts, and Methods

2

AVOIDING THE SECURITY TRAP

The Contributions of Terence Hopkins and World-Systems as Methodology for Critical Police Studies

Brendan McQuade and Stuart Schrader

The last 20 years—a conjuncture defined in obvious and profound ways by the "Global War on Terror"—have made "security" and related concepts such as "police," "counterinsurgency," and "surveillance" unavoidable topics. Books on these topics proliferate endlessly, often with a critical tone. Many predictably repeat the same points, however, liberty is under threat from security, surveillance is expanding, numbers of prisoners are rising, police are becoming too powerful, and so on.

These types of arguments endlessly reappear because they accept the logic of security. They make the "realist," Hobbesian assumption that we exist in a condition of scarcity: We—as individuals and households, as peoples and nations—always and already are at "war" with each other. This condition presupposes that our safety needs to be "secured" against hostile actors (the amorphous and ever-shifting enemies of order) or harsh circumstances (softer notions of "human security," "health security," "food security," or endless other basic needs to be "secured").

This is the security trap. The pattern is clear. Someone conducts thorough research, often with the odds otherwise stacked against them; they document the abuses of the security apparatus, providing original analyses of its causes, effects, or significance; when the time comes to recommend "solutions," however, horizons narrow down to reforming the problem specific to their object of study and category of analysis. What follows is the conservative, technocratic tinkering of liberal reforms, which is to say, changes that expand the reach and legitimacy of security apparatuses.

Reifying or isolating a category of analysis sets an analytic trap. The bait is the assumption of the unity and autonomy of its subject. Rather than demonstrating the historically contingent and politically contested character of that

DOI: 10.4324/9781003325109-3

unity and autonomy, one "falls" for the trap that a category of analysis stands on its own as a "natural" entity that needs no explanation or context. As such, scholars obscure what they should explain and naturalize what they should reveal, if not unsettle: the historical construction of social things.

For example, territorial (Agnew 1994) or scalar traps (Jessop 2009), respectively, isolate territory and scale from one another, and from other analytic dimensions of geographic space such as place and networks (Jessop, Brenner, and Jones 2008). This is not to say that there are no reasons to focus on a particular instance or relation for analytic purposes. The important question is why territory, for instance, appears to be the most important sociospatial dimension. We "fall" for methodological nationalism, the most common territorial trap, because institutional practices—within and beyond the university—are premised on the "natural" acceptance of nation-states and their institutional domination.

The security trap corresponds to the security effect. Closely related to the state effect (Mitchell 1999), the security effect posits security as the primary goal, subordinating other contending goals. The security effect leads to the commonsense thinking that security challenges or problems can be solved without changing social relations. The security effect proposes policing, incarceration, surveillance, and more subtle social policing as the only responses to insecurity. The security trap swallows researchers who focus on reforming security institutions while leaving other practices of governance and capital accumulation untouched.

The most important questions are rarely considered: What is the content of security? What is to be secured? Remember that Marx (1978) called security "the supreme social concept" of bourgeois civilization, an order that "exists only in order to guarantee for each of its members the preservation of his person, his rights, and his property" (43). To be caught in the security trap, then, is to accept bourgeois idiocy and egoism—the right to live private lives apart, mediated and connected only through the cash nexus—as natural, desirable, and worthy of defense.

Hence, the constant churn of the same essential arguments. Of course, the punishment of criminals is necessary, but we need to punish the right criminals the right way. Of course, policing is necessary to control crime, but it must be carefully regulated by law. Of course, surveillance protects us, but it must respect rights. Even when hedged with "pragmatism," "nuance," or even a certain kind of critical distance, these accounts accept the current order of things.

The most profound "of course" clauses are the ones that cannot be countenanced: Of course, the reproduction and expansion capital is the central principle of social order; of course, the work of politics is to modulate an equilibrium that prevents "violence" and directs social change; of course, global inequalities over spatial, racialized, or gendered divides will never be resolved without fundamentally fracturing social order. Security obscures these deeper relations (Neocleous 2008). It is a fetish that reinforces capitalist social relations by negating the structural causes of social injuries with fear of the other: the theatrics of crime and punishment and the spectacle of war and terror.

The way to escape the security trap is, at the very least, to foreground it. But it also requires a disposition that we have found in an unlikely place, the writings of Terence Hopkins, the "methodologist in chief" of the world-systems school (Wallerstein and Tamdgidi 2017). While other world-systems scholars are better known, Hopkins' methodological writings and work as director of graduate studies for Binghamton University's sociology program made a profound impact on the field. Hopkins not only taught world-systems as method to his students, like Philip McMichael and Beverly Silver, but also influenced contemporaries, including Giovanni Arrighi and Immanuel Wallerstein, and colleagues, including Cedric Robinson and Dale Tomich (who began working at Binghamton in 1973 and 1976, respectively). As Wallerstein wrote in the acknowledgements to the first volume of *The Modern World-System* "As for Terence Hopkins, my debt is to our twenty years of intellectual discussion and collaboration. There is no sentence that can summarize this debt" (1974b, xi).

Our debt to Hopkins is less personal, as we began to read him more than a decade after his death in 1997, but he is no less meaningful for our work. In different ways, this method allowed us to start with something small, a single "security" program—Cold War-era police training (Schrader 2019) and post-9/11 police intelligence systems (McQuade 2019)—and move outward to construct the social relations that unfold kaleidoscopically around our chosen empirical object: security, police, the state, class, racism, capital.

This procedure offers glimpses of the totality of historical capitalism. It demands we start with a part and understand it as a theoretical process, and to then build to a concrete "level of conceptualization" (Hopkins 1982b, 146). Schrader (2019) takes the historical ground of Cold War US police assistance to reveal that the "national security state" and "carceral state" are both condensations of the color lines that constituted the structures of US hegemony. For McQuade (2019), police intelligence centers become a point of departure to trace out a series of interlinked developments—economic crisis and austerity, decarceration, increased resistance, and repression—and to identify an emergent reformulation of state strategy, the end of mass incarceration, and reconfiguration of pacification around mass supervision.

This approach not only broadens the discussion but also avoids the trap of security. Schrader shows that "de-militarizing" the police is an inadequate slogan and the only way to address police violence and the carceral state is to dismantle US empire. The antithesis of security is solidarity. Internationalism is the only political antidote to US empire, to the "global policeman," because the security apparatus relies on its own unquestioned border-crossing abilities. McQuade concludes that surveillance (and police) does not stand in opposition

20 Brendan McQuade and Stuart Schrader

to "rights" but rather produces the differential application of them. Hence, the only answer to surveillance is abolition, understood as the construction of democratically self-administered forms of institutional legibility. The antithesis of police is the commons.

As authors, much of our adult lives have occurred during the "war on terror." Yet we also remember the twilight of the Cold War and the heady days of "globalization," when, as children, we saw the fear-mongering about the threat of the Soviet Union and Communism shift to new enemies. Coming of age also meant coming to terms with this amorphous forever war and coming to see that this war was never confined to "over there."

Our experiences are singular but not unique. They are generational and this collective reckoning is reflected in the recent proliferation of critical police studies (Linnemann 2016; Correia and Wall 2018; Seigel 2018; Balto 2019; LeBrón 2019; Jefferson 2020; Felker-Kantor 2018; Paik 2020). In different ways, this scholarship avoids the security trap by historicizing. Some of these works, written in conventional historiographical terms, leave methodological and conceptual questions implicit or understated. Others draw on Marxism, the Black Radical Tradition, and decolonial approaches. Despite their varied presentations and positionings, all these works have different, unstated, and hence undeveloped affinities with the methodological imperatives laid out by Terence Hopkins.

Security as the Guarantor of the Wholeness of the Whole

The way to break free of analytic traps is to reject reification, rethink once-isolated "cases" as "parts" of a larger whole, and begin to think through the mutual constitution of these part–whole relations. "Security" is not an interchangeable part but an integral one. It is the guarantor, in fact, of the wholeness of the whole. This does not mean, however, simply considering a particular security program in relation to related ones, even in relation to a particular state apparatus (the oft-obscured link between "social" and "national" security). It means situating an instance of security immanently within the totality of social relations, which is to say in relation to modernity or—better—capitalism as a historical system:

> [A] concrete, time-bounded, space-bounded integrated locus of productive activities within which the endless accumulation of capital has been the economic objective or "law" that has governed or prevailed in fundamental economic activity. It's that social system in which those who have operated by such rules have had such great impact on the whole as to create conditions wherein the others have been forced to conform to the patterns or suffer the consequences. It is that social system in which the scope of these rules (the law of value) has grown ever wider, the enforcers

of these rules ever more transigent, the penetrations of these rules into the social fabric ever greater, even while social opposition to these rules has grown ever louder and more organized.

(Wallerstein 1983, 19)

In other words, capitalism is both an abstract system of impersonal social domination, where social life is "form determined" by the law of value (Postone 1996), *and* a globally involving relational system—heterogeneous and conflictive—that has integrated, in uneven and varying degrees, all historically known forms of labor control under the law of value (Quijano 2000). Capitalism is also a social system that requires "a politics of security" to "enforce the rules" in the face of both social struggles to transform the parameters of the system *and* the endemic "insecurity" that is the unavoidable outcome of capital accumulation (Neocleous 2011). By producing insecurity that people feel intimately on a daily basis, capitalism's impersonal forces also summon highly personal forms of domination to enforce those rules: the security apparatus.

Situating the "case" within the totality, however, is not an easy task. Traditionally, social scientists abstract seemingly similar "cases" out of history to compare their points of agreement and disagreement. This approach retreats from questions of totality in favor of questions of abstracted causation: What common circumstances hold across shared outcomes? What differences separate divergent paths? To foreground the systematic relations traditionally obscured by comparative historical research, a different approach begins by situating cases within transhistorical structures. How are sets of "cases" positioned, for example, within the world-economy or interstate system? Such encompassing comparisons, however, "*presume* a 'whole' that governs its 'parts'" (McMichael 1990, 386, original emphasis). It highlights connections between cases by theoretically prefiguring history. This is world-systems as rarefied Theory, which Hopkins rejected and trained students at Binghamton to avoid during his two decades as director of graduate studies from 1971 to 1993.

An alternative approach, however, incorporates comparison within historically specific structures and processes, reframing "cases" as "'instances' . . . distinct mutually-conditioning moments of singular phenomenon posited as self-forming whole" (McMichael 1990, 391; Hopkins 1982b, 154). This is "world-systems analysis as a methodology" (Gates and Deniz 2019). Not only is this approach a more subtle and dialectical approach to theorization but it also expands the field of "cases." Where Tomich (1994) made "huge comparisons" with "small islands," we start with small security programs to construct global pacification projects. The justification for this analytic move is the mutual conditioning and historical interrelationship of "cases" discerned through empirical research and theorized in our analyses.

In this way, our reliance on Hopkins is a "return to the source" in Amilcar Cabral's (1973) sense: not an escape into an autonomous domain of "culture" as primordial *or* as the antidote to foundationalism but as a political process that starts from an acute awareness of somewhere, of the historical ground (and its relationality). Instead of beginning with ideal-typical categories that are said to align with empirical data, a movement of thought from concept to indicator, we, following Hopkins, construct the whole, the totality, by "moving out by successive determinations, bringing in successive parts—themselves abstract processes—in constant juxtaposition" (Hopkins 1982b, 147).

For these reasons, Hopkins's methods are particularly resonant with critical scholarship on police and security. Non-positivist, relational, and historical research into policing confronts many of the same issues as world-systems: the polarization of "core" and "periphery," the inseparability of "race" and "labor," and global phasings of social processes, both the accumulation of capital across commodity chains and the enforcement of the law of value by actors across the police–military continuum. Some of the best work using world-systems as a method is accomplished without conscious reference to the tradition. Our intention in this piece is to increase this awareness by explaining how we used world-systems analysis as a method to conduct research into topics not normally considered in these terms.

Not Security or Police But What Is Secured or Policed

One of the key methodological tools that Hopkins described is the figure-ground movement. Hopkins (1982a, 20) wrote that "in world-system studies the core–periphery relation itself is central to the operation and development of the capitalist world-economy. It itself is a major focus of attention. Thus, what is 'ground' in dependency studies becomes 'figure' in world-system studies." Elsewhere, he expanded this methodological discussion. "I have in mind the figure-ground movement where if one refocuses, what was figure becomes ground and when one refocuses again, what was ground becomes figure. For us, the figure-ground movement seems to take place centrally between social relations and agencies of action, between role and role relation . . . . our acting units or agencies can only be thought of as *formed*, and continually re-formed, by the relations between them" (Hopkins 1982b, 149).

"Figure-ground movement" for Hopkins is a methodological maneuver that, to adopt the sight-based metaphor, refocuses the lens, so that the blurry background becomes sharper. The goal is not to ignore the object in the foreground but to re-evaluate, on the one hand, how it is connected to the background, and on the other hand, thus how it is an emergent part of a whole that includes both foreground and background in structurally interdependent ways.

Figure-ground movement is not about a figure-ground binary in ontology, about a primary versus secondary level of social life. It instead asks us to be explicit about what choices we make in our analyses that lead to specific emphases and specific elisions or occlusions. Hopkins's proposition hinged on a key point: The object in the foreground is typically the case, and the embedded assumption is that the case and the unit of analysis align. But the analyst either leaves out an explanation of why that should be true or why the unit and case as such exist as "end points" that accurately represent the key social relations. Instead, he argued that the relations make the units. World-systemic processes make nation-states. But that does not mean that nation-states are the correct units of analysis to grasp world-systemic processes.

Although Hopkins offered this methodological injunction in a specific discussion of debates in the literature that are now decades old, it provides a useful way to describe how to avoid the security trap, as well as other analytic traps. Moreover, this approach helps highlight the interconnection among analytic traps. In short, security is fundamentally a process of circumscription: Through law, policy, and state violence, borders and cages, nightsticks and handcuffs become the tools of the fabrication of social order. The security effect becomes a territorial effect, and it tempts its analysts into methodological nationalism and security reformism.

In *Badges Without Borders*, Schrader analyzes the rise of the carceral state as an effect of the US empire and the prosecution of the global Cold War. In *Pacifying the Homeland*, McQuade tracks the transformation of that same carceral state in relation to the shifting historical ground of US imperial decline. Schrader shows how US overseas police assistance to prevent Communist revolution reverberated domestically to shape law enforcement and foster the expansion and intensification of policing in the context of the political and social turmoil of the 1960s, particularly Black freedom movements. In situating U.S. policing "in the world," it provides a deeply archival investigation of the unity that many Black radicals denounced: Between state security practices found in Harlem as much as in Saigon. McQuade picks up the same process decades later when intelligence systems put into place as part of the global war on terrorism interacted with austerity and mounting inequality to produce an unplanned security fix. While carried out in the name of "counterterrorism," the rapid expansion of domestic intelligence interacted with and enabled an unexpected decarceration that reduced prison populations but did not rectify the social problems at the core of mass incarceration.

Badges Without Borders opens by drawing on Hopkins to make a "figure-ground inversion" (Hopkins 1982b, 152) to move away from the methodologically nationalist framing of the carceral state. It proposed seeing the carceral state as a figure against the ground of US empire, and then, refocusing or recalibrating the resolution of the analysis to bring that background of empire and the national security state itself into the foreground. Similarly, *Pacifying the Homeland* opens by separating the figure of fusion centers from the common-sense context of counterterrorism and locating them in relation to the ground of the carceral state. While the extant literature fixated on the apparent failures of fusion centers as a counterterrorism program, McQuade found that fusion centers focused on managing acute poverty and extreme violence underpinning the drug trade in internal peripheries on the losing end of neoliberal restructuring, in places like Camden, NJ, where the police chief sardonically described the city's violence as falling "somewhere between Honduras and Somalia." Our world-systems approach takes this joke seriously and constructs its units of analysis from the social processes that plot these locales on a continuum rather than trying to separate them to evaluate the accuracy of the claim and find security solutions that would rescue Camden from its placement on the continuum, leaving the others untouched.

Furthermore, in shifting from security or police to what is secured or what is policed, our analyses focus on historically embedded but fluctuating and evolving part–whole relationships. For instance, the term carceral state largely remains undefined in the literature. One tension relates precisely to part–whole relations. Is the carceral state a part or branch of the state or is the carceral state a process through which the state itself has undergone "carceralization"? Further is the whole the national security state (or security and counterterror apparatus), with the carceral state as a part? Is the whole US empire, with both the national security state and the carceral state as parts, or does all of this comprise a single differentiated unit?

The carceral state and US empire are interrelated, Schrader shows, in ways that are not purely coincidental but in fact make the one unimaginable without the other. US empire racializes the globe through state violence, and this process of state violence is a primary driver of racialization at home. It is impossible to imagine US hegemony globally during the post-1945 period without the recourse to police-led state violence in dozens of allied and proxy states, and this type of state violence was (and is) also the means of defeating revolutionary movements at home, which, in turn, developed ties and alliances with the global revolutionary movements the national security state was trying to defeat abroad. The efflux of this cycle, in part, was "mass incarceration."

Subsequent turns of this cycle, moreover, are oriented by the historical ground they passed through. Hence, the decline of US hegemony began amid the world-historic nadir of the left and accelerated in relation to imperial overextension, which, in turn, helped push a booming but thoroughly financialized world-economy to go bust. As social struggle intensified across the globe, technologies developed in part on the smoldering battlefields of the war on terror were, as McQuade maintains, put to work to manage the rising costs of mass incarceration, producing a punitive decarceration effort centered on police surveillance. This apparatus simultaneously contains the violence and harms of mounting immiseration and monitors the rising rebellions in streets and squares.

Connections Over Cases

In situating our object of analyses on their constitutive historical ground, we emphasize connections over cases. Our analyses could not be conventionally comparative in variation-finding terms (McMichael 1990; Tilly 1984). For Schrader, individualizing comparison would have meant isolating cases, say, of US security assistance to Brazil and Uruguay, or Uruguay and South Vietnam for that matter, to then comparing them. Case comparison would not have been satisfactory because, historically, practically interconnected cases would have been artificially separated, leaving out or obscuring how each was part of a self-forming whole. For McQuade, an individualizing comparison would have prevented a reckoning with the full scope of his research. The case was "a fusion center" but these sites were connected by a broader process, the institutionalization of intelligence fusion, which extends beyond *both* the institutional domain of DHS-recognized fusion centers *and* the historical boundaries of the war on terror. As McMichael (2000a, 671) puts it, "comparison is 'internal' to historical inquiry, where process-instances are comparable because they are historically connected and mutually conditioning."

Another type of comparison we could have made would have been the encompassing approach (McMichael 1990; cf. Tilly 1984). It would have meant, for Schrader, comparing the buildup of policing and penal capacities accomplished through police assistance in other countries with the same type of buildup within the United States and, for McQuade, comparing the creation of fusion centers among different US states. In encompassing comparison, a different but related inadequacy would arise. Even stipulating the analytic primacy of carceral capacity-building or intelligence expansion, encompassing comparison would have turned particular security apparatuses into instances of a generalized and abstract process. This proposition has some appeal, but it is empirically unsustainable, in part because in its abstraction it gives agency to an entity that can never be pinned down.

Instead, we both pursued "incorporated comparison" (McMichael 1990), which means elucidating what and how particular part–whole relations emerged. In *Badges Without Borders*, police technical assistance was not the only connective tissue. It was the integument surrounding interrelated state-building projects. For example, Uruguay, South Vietnam, and the United States all shared single technologies of biodata creation and archiving through identification card programs designed by a single expert body and manufactured according to the same specifications by the same firms. Looking at individuals revealed what connected Brazil to Uruguay, as the same person, Dan Mitrione, brought some of these forms of technical assistance to both (as a footnote, he was assassinated by left-wing militants in Uruguay, who accused him of teaching torture in Brazil).

Similarly, *Pacifying the Homeland* incorporates a comparison of different police intelligence hubs in New York and New Jersey and focuses on the organic links among surveillance, policing, and the carceral state. A focus on the nominal case, the DHS-recognized fusion centers, would present a false picture, where New Jersey is a model and New York a laggard. A broader focus on relevant moments of institutionalized intelligence fusion, regardless of their specific position in the state-apparatus revealed something different. The nationwide attempt to institutionalize intelligence fusion through DHS counterterrorism initiatives is part of a larger structural transformation that some of the policing innovations in New York City prefigure.

Hopkins provided a set of framing devices and tools with which to make sense of connections we encountered. Hopkins helped us find new angles for the critique of security and the historical analysis of both US imperial state-formation and carceral state-formation such that the two can be conceived relationally. We have identified the security trap as the analytic problem, and the security effect as the historical ground for this problem. Our work employs tools from Hopkins to avoid the trap for the purpose of contributing to the abolition of the effect.

Conclusion

We therefore urge greater collaboration between thinkers using the world-systems approach and those developing the critique of security. Capital accumulation has to be secured at every moment of the valorization process, and every moment of the valorization process creates insecurity. This is the true demand-side reason for security interventions that take the form of police, incarceration, and counterterrorism. And this situation is global in scope and scale. The security effect relies on national borders for the efficacy of its interventions, but it transcends them in its demand that all governments adhere to its protocol of identifying the social injuries of capitalism as insecurity.

To identify the security trap as an analytic pitfall is also to suggest that specific methodological tools can help overcome it. The work of Hopkins and his followers provides one such set of tools, though others are available. The world-systems approach, however, has fallen short in the past, typically by excluding questions of security from its investigations. Such an exclusion is no longer tenable.

Yet this exclusion itself was surprising from the outset. Although the original world-systems thinkers such as Hopkins, Wallerstein, Amin, and Gunder Frank (and before them Dobb, Cox, and Du Bois) focused on questions of world-economy, above all they were challenging the modernization paradigm. Wallerstein himself was the exterminating angel of modernization theory, who issued its death certificate. His work struck the fatal blow at the intellectual level to modernization as movements of national liberation often tried to strike fatal blows in practice. Modernization was never merely an economic approach, and its practitioners always recognized the necessity of security interventions both to clear the ground and then to hold it while the maelstrom of modernization unfolded (what Neocleous and others have called pacification).

Furthermore, at a strategic and administrative level, the era's national security experts were themselves theorists of a world-system, so to speak. Even as figures like Robert W. Komer worked within the modernization paradigm, they were not methodologically nationalist in their assessments of the relationship of the United States to the globe but instead appreciated the interconnectedness of a global fabric (Schrader 2019; Barkawi and Schrader 2020). Modernization theory's methodological nationalism was inadequate for analyzing US power, according to some charged with protecting that power. For this reason, the world-systems approach, with its thorough critique of methodological nationalism, remains vitally important, if underused, in analyzing schemes of protection and enforcement of rules by security apparatuses.

Overall, our work demonstrates that studies of security fail to critique security adequately if they take security as an analytic category. We have used Hopkins in different ways to develop this approach. The world-system, for Hopkins, was not a receptacle for global histories. It was a way to identify the processes shaping social reality. A central premise of Hopkins' methodological imperative was to recognize that analyst and object of analysis are co-produced. Furthermore, so too are fields of study. A critique of security requires seeing security studies itself as a process-instance of security, which then demands historicizing its emergence. Our work, we hope, illustrates how to begin this work. Nothing less than everything is at stake.

3

TERENCE K. HOPKINS AND CONCEPTS AS RELATIONAL CATEGORIES

Different Manifestations of the Relationship Between Religion and Neoliberalism in the Global South

Gamze Evcimen

Introduction[1]

We are witnessing a critical juncture in which not only the field of world-systems analysis but also sociology as a discipline is undergoing radical change. Scholars like Gurminder Bhambra (2007) and Julian Go (2016) call for the development of a global historical sociology and urge researchers to rethink and reformulate theoretical concepts by incorporating excluded and marginalized voices from the Global South. The lineages of world-systems analysis have a lot to offer to meet this call.

More than four decades ago, Terence K. Hopkins (1978a) proposed an alternative perspective on concepts as *relational categories*. In her recent piece, Leslie Gates (2018) similarly offers a relational methodology of comparisons to address the surge of populist politics. These works offer crucial methodological interventions that open room for bringing world-systems analysis into conversation with other critical perspectives for addressing the multifaceted challenges of the current juncture.

In this chapter, I draw from the methodological contributions of Hopkins and other key scholars of world-systems analysis to construct a relational perspective for studying seemingly distinct instances of the relationship between religion and neoliberal capitalism in the Global South. Distinguishing between systemic and anti-systemic manifestations of the assemblages between religion and neoliberalism, I analyze Hindu nationalism in India, political Islam and Islamic Calvinists in Turkey, pious neoliberalism in Egypt, and neo-Pentecostalism in Latin America and Africa as *systemic tendencies* and Liberation Theology in Latin America and anti-capitalist Muslims in Turkey as *anti-systemic tendencies*.

DOI: 10.4324/9781003325109-4

My analysis illustrates that religion and neoliberalism operate as relational categories à la Hopkins by examining how religious discourses and practices affect and are affected by support for or opposition to neoliberal ideas and policies. Moreover, it unveils the agency of different social forces in these processes and helps identify how various social actors constitute and are constituted by the relationships between religion and neoliberal capitalism. This study also opens room for transforming theory-building processes and our perspectives by including evidence and experiences from the Global South.

Centering the Global South

This study focuses on the relationship between religion and neoliberalism in the Global South to address the particular ways in which neoliberal restructuring has coalesced with a surge in religious discourses and practices in both semi-peripheral and peripheral societies. The coalescence of religion and neoliberalism has operated differently in (semi-)peripheral and core societies in two critical ways. First, the historical legacies of social service provisions in the Global South enabled a combination of neoliberal policies and informal practices of social help and charity in (semi-)peripheral societies. Although these societies improved their implementation of infrastructural projects and social services in the state-led developmental era, such processes have not brought about promised changes in the public infrastructure of countries like India (Aneesh 2015) or in the institutionalization of social assistance, particularly in peripheral societies like Zambia (Ferguson 1999). In contrast, core countries benefitted from extensive welfare systems and, although the neoliberal shift has been dismantling social provisions (Wacquant 2010), the Global North's economically marginalized sectors continue receiving institutionalized social assistance compared to their counterparts in the (semi-)periphery. Due to this divergence, the relationship between neoliberalism and religion in the (semi-) periphery aims to incorporate losers of neoliberal globalization through informal practices of social help and charity while lack of institutional welfare also opens room for opposition and resistance to neoliberalism.

Second, class formation processes driven by the neoliberal turn have taken different forms in the Global North and South, with differentiated effects on the class relations and inequalities in each. Due to global outsourcing of manufacturing jobs, core countries like the United States experienced a decline in the privileged sectors of workers, who were considered as middle class based on purchasing power and job benefits (Taft 2016). In contrast, with policies like privatization and deregulation, which reduced public employment and motivated entrepreneurial activities, the Global South witnessed the emergence of a new bourgeoisie, exemplified by instances like the rise of pious small- and medium-sized enterprise owners as the Islamic bourgeoisie in Turkey (Adaş 2006) and the rise of India's upper caste members as new entrepreneurs that

30 Gamze Evcimen

support Hindu nationalism (Fernandes and Heller 2006). The concomitant rise of inequalities in these societies motivated such actors to adopt neoliberal principles in their religious discourses and practices in order to sacralize and justify their newly accumulated wealth as well as to legitimize and depoliticize increasing inequalities.

These two processes, exacerbating inequalities due to the retrenchment of social provisions and increasing wealth as reflected in the growing middle classes, shape the manifestations of the relationship between religion and neo-liberalism in (semi-)peripheral societies. Following the calls for democratiz-ing theory building by incorporating excluded and marginalized voices from the Global South (Bhambra 2007; Go 2016), this study starts from the (semi-) periphery and centers the experiences of these societies in both theory building and empirical research. Although some core countries like the United States have recently been experiencing a similar religious surge with the rise of far-right politics, the sociopolitical rise of religion in the Global South is not only the result of divergent conditions mentioned earlier but also preceded similar tendencies in the core. In light of these issues, this chapter focuses on the rise of religious discourses and practices in semi-peripheral societies, which are central to an analysis of the world-system (Dunaway and Clelland 2017). It also devel-ops an alternative way of theory building by employing insights from (semi-) peripheral societies to understand similar processes and practices in the core.

Religion and Neoliberalism in the Global South

Current scholarship points to a surge in religious discourses and practices in the Global South in the neoliberal era. Rudnyckyj (2009) argues that spiri-tual economies in Indonesia create pious and economically productive work-ing subjects. Atia (2012) also shows how pious neoliberalism in Egypt creates middle-class subjects engaged in charity to overcome the moral ambiguities of newly gained wealth. Similarly, Atasoy (2009) argues that Islam's marriage with neoliberalism in Turkey explains the simultaneous rise of political Islam and neoliberal restructuring of the state and economy. These works highlight the political–economic and socio-cultural processes through which middle-class actors play role in the coalescence of neoliberal capitalism and Islam in (semi-)peripheral societies.

This assemblage between religion and neoliberalism transcends Islamic dis-courses and practices. Neo-Pentecostalism with its prosperity theology and gospel is on the rise in Latin America and Africa, especially in countries such as Brazil (Freston 1995), Ghana (Meyer 1998), South Africa (Anderson 2005), and Nigeria (Adeboye 2004; Hackett 2003). Most situate this recent rise of neo-Pentecostalism in structural adjustment and neoliberal policies; while some address how neo-Pentecostalism facilitates community building and pro-vision of social services (Barker 2007; Comaroff 2012; Dilger 2007), others also emphasize its role as a new spirit of neoliberal capitalism (Comaroff and Comaroff 2000; Freeman 2012). The rise of Hindu nationalism in India indicates a similar affiliation between neoliberalism and religion as the state employs religious discourses and practices to legitimize neoliberal transformations and policies (Nanda 2012; Rajagopal 2001; Teltumbde 2006; Vanaik 2001).

Although such works study the relationship between religious discourses and neoliberalism, they rarely pay attention to the fact that similar processes are unfolding in different societies or consider instances of neoliberalism and different religious traditions as part of the same process. Indeed, different articulations of rising piety and neoliberalism illustrate a systemic relationship between religion and neoliberal capitalism. Moreover, since these works define religion in different ways—including moral regulation and creation of pious and neoliberal subjects, cultural accommodation and re-enchantment against anomie and deprivation, ideological legitimation of neoliberal hegemony—they lack a perspective on the convergence of religion and neoliberalism as a systemic process experienced in (semi-)peripheral societies in different ways. Ignoring this convergence obscures how seemingly distinct, local processes remain inextricably interlinked to each other and to the world-system.

How can we study these different instances of the relationship between religion and neoliberalism in the Global South as connected to each other and as part of the world-system? How can we develop a systematic approach to analyze the world-historical significance of the surge of religion and neoliberalism in the Global South? To address these questions, I draw from Hopkins's methodological contribution and other key works of world-systems analysis.

Theoretical Underpinnings of an Alternative Framework

World-systems scholars provide nuanced methodologies for historical analysis. Philip McMichael (1990) offers incorporated comparison as a strategy to bring together theory and history and to study both particularity and generality of cases in historical comparisons. Similarly, Dale Tomich (1994) develops a method of substantive comparison that considers interdependency and diversity of cases by addressing historical processes, which form relations between cases while also influencing changing patterns of these relations and cases. Leslie Gates (2018) regards such contributions as a logic of comparison for concrete historical analysis, and by building on these conceptualizations, offers a relational methodology of comparisons.

By defining theoretical concepts as relational categories, Terence Hopkins (1978a) offers an earlier methodological intervention. Hopkins (1978a) theorizes *concepts* as constantly constituted through the *relations between them*; such relationships form *categories*, which are continuously produced by these relational processes. Rethinking his conceptualization in the light of subsequent methodological contributions opens room for not only studying comparisons of cases in historical analysis but also redefining theoretical concepts based on their interrelationships. For instance, we can employ Tomich's definition of factors as "historically formed social relations that are constituted differently in each instance within the emerging patterns of production, exchange and consumption of the larger world economy" (1994, 344) to conceptualize theoretical concepts as relational categories.

Using this perspective, I define the concepts of religion and neoliberalism as constituted through the relationship between them. These two concepts have a myriad of definitions; studies focus on the role religious discourses and practices play in processes such as cultural accommodation, moral regulation, or political legitimation of power; while others define neoliberalism as projects of political and economic elites, policies implemented by state, values internalized and reproduced by individuals, or discourses contested by oppositional forces. In contrast to such distinct conceptualizations, I suggest focusing on the dialectical relationship between these mutually constitutive and reinforcing concepts as constitutive of the different manifestations of religion and neoliberalism in (semi-)peripheral societies.

Religious movements entail both progressive and reactionary elements and aims that can conflict with each other (Billings and Scott 1994; Frank and Fuentes 1990, 173). Similarly, the relationship between religion and neoliberalism proves dialectical. On the one hand, religion can operate in the service of systemic tendencies as pro-systemic forces use it for building and maintaining capitalist hegemony. On the other hand, religion can play a role in anti-systemic, and potentially counterhegemonic, movements since oppositional forces can employ it for challenging hegemonic order and building alternatives. Such movements aim at systemic transformation by building an egalitarian and democratic world (Arrighi 2004, 79; Wallerstein 1990, 51). These two faces and processes are in constant conflict with each other as pro- and anti-systemic forces use similar sources, religious discourses and practices, to build opposing conceptions of the world.

Furthering Hopkins's methodological contribution, this framework also focuses on the constant interactions between structure and agency by addressing how pro- and anti-systemic forces both constitute and get constituted by these different manifestations of the relationship between religion and capitalism. A world-systemic perspective on the relationship between religion and neoliberalism regards "structure as formed through specific historical relations" (McMichael 2000a, 670). Social forces get constituted through such relations, or through "processes by which groups (and institutions) are constantly recreated, remolded, and eliminated in the ongoing operations of the capitalist world-economy" (Arrighi, Hopkins, and Wallerstein 1989, 22). Simultaneously, social forces play an active role in shaping these relations as "agents of change, led forth by values, hope, anger, analyses, or strategies" (Touraine 2000, 915). Regarding capitalism "as a dynamic—albeit highly structured—system that political struggles continuously form and re-form" (Gates and Deniz 2019, 77), this approach emphasizes agential processes within the capitalist world-economy.

This perspective opens room for studying the processes through which formation of local social forces simultaneously affects and is affected by world-systemic processes. Capitalism gives rise to social groups that actively support or oppose its processes; in other words, it both constrains and facilitates pro- and anti-systemic forces.[2] This dialectic of structure and agency also plays out in the relationship between religion and capitalism, which takes different forms based on sociohistorical contexts. On the one hand, neoliberalism and religion play a role in the emergence of new pro- and anti-systemic forces that form and promote particular readings of religious texts and rituals. On the other hand, as their religious discourses and practices reproduce or challenge hegemonic articulations of neoliberalism and religion, these social forces play an active role in the making and disrupting of neoliberalism.

In many (semi-)peripheral societies, pro-systemic actors such as political parties, religious institutions, and faith-based organizations as well as anti-systemic actors such as non-governmental organizations and religious groups weave neoliberalism and religion. In a similar vein with semi-peripheral societies mediating the relations between core and periphery (Babones 2015, 9; Galtung 1971, 104; Wallerstein 1974b, 349–50), these middle-class actors mediate between capitalist and working classes in their respective societies. They play an active role in building or opposing hegemony by developing conceptions of the world that aim to capture the hearts and minds of pious populaces (Gramsci 1971). While pro-systemic actors form hegemonic worldviews by appealing to the oppressed and disadvantaged social groups and creating consent for hegemony, anti-systemic forces resist the hegemonic articulation of religion and neoliberalism by opposing capitalism and by offering alternative worldviews with counterhegemonic potential.

This alternative framework focuses on how neoliberalism and religion affect the formation of new social forces while these actors also construct and contest the neoliberal world-system. It addresses the co-constitutive relationship between religion and neoliberalism by investigating the ways in which particular religious discourses and practices of social forces legitimize or challenge neoliberalism while neoliberalism reinforces or undermines such interpretations of religion and their agents. With this focus, this chapter reformulates Hopkins's methodological contribution of concepts as relational categories also as an epistemological intervention: Social forces constitute the relationships between concepts while simultaneously getting constituted by such relationships. In this way, it opens room for tracing the agency of different social forces and their particular roles in the articulations of religion and neoliberalism.

34 Gamze Evcimen

Analyzing Different Instances of Religion and Neoliberalism in the Global South

The manifestations of the relationship between religion and neoliberalism in the Global South take two particular forms: pro-systemic articulations and anti-systemic alternatives. In the first instance, political actors, such as governments and political parties, and civil society actors, such as religious institutions, non-governmental organizations and faith-based associations, fuse religious discourses and practices with neoliberal principles and policies to create cross-class coalitions and to build a hegemonic conception of religion and neoliberal capitalism. In contrast, other religious institutions, non-governmental organizations, and religious groups offer alternative readings of religion that challenge and resist dominant religious understandings and that develop piety as opposition to neoliberal capitalism. In both pro-systemic articulations and anti-systemic alternatives, religion and neoliberalism mutually shape each other; while neoliberalism transforms religious discourses and practices, particular interpretations of religion also influence the implementation of neoliberal capitalism in different societies.

Pro-systemic Articulations

The recent surge of piety in India, Turkey, Egypt, and several countries in Latin America and Africa has coalesced with the neoliberal shift. Neoliberalism and Hindu nationalism or Hindutva rose simultaneously in India as cultural hegemonic projects that are indispensably linked to globalization and neoliberal capitalism (Chatterjee 2010, 628; Gopalakrishnan 2006; Rajagopal 2001, 42; Teltumbde 2006). Turkey has also experienced a similar rise of political Islam linked to neoliberal capitalism through "a dialectical process wherein capitalism and Islamic culture interpenetrate and transform each other" (Adaş 2006, 115).

Similarly, the coalescence of Islamic piety and neoliberal values in Egypt arose as a political project accompanying neoliberalization, whereby the revival of Islamism occurred as "both a response to and a product of neoliberalism" (Atia 2012, 814). In Indonesia, spiritual economies link religious practices to neoliberal transformation and constitute "an unprecedented assemblage that is as much the Islamization of neoliberalism as it is the neoliberalization of Islam" (Rudnyckyj 2009, 131). Neo-Pentecostalism in Africa and Latin America also rose as a product of the neoliberal turn and relates to structural adjustment and worsening economic conditions with increasing unemployment and poverty in these societies (Adeboye 2004, 141, 143; Bornstein 2003, 16–17; Freeman 2012, 4, 10, 24; Freston 1995, 120, 132; Hackett 2003, 205; Hasu 2012, 69).

A variety of actors mediate the relationship between religion and neoliberalism in these societies as they get constituted by and come to constitute the neoliberal order. The Indian state has combined structural adjustment with the ideology of Hindu nationalism (Chatterjee 2010, 621, 627) as "the political organs of Hindu fundamentalism have embraced the neoliberal economic agenda as fervently as any neoliberal evangelist" (Teltumbde 2006, 248). Also, India's middle classes, the main beneficiaries of neoliberal reforms, constitute the backbone of rising Hindutva and support the Bharatiya Janata Party (BJP), both of which articulate a discourse that further promotes their class interests (Nanda 2012, 65).

The rise of political Islam in Turkey also occurred as the Justice and Development Party (AKP) utilized religion as a politico-ideological instrument to legitimize and de-politicize its neoliberal economic policies while also undermining or co-opting oppositional tendencies (Bozkurt 2013; Yalman 2012). Turkey's newly rising Islamic bourgeoisie, which organize in faith-based associations such as Independent Industrialists' and Businessmen's Association (MUSIAD), also reproduce neoliberalism with their discourses and practices that link religious values to the capitalist economy and undertake "Islamization of capitalism and the construction of entrepreneurial Islam" (Adaş 2006, 113).

A combination of religious actors, faith-based organizations, and non-governmental groups in Egypt also bring together Islamic piety and charity with neoliberal values for creating religious solutions to social problems caused by neoliberalism (Atia 2012, 812, 808). Similarly, Indonesia's corporate, state and religious actors "sought to enact a set of neoliberal practices by creating a new type of subject, a worshipping worker for whom labor was a matter of religious duty" (Rudnyckyj 2009, 107). In many societies of Africa and Latin America, neo-Pentecostal churches refashion development in terms of a prosperity gospel while providing social services and sense of community to members (Freeman 2012, 2; Hasu 2012, 83; Robbins 2004, 131).

These actors form, follow, and promote certain discourses and practices, which link and shape piety and neoliberal capitalism. They advocate religion for material success along with the formation of both pious and neoliberal, or economically productive, selves. In India, "the public sphere is replete with these messages of becoming more Hindu in order to become more successful in the global race for money and power" (Nanda 2012, 106). Similarly, in Turkey, Homo Islamicus arises as a new economic actor who blends in entrepreneurialism and economic activities with religion and morality by embodying Islamic ethical values and norms (Adaş 2006, 116, 127, 130, 133).

Egypt's Islamic development organizations also promote values and activities such as financial investment, entrepreneurship, self-improvement, and productivity as constituents of a pious identity and as crucial elements of both material and spiritual success (Atia 2012, 808, 809, 811). Similarly, in Indonesia, norms such as efficiency, productivity, accountability, and transparency coalesce with Islam for redefining work and labor as practices of religious worship (Rudnyckyj 2009, 118, 123). Prosperity gospel and theology in Latin America and

Africa also serve as the new spirit of capitalism by providing a moral framework for neoliberalism and motivating new behaviors such as entrepreneurial ambition, hard work, desire for wealth, self-control, and time management while also legitimating these behaviors by classifying them as sacred (Comaroff 2012, 52; Freeman 2012, 20; Freston 1995, 131; Van Dijk 2012, 96).

Although such values and behaviors seem aspirational and applicable for all members of these religions, indeed they remain tailored particularly for the winners of neoliberal capitalism in these societies. These groups further legitimize their economic success and profit motives through particular religious discourses and practices. India's middle classes associate their consumption practices with Hindu nationalism and employ piety to overcome the moral ambivalence of newly gained wealth (Gopalakrishnan 2006, 2807; Nanda 2012, 104–05). Similarly, faith-based voluntary organizations in Turkey promote charitable work for social assistance and welfare provisioning (Kaya 2015). Egypt's religious associations also form "a pious neoliberalism by drawing on a globalized religious discourse of volunteerism and faith and combining it with widespread individualism and entrepreneurship" (Atia 2012, 811). Neo-Pentecostal churches balance such opposing tendencies by promoting "conspicuous" consumption and charity simultaneously (Maxwell 1998, 363).

The actors that mediate religion and neoliberalism in these societies also form customized messages and responses for the losers of neoliberalism. The Indian state aims to co-opt lower castes and Dalits into Hindutva discourse and neoliberal hegemony particularly by promoting a unified Hindu identity against the Muslims in India (Gopalakrishnan 2006, 2808; Rajagopal 2001, 34). Turkey's AKP also encourages the poor to rationalize their suffering by seeing "poverty as a blessing and a test" (Tuğal 2009, 218, 224) while preaching morality and family structure as response to market deprivation.

Similarly, in order to provide the society, especially the urban poor, with a moral framework against moral breakdown and feelings of deprivation, neo-Pentecostalism promotes personal transformation as a key theme for "a shift from seeing oneself as victim to seeing oneself as victor" (Freeman 2012, 12), or as a "conqueror" through taking control of one's life (Van Dijk 2012, 104). Moreover, it promotes survival entrepreneurship and penny capitalism or informal economic activities for the losers of global neoliberalism (Maxwell 1998, 355; Martin 1990, 206; Martin 1995, 111) while also promoting community formation on the basis of faith through social work and charity to develop collective but informal responses to the societal problems created by neoliberalism (Adeboye 2004, 149–50; Dilger 2007, 72; Barker 2007, 427; Robbins 2004, 131).

The declining role of the state due to neoliberal policies in these societies has created a void in material and cultural provisions for their citizens; civil society organizations and religious institutions become main agents that provide social services and create a sense of belonging and conscience. These instances also illustrate how middle-class actors in religious institutions and faith-based organizations as well as in politics and the corporate sector play a crucial role in pro-systemic articulations of religion and neoliberalism. Such articulations owe their hegemonic success to customized religious messages for the winners and losers of neoliberal capitalism; they simultaneously delink individuals from society with discourses such as individual prosperity for the middle class and self-control for the lower class, while also creating a sense of community with practices such as charity for the middle class along with care and support networks for the lower class. Religious discourses and practices normalize and de-politicize neoliberalism, which ascribes the responsibility for correcting its systemic problems to piety. In this way, pro-systemic articulations bring diverse sectors together and build cross-class coalitions that actively form and support a pious and neoliberal order.

Anti-systemic Alternatives

Religion also takes part in anti-systemic movements, which construct and promote alternative worldviews that incorporate religious discourses and practices to challenge neoliberal capitalism. The rise of Liberation Theology in countries such as El Salvador and Nicaragua exemplifies an instance of an anti-systemic alternative to the capitalist system through religious ideology and organization (Billings and Scott 1994; Nepstad 1996). Emerging as both a product of and a response to the processes of secularization and industrialization, Liberation Theology in Latin America aims "to redefine the sacred as a set of moral principles which should be invoked in the wider society to reduce social inequalities and justice" (Jules-Rosette 1985, 223–24). It targets "the inequalities in the world-system of stratification; much of 'the space' for Liberation Theology has been created by the global interest in radical international inequality" (Robertson 1985, 354).

Political Islam also plays a role in anti-systemic religious movements by posing "a challenge to the central values that describe the dominant neo-liberal world order, particularly those values that legitimate the global political economy" (Evans 2011, 1751). Such movements employ "Islam as a 'revolutionary' ideology to attack, criticize, and de-legitimize the ruling elites and the power structure on which their authority and legitimacy is based" (Butko 2004, 41). A recent example is Turkey's anti-capitalist Muslims, who offer an alternative, leftist reading of Islamic texts and rituals against the government's hegemonic discourses that legitimize neoliberal capitalism through religious interpretations and practices (Evcimen 2017; Uestebay 2019).

Civil society actors such as religious institutions and non-governmental organizations mediate anti-systemic readings of religion. With their discourses and practices, Christian base communities in Latin America have challenged capitalist exploitation and authoritarian regimes (Billings and Scott 1994, 182).

They enabled grassroots mobilization of poor masses for transformative change by integrating revolutionary ideas within Catholic discourses and practices (Nepstad 1996, 105). By supporting the growth of such a religious interpretation against the official religion of traditional intellectuals, Nicaraguan and Salvadoran churches acted as organic intellectuals for counterhegemonic movements (Nepstad 1996, 109–10).

Similarly, religious actors and interpretations outside of Turkey's hegemonic religious institutions, which ally with political and corporate actors in supporting the marriage of Islam and neoliberalism, inform anti-capitalist Muslims. By forming their own religious discourses and practices, anti-capitalist Muslims also become organic intellectuals of Islamic leftism in Turkey (Evcimen 2017). The group draws members mainly from the youth and particularly appeals to university students (Uestebay 2019). Anti-capitalist Muslims bring together Islamic and leftist works both to build consciousness among existing members and to mobilize new members (Evcimen 2017; Uestebay 2019).

These actors create and advocate particular discourses and practices that mobilize pious sectors against neoliberal capitalism. For this purpose, Latin America's Liberation Theology promotes the following main principles: Theology should be contextually situated; the redefinition of sin as "structural oppression" rather than individual misdeed; and salvation is to be achieved in this world through a just society (Nepstad 1996, 110–11). Similarly, anti-capitalist Muslims in Turkey create a resistant form of political agency, particularly through practices like building solidarity with other oppositional sectors and implementing principles of radical democracy in their internal organization and interactions with other groups, and hence, challenge the pro-systemic articulation of Islam and neoliberalism in Turkey (Evcimen 2017). Members of this group also expressed critical politics and grassroots mobilization with their participation in Turkey's 2013 Gezi protests, which further facilitated their influence and organization (Uestebay 2019). With such discourses and practices, these agents oppose neoliberal hegemony and offer alternative worldviews with counterhegemonic potential.

Current Assemblages and Future Trajectories

How can we understand recent instances of the relationship between religion and neoliberalism and the current manifestations of pro- and anti-systemic forces in these processes? First of all, we are witnessing the rise of pro-systemic religious tendencies in the core and (semi-)periphery alike, especially with the surge in far-right politics and right-wing populism in countries such as the United States, Brazil, and Poland, along with the continuing dominance of neoliberal religious forces in societies like Turkey and India.

In the United States, the affiliations between contemporary evangelicalism and capitalism (Brown 2019) reinforce pro-systemic religious tendencies while the religious right's indispensable support for Trump presidency (Harris, Davidson, Fletcher, and Harris 2017) indicate the sociopolitical significance of religion for the reorganization of neoliberalism. Likewise, evangelicalism has been on the rise against liberation theology in Brazil and evangelicals played essential role in the election of far-right candidate Jair Bolsonaro to presidency (Antonopoulos, Ribeiro, and Cottle 2021). Also, the nationalist right in Poland and its conservative agendas against the LGBT community and the right to abortion reflects the rise of right-wing populism in complicity with the Catholic church and the ideological alliances among the Church leaders, right-wing columnists and radical nationalist right (Żuk and Żuk 2020). These instances accompany the strengthening of existing pro-systemic religious forces like Turkey's AKP regime (Mutluer 2019) and India's BJP rule (Bhatty and Sundar 2020). They also illustrate the processes through which pro-systemic religious discourses and practices are also gaining sociopolitical visibility and significance in the Global North, especially with the current rise of far-right politics in several core countries.[3]

More importantly, these instances indicate the current critical juncture as a crisis of neoliberal hegemony, a crisis in which hegemonic forces intensify sociopolitical polarizations to reorganize hegemonic blocs—the alliances among divergent groups—and ultimately to maintain their dominance. For instance, far-right politics in the United States arose as a mobilization of "white (male) rancor" (Brown 2019, 60) and as an alliance of neoliberal fundamentalists, the religious right and white nationalists from middle class, working class, and rural poor sectors (Harris, Davidson, Fletcher, and Harris 2017) against the existing neoliberal-democratic consensus, whose underpinnings encountered an existential shock with the current crisis of capitalist world-system. In other words, right-wing populists employ religious discourses and practices to overcome the crisis of capitalism, to offer an alternative pro-systemic vision to inoperative neoliberal-democratic consensus, and to restructure neoliberal hegemony. Such alternative constellations necessarily constitute and get constituted by sociopolitical polarizations that strengthen the rise of far-right politics as pro-systemic movements while also opening room for oppositional forces to build anti-systemic visions.

So, second, and relatedly, we are also witnessing the persistence of anti-systemic religious tendencies in core and (semi-)peripheral societies alike. These anti-neoliberal religious forces develop and enact both theories and practices of resistance and oppositional alternatives. For instance, resonating with the earlier iterations of liberation theology, Keri Day (2015) offers womanist and Black feminist theologies and experiences for forming resistance to neoliberal discourses and policies. In a similar vein, considering how religious leaders held candles and knelt in prayer in Ferguson protests (Ransby 2018), the role of religion in recent Black Lives Matter Movement or Movement for Black Lives in the U.S. also emerges as a potential instance of anti-systemic

40 Gamze Evcimen

groups that incorporate religious discourses and practices in their opposition to racial capitalism. Likewise, anti-capitalist Muslims in Turkey challenge and oppose the AKP's neoliberal hegemony while also forming alliances with other oppositional sectors as reflected in their slogans and activities in the 2013 Gezi protests (Evcimen 2017; Uestebay 2019).

These recent instances of anti-systemic religious views and tendencies point to the need for further research on the role of religious discourses and practices in the early twenty-first century protests, which have been bringing together divergent sociopolitical sectors, and hence, opening room for forming oppositional coalitions that can build resistance and alternatives to both the declining neoliberal-democratic consensus and the rising far-right constellations of neoliberal hegemony. This research can particularly address the counterhegemonic potential of anti-systemic religious forces by focusing on whether they promote and enact notions and practices like social peace and coexistence as venues for forming solidarity among widely divergent oppositional groups and as antidotes to the discourses of pro-systemic forces that employ religion to exacerbate societal polarizations. This focus arises a crucial research agenda and a political task in the current critical juncture that reflects the crisis of neoliberal hegemony.

Conclusions

Although (semi-)peripheral societies have been experiencing a surge in piety with the neoliberal turn, varied conceptualizations of religion and neoliberalism conceal the systemicity of such experiences. Reviving Terence Hopkins's methodological contribution opens room for regarding these concepts as relational categories and for studying the multifaceted articulations of the dynamic relationship between rising piety and neoliberalism in different (semi-)peripheral societies as part of the same systemic process. In this chapter, I developed and employed this perspective to illustrate how the discourses and practices of religion and neoliberal capitalism mutually constitute each other in these societies while also taking different forms based on particular sociohistorical contexts. My analysis also sheds light on how this systemic relationship also relates to, influences and is affected by the formation of new systemic and anti-systemic social forces in (semi-)peripheral societies.

This chapter offers a twofold intervention at this critical juncture: A theoretical and an epistemological rethinking of Hopkins's methodological contribution as a key lineage of world-systems analysis. Adopting a historical-relational approach to illustrate the systemic linkage of religion and neoliberalism, this chapter opens room for studying other manifestations of this relationship as a crucial agenda for world-systems analysis. Addressing particular discourses and practices of religion and neoliberalism that were developed and promoted by particular social forces, this approach also helps unveil and trace the constitutive agency of social actors in the assemblages of religion and neoliberalism in the Global South.

Notes

1. This chapter benefitted from the questions and feedback I received during my presentation at the 44th Annual Conference on the Political Economy of the World-System; many thanks to Patricio Korzeniewicz, Beverly Silver, and Corey Payne for organizing the PEWS 2020 conference amidst the COVID-19 pandemic. I am also indebted to Beverly Silver and Corey Payne for their extensive and insightful feedback on a previous version of this chapter. All errors are my own.
2. As Blackledge (2013) also suggests, this dialectic approach resonates with Linebaugh and Rediker's point on how slave ships served both as an engine of capitalism and a setting for resistance (2000: 144).
3. It is important to mention the divergence and the parallels in far-right's religious discourses and practices in the United States and European countries. The religious right and their social-conservative discourses are more visible in the former than the latter considering how the far-right in most European countries adopt a rigid, Eurocentric stance on secularism, and situate themselves against the religious freedoms of Muslim citizens and immigrants. Rogers Brubaker (2017) elaborates on how the contemporary European far-right politics deploys Christianity as a civilizational identity as follows: "Christianity is embraced not only as a religion but also as a civilizational identity understood in antithetical opposition to Islam. Secularism is embraced as a way of minimizing the visibility of Islam in the public sphere. Liberalism—specifically, philosemitism, gender equality, gay rights, and freedom of speech—is selectively embraced as a characterization of 'our' way of life in constitutive opposition to the illiberalism that is represented as inherent in Islam" (Brubaker 2017: 1194).

4

SYMBOLIC POWER AND GEOCULTURE IN THE WORLD-SYSTEM

Ottoman and Russian Perspectives

Juho Korhonen

Introduction

In this chapter, drawing from recent historical works, I use the examples of late Ottoman and Russian empires to explore how symbolic power has served to shape the world-system's geoculture and the core's hegemony. The world-system's geoculture is defined by Immanuel Wallerstein (2011, 220; 277) as forms of analyzing, perceiving, and categorizing the world, which in the long nineteenth century imposed its ideology "in three crucial spheres" of statehood, citizenship, and the historical social sciences.

By introducing Pierre Bourdieu's concept of "symbolic power" into world-systems analysis, I aim to draw attention to how the geoculture of the system was challenged and in fact developed through contestations for the symbolic meanings and definitions of the three spheres in the long nineteenth century. In this regard, I engage with Wallerstein's fourth volume on the history of the modern world-system, which takes as its central point the analysis of how the West culturally came to bridge the disjuncture between the world-system's political economy and its discursive rhetoric (2011). In the volume, Wallerstein prioritizes the importance of culture in understanding the transformations leading up to the First World War (1789–1914) and writes that

> the real social world changed remarkably during the nineteenth century. But the ways in which we perceived, analyzed and categorized the world changed even more. To the extent that we do not take cognizance of the latter, we exaggerate the former.
>
> *(Wallerstein 2011, 220)*

DOI: 10.4324/9781003325109-5

In a similar manner, for Bourdieu symbolic power refers to the forms of "the legitimate imposition of principles of visions and division of the social world" (Swartz 2013, 61–69). A "recognized authority" of symbolic power refers to "esteem, recognition, belief, credit, confidence of others" as publicly recognized social authority (Swartz 2013, 84). For example, historian Jane Burbank (2006, 398) notes that Bourdieu's approach can work well to analyze the "unrecognized, self-reproducing, and adjusting field of practiced empire" specifically in terms of how it changed as part of the world order.

I seek to show this through reviewing historical analyses of the Ottoman and Russian Empires that emphasize symbolic contestations. Recent historical research on these empires contradicts earlier retrospective analyses based on the core's geoculture. These examples show the importance and role of symbolic power in the political transformations that the lead to dominance of the core's geoculture for the twentieth century, as Wallerstein accounts (2011). They include contestations over issues such as redefinitions of sovereignty, the creation of the nation-state, international law, and the historical social sciences.

These two empires are chosen because they straddled the border of the core and the rest of the world-system in this period (1789–1914), during which symbolic control over the borderlands and peripheries became one of the key aims of the world-system's geoculture, as Wallerstein describes especially regarding the role of the historical social sciences. More specifically, it is in the responses of the geoculture to the symbolic power leveraged by alternative forms of analyzing, perceiving, and categorizing the world, which we can locate how that geoculture gained dominance and contained antisystemic movements, as well as dictated the ways in which we define, interpret, and thereby can challenge the world-system. In this period, a multiplicity of alternatives that contested the core's geoculture arose within and in interaction with the Russian and Ottoman Empires.

Geoculture in the Modern World-System 1789–1914

Before discussing historical examples, I will first describe briefly why the concept of geoculture calls for a focus on symbolic power. In the period leading up to WWI, Wallerstein (2011, xvi) takes as the "key happening" the creation of "a set of ideas, values, and norms" that came to constrain "social action." He identifies several key mechanisms of this geoculture; a particular definition of sovereignty that binds states and nations together and overlaps ideologies with states (instead of transnationally based ideologies), defines and limits what antisystemic movements can look like (especially regarding rights of subjecthood, i.e., citizenship), and finally, takes the historical social sciences as the guarantor of legitimizing this culture over others. As Wallerstein (2011, 277) summarizes, it was a configuration of values that bring together a particular understanding of states, citizens, and "modes of enabling dominant groups to control the dominated strata."

These mechanisms served to make the political symbolism and cultural memory of peoples' sovereignty a tool for "the privileged strata of the world-system" to "incorporate it institutionally in ways that would contain its potential for the radical dislocation of existing hierarchies" (Wallerstein 2011, 156–57). As shown in the following, it is often in alternatives to forms of polities, to the relation of sovereignty with subjecthood, and to local autonomy symptomatic of the West that we find the most pertinent symbolic contestations in the Ottoman and Russian Empires. Once alternatives are defined as impossible or inferior, the historical social sciences follow suit in confirming the West's model as the original one for inducing historical chance and development and occlude others from sight. Ultimately, the core's geoculture took the form of knowledge production and control that monopolized definitions of what political strategies, ways to describe the world, and ways to further change could look like (in order to actively control and limit it) (Wallerstein 2011). This symbolic power transformed how people perceived, analyzed, and categorized the world and thereby changed the world as much as "real social change" (Wallerstein 2011, xvi; 220).

As we learn from the examples that Wallerstein raises, from citizenship rights and women's suffrage to Orientalism and the creation of nationalist histories and myths, this process was in no sense uncontentious, smooth, or unilinear. Yet, due to the nature of the geoculture as part and parcel of the historical social sciences, we must analyze alternative and relational histories, those made irrelevant in the very process of the making of the geoculture's hegemony. Therefore, observing the symbolic contestations and alternatives that emerged in the Russian and Ottoman Empires informs us of the development and trajectory of the current geoculture. The historical examples discussed next aim to shed light on what that "disjunction" Wallerstein speaks of really meant, to specify the kinds of "social action" that were contained in bridging the disjunction, and, in doing so, speak specifically to how the three pillars of geoculture—polity, subjecthood, and the ways in which we analyze them—became interlinked.

Ottoman and Russian Examples

This section recounts a variety of intersecting historical examples from sovereignty and rule to identity and law that run counter to historical readings that take the geoculture's own historical and analytical narrative at face value. Ottoman and Russian Empires actively compared each other, and especially their respected relationships with empires of the Atlantic (Taki 2011). They both experienced a mismatch in terms of domestic sovereignty, subjecthood, and sovereign relations vis-à-vis Atlantic empires (Stephanov 2019). The narratives that the Russian and Ottoman Empires failed to reform their systems of rule, or that forces of nationalism and modernism were too much for them to resist, intentionally overlook the geocultural origins of the analytical lenses needed to produce such a view. Extensive and increasing work in the last decades has shown that this was not the case. Interactions were mutual, entangled, and interlaced inter-imperially. Many of the ideas that we now recognize as modern arose and first took shape in the imperial borderlands, already then as the result of earlier reconfigurations and reformulations that borrowed from and connected multiple locations and ideas across intra- and inter-imperial dimensions (Snyder and Younger 2018).

Mikhail and Philliou (2012, 723) correctly point out that "trying in vain to imitate the British or to call attention to their Mongol predecessors would hardly have garnered them [the Ottomans] any cache on the stage of world history." With this Mikhail and Philliou (2012, 723–24) point to the need for treating the Ottoman case much like Dominic Lieven's (2001) analysis of the Russian Empire, where the nature of power is analyzable only via and changes "in response to conflicts and tensions" with other empires of the world-system. Even if a particular geoculture was forming during the long nineteenth century based on and aligning with the political economic core of the Atlantic empires, this process nevertheless took place in reference to and within an international order that already included the Chinese, Russian, Ottoman, Persian, and other cases. There was never a spread or diffusion of the geoculture from the core to the rest. Focusing on Ottoman and Russian governance, identities, and their position within international law, we can highlight some conflicts of symbolic power related to the historical development of the geoculture in the long nineteenth century.

Identities

In the Ottoman Balkans fluid identities allowed for nationalism to be leveraged in favor of the imperial status quo and against attempts at constructing a liberal state of the Atlantic imperial variant (Sohrabi 2018). "Ottoman reality at the end of empire" was one of "overlapping, hybrid" citizenship claims, "with movement allowed more easily from one identity category into another" (Sohrabi 2018, 33). Sohrabi continues that "the Balkan nationalisms in general and Albanian nationalism in particular were interesting portrayals of what Brubaker has called ethnicity without groups (Brubaker 2002) or, better yet, ethnicities preceding groups" (ibid.) and as such contrary to, and even exhibiting a political movement that could undermine the exclusionist connection of citizenship with a national state as a central feature of the world-system's geoculture (Wallerstein 2011). The process of denying this alternative subjecthood arrived in waves to Ottoman Balkans: "With modernity coming in the form of nationalist low-scale feuds culminating into international warfare, territorial claims that imagined definitive borders and other pressures to bear fixed identities, the possibility of remaining ungoverned (Scott 2009) or permanently 'hybrid' was rapidly being ruled out" (Sohrabi 2018, 33).

Similarly, Deringil (2003, 341) observes in Ottoman Syria how subjects of the empire feared that the state could no longer protect them against "real colonialism": "Syria is Ottoman first, Arab second, and rejects any foreign interference. The Syrian nation holds fast to its Ottomanism and . . . does not wish for the policy of colonization to put an end to its national life." Against this, then, instead of an endogenous awakening, the particularly exclusive form of national subjecthood was a product of the symbolic power of imposing definitions and connections against a local national subjecthood, such as that in Ottoman Syria. Finally, "when the empire broke down, many of the publics it left behind were already politicized along ethnic lines" (Deringil 2003, 34). Where populations were not willing to accept a core-type nationalism tied to the state and notions of development and sovereignty, they were deemed not ready for national self-determination.

The Russian Empire similarly challenges "the notion that citizenship—both as a practice and a construct—need be restricted to polities that declare themselves founded on the principles of shared nationality and uniform rights—based on ethnicized or other homogenizing identifications of their populations," because such considerations, which Wallerstein considers one of the pillars of the geoculture, would set us astray "if we want to describe the modes of political expression, claim, and exercise of rights characteristic of the Russian Empire" (Burbank 2006, 397).

In the Russian Empire, contrary to the geoculture, "a kind of citizenship, enabled by governance based on differentiated rights, functioned" (Burbank 2006, 39). Much like with the Ottomans, this capacity of the sovereign polity of the Russian Empire led to problematic situations for the geoculture. How was it possible, that subjects of the Tsar were the first to enact a fully democratic state in the world? How could the core liberal states deal with the fact that these sovereign polities could at will privilege their political and economic peripheries against the core state? This ran counter to the aim of the geoculture to constrain social action that would hinder the expansion of the capitalist world-economy in line with Western national cores, such as the delineation between Europe and the rest and the justification of racialized imperialism, "crucial to the geopolitics and geoculture of the post-1789 world" (Wallerstein 2011, 58), and of course its associated universalist claims. In the Russian Empire "governance through social difference and through the imperial rights regime gave both rulers and subjects perspectives on politics that differ from those fortified by the ideals (and tensions) of natural and universal rights" (Burbank 2006, 430).

International Law

Unlike the Atlantic powers, who could depend on their position in the core of the world-economy, the Ottomans perceived the "the survival of the state and the survival of the empire" as one and the same and by 1914 European powers had set the Ottoman Empire under international isolation (Aksakal 2008, 2; 59). The Atlantic powers treated sovereign actors elsewhere in a manner that Horowitz calls "treaties and patterns of relations" that "would come to form a fundamental infrastructure of semicolonial political systems," where international law developed hand in hand with sovereign coercion; colonial occupation was avoided "at the cost of humiliating treaties" (Horowitz 2004, 447–48).

This was a slow movement of imposition that responded with one arm of the core's geoculture, when the other failed. Horowitz (2004, 448) shows how British actors characterized international law as an objective political science that "embodied key concepts about law, administrative organization, territoriality, and national identity" to which Ottoman and other non-core actors "adapted to maximize their autonomy" and increasingly approximated "the European models of a national state by the early twentieth century." Indeed, in the nineteenth century, international law was reconfigured from a naturalist conception to an idea that "international law was Christian in its origins and that only those non-Christian states that had reached a comparable level of 'civilization' could be treated as full participants in international law" (Horowitz 2004, 453). This effectively ruled out the recognition of any peripheral autonomous development. Horowitz points out the connection between international law and statehood: International law that was "embodied in unequal treaties and the associated discourse about civilization provided powerful external incentives for indigenous political elites to comply with this 'standard' European model of a national state" and a territorial and nationally defined conception of sovereignty (Horowitz 2004, 484–85).

In the Ottoman case, Atlantic Empires used this pretext to intervene in the Empire's domestic affairs. European consulates and embassies provided

> non-Muslim communities of the Empire with judicial immunity . . . the Ottoman ruling elite attempted to prevent European intervention via extraterritoriality by employing officials who had mastered European international law. Ironically, therefore, the Ottomans attempted to resist extraterritoriality by adopting European international law, requiring further emphasis on the teaching of this field of law.
>
> *(Palabiyik 2014, 7)*

Laws of extraterritoriality and capitulations in the Ottoman realm were not a direct colonial tool. After the Treaty of Paris in 1865, the Ottoman Empire had, at least symbolically, been accepted as part of the Great Powers. Indeed, a realistic account of the capitulations, according to Özs (2012, 429), "captures the distinctive fluidity of Ottoman-European relations . . . developed on the back of the insight that each capitulatory document was first and foremost a site of contestation." Ottoman–European relations were one of the key developing grounds of a particular international law as part of the geoculture, related as they were to the contested status of the Ottoman Empire itself both economically and as part of the world order. Even though the lower civilizational status of both Ottomans and Eastern Europeans featured in European debates over international law (Korhonen 2019) Russia engaged in similar contestations from a symbolically more powerful position as a Christian nation with Pan-Slavic claims across Europe and a stronger historical footing in the Concert of Europe.

Much like the Ottomans trained officials in European law, Russia used it symbolically in its favor. During the 1877 intervention of Russia in Turkey, the matter was considered as follows in favor of Russia by scholars of international law: "If some powers are unwilling to take the burden of humanity, this cannot mean that no other power may do this. After all 'fundamental principles of international law' are at issue" (Martens quoted in Koskenniemi 2005, 114). The criteria for excellence in international law were and are set by Europeans. It is a form of thought, just like the geoculture described by Wallerstein that generalizes European localities into a "representative of the universal" (Koskenniemi 2005, 114) specifically through symbolic intervention in the interfaces of contestation and difference.

Imperial Rule

From the Balkans and extraterritoriality, to Ottoman Egypt under British occupation, recent findings have shown "that nineteenth and early twentieth century European and Ottoman political practices and ideas were inextricably intertwined. The Ottoman Empire contributed to and was perhaps the key testing ground for enduring political and administrative experiments in the post-imperial international order" (Genell 2013, 6). Moreover, the question of Ottoman Egypt bears remarkable similarity to the question of Russian Finland that emerged just a little later in inter-imperial considerations. Egypt was ruled by the British under Ottoman sovereignty and Finland developed democratic statehood under Russian sovereignty after 1905. As Genell (2013, 3–5) has shown, the status of Egypt became entangled with "inter-imperial arguments about sovereignty, territory, and international law" and with "how we define state and sovereignty today."

And just like the Finnish Question under the Russian Empire, in retrospect the historiographies of the cases have become aligned with the geoculture of the world-system, that is, writing out the alternative Russian and Ottoman perspectives on sovereignty in favor of an understanding of the spread of the national state in the Atlantic metropolitan model to new regions of the world-system. This later understanding has occluded from sight how the Egyptian and Finnish Questions led to "a new model of client-state sovereignty" that "emerged out of the intense imperial rivalry between the Ottoman [and Russian] and European Empires in Egypt [and Finland] and had lasting significance more generally for how we define states and sovereignty today" (Genell 2013, 3).

Similarly, the Finnish Question, of how international law should treat a democratic polity under the Russian Empire, became entangled with the geoculture's alignments with sovereignty, civilization, statehood, and race. Volumes were written and conferences convened in the West, most famously the London Conference in 1910. Among the signatories of that conference's outcome were professors of law from Oxford, Cambridge, Berlin, Göttingen, Paris, Grenoble, and Leiden (Finnland und Russland: Die internationale Londoner Konferenz 1911). Their "scientific explanation" boiled in the end down to race, temperament, and customs "giving form to political freedom, which cannot be removed from its substance" (ibid., 103). The ultimate grounding of their argument was that it is a legal question of a racial kind, and therefore arguing in favor of the interests of the Empire is not correct, since the question is not one of politics or interests, but of "social development." The important difference here is that these legal scholars state explicitly that the historical, racial, temperamental, and customary right of Finnish autonomy, is in no way connected to its statehood, which it has rather achieved due to its connection to the inferior Russians (ibid. 112), thus suggesting that under Western sovereignty Finland would have naturally appeared relatively less autonomous, that is, it would not even have had the need to develop peripheral autonomy.

Where one aspect of the geoculture would fail, liberal statehood in this case, the other two, Western subjecthood rights and legal and social sciences would join hands to lift the third from the ground. What was overlooked, was the position of peripheral actors themselves, in this case the Finns, who, not unlike the Syrians or Albanians discussed earlier, were not arguing against the Empire or its sovereignty, but simply for local autonomy and democracy as part of it, delinked from matters of the core and from inter-imperial sovereignty, something that has become unthinkable with the geoculture's hegemony.

Ultimately, encounters with these forms of non-sovereign power, in the geoculture's sense, aided in developing dominance without exposing weaknesses and led to the mandates system of the League of Nations and to Soviet nationalities policies. Both for Egypt (1922) and for Finland (1919), the recognition of formal independence from Britain and the US came only in the form of externally modeled statehood. This was the universalization of "global territorialization of sovereignty" (Genell 2013, 224) by the geoculture: "formal

50 Juho Korhonen

sovereignty could reside in Egypt, as it had in the Ottoman Sultan during the occupation, while Britain administered core functions of the state" (Ibid., 225).

Tellingly, in both cases, the form of sovereign independence was unilaterally imposed by the Allies. Yet, this solution stemmed from the very core problemacy that had made the Finnish and Egyptian questions so debated, this independence "paradoxically removed Egypt from the sphere of international politics and legal contest and publicity" (Genell 2013, 226), as it did for Finland.

What comes to subjecthood rights applies similarly to the connected issue of constitutionalism in the Russian and Ottoman Empires. Ottoman and Russian constitutions were founded upon their own polities of imperial diversity and composite rule, which was "at the center of political practices and imaginaries" (Semyonov 2020, 30) of these reforms, reflecting the different citizenship regimes. As such they lacked similar exclusionist elements that Wallerstein puts at the center of the core liberal states' constitutional citizenship regimes (Wallerstein 2011). Furthermore, these constitutionalisms equally aimed to straddle the "global transformation of political life" in the early twentieth century and "nested possibilities of compromise and redefinition of political solidarity in the space of diversity" (Semyonov 2020, 30), and thus presented a challenge to the symbolic power of the geoculture. Returning to the case of Finnish democratization as part of the Russian constitutional reforms offers a clear-cut example of this: "Retained and reshaped in 1906 the traditional logic of [Russian] imperial sovereignty helped quite paradoxically to achieve universal suffrage in the reformed Sejm of the Grand Duchy of Finland" (Semyonov 2020, 32). This, in fact, moved the Grand Duchy in a revolutionary transformation from the most antiquated system of representation in Europe to the most progressive in the world, providing a further counterargument to claims of diffusion, civilizational development modeled on the core's trajectory.

These challenges to the geoculture thus come in the form of shattering its symbolic universalism and narratives of development by the means of showing an alternative perception and categorization of the relations of sovereignty, citizenship rights, and international law. This compromises the interlinked effects of the geoculture's three pillars in defining forms of polities, forms of subjecthood, and the historical social sciences, and the ways in which these can be analyzed and linked to each other

As Semyonov further summarizes, this

> renewed logic of imperial sovereignty cast the Finnish situation in a legal perspective and foregrounded the individual treatment of this part of the imperial realm in accordance with local peculiarities of the Duchy and the pluralism of the imperial space as a whole.
>
> *(Semyonov 2020, 33)*

The Russian and Ottoman cases present an alternative to the geoculture that allows us more analytical leverage in analyzing it:

> The idea that western European countries by the early 20th century had a working democratic government thanks to the formation of nation-state in the metropole of the colonial empire needs to be reconsidered together with the idea of symbiotic relations between nation and democracy.
> *(Semyonov 2020, 37; see also Korhonen 2019)*

The forms of government based on political rights of all citizens took their own decidedly different and for the core liberal states possibly compromising forms in the Russian and Ottoman realms in that they "coexisted with a commitment to communal rights or at least communal governance. In both the Ottoman and Russian empires, these notions of rights coexisted in tandem, often without conflict but with some tension" (Khoury and Glebov 2017, 53). Indeed, as the geoculture of world-economy consolidated its position, it did so based on the alternatives it learned from and sought to eliminate and appropriate on its way. The geoculture of the core was made and its main claims and the mutually reinforcing relations of its constituent parts, as Wallerstein recounts them (the universalistic assumptions of the connections between polity, subjecthood, and the analysis of the two through the historical social sciences), emerged from inter-imperial symbolic contestations.

In the end, the ultimate power of the particular geoculture of the world-system was not in its difference and separation from the non-core empires, or in its reliance on the core against the rest, but in its embeddedness with the non-core. Through an understanding of the "malleable compacts established between state and social actors" (Barkey 2008, 6, quoted in Mikhail and Philliou 2012, 733) in the Ottoman empire, the Atlantic empires, not least through their application of international law for the Ottoman and Russian realms, tested and formulated an inextricable link between subjecthood, states and their definitions, and analysis of them. A descriptive analogy, though one not to be taken too straightforwardly, is of the Ottoman Empire as a laboratory (Mikhail and Philliou 2012, 744), not as the object of tests, but as an environment in which the developing geoculture of the world-system was tested, scrutinized, rethought, and propelled forward. In this regard, Kolluoğlu (2013, 535–36) has shown how population movements in the Ottoman Empire "prepared the historical background that made internationally sanctioned forced population transfers both a viable and a thinkable possibility" and crucially contributed to the definition of "refugee."

Mikhail and Philliou (2012, 743) suggest that we need to "begin to think beyond these [two-dimensional] images to examine the positive processes going on in the space 'between'—not the assumed void, but an arena of intense contestation between a panoply of forces, actors, and places." Deringil (2003,

52 Juho Korhonen

312) brings forth a similar argument in how the late Ottoman empire aimed to compete on the world-stage that was set by the core of world-system, to gain the same symbolic power, but did so with their own "grab bag of concepts, methods and tools of statecraft, prejudices, and practices." This greatly contributed to the consolidation of the geoculture. For example, the greater negotiation power of the Ottoman and Russian subjects was closely monitored and even exploited by the Atlantic empires.

Conclusion—Symbolic Power in the World-System

Wallerstein (2011, 267) describes geocultural dominance and its function as follows: It aided "the powerful to govern their charges and/or deal with other civilizations more intelligently and more effectively" and "abetted reforms that served to limit conflict and above all radical subversion of the status quo of pan-European geopolitical power." This becomes clearer specifically in its applications vis-à-vis the non-core, where, Wallerstein (2011, 265) writes, it served the connected purpose of rendering the particular political relations and dynamics there as ahistorical, "meaning that they had not changed, developed, progressed over historical time."

The examples discussed earlier show the importance of analyzing conflicts over symbolic power and that this cannot be done without being historically reflexive about the core's geoculture, including the social sciences. Indeed, Bourdieu's symbolic power refers to "the more subtle and influential forms of power that operate through cultural resources and symbolic classifications that interweave everyday life with prevailing institutional arrangements" (Swartz 2013, 233). These are also the analyses, perceptions, and categorizations of the world that Wallerstein discusses, showing how they lead to control over the variety of emerging options and to the occlusion of past and present alternatives. He refers to transformational "TimeSpace," a concept that seeks to capture

> the struggle within the world of knowledge, which determines whether we can clarify the historical alternatives that we face, make more lucid our choices, both criticize and empower those who are engaged in the political struggle (from which of course the world of knowledge is unable to dissociate itself).
>
> *(Wallerstein, Lemert, and Rojas 2013, 181)*

Any analytical efforts to achieve this, must thereby be imbued with enough historical self-reflexivity to escape the confines of the world-systems' geoculture dominated by the core. A symbolic power-centered approach is one way to achieve this as it is a core mechanism of the geoculture to enforce its own interpretation over alternatives.

Contested moments of transformation at the borders of the geoculture in the long nineteenth century offer a historical perspective into analyzing acts of omission and appropriation by the geoculture through symbolic power. Analytically we can approach this by considering Wallerstein and Bourdieu together: The core's geoculture achieved this kind of control by monopolizing idées-forces. Steinmetz (2008, 607) introduces the concept of idées-forces from Bourdieu's *Propos sur le champ politique*. An idée-force directly addresses or intervenes in the political field's definitional struggles; it sets the stakes. These are the performative ideas used to compete for symbolic power in the political field with varying connections to other fields, including power. Wallerstein calls the equivalent of this "political metastrategies" (2011, 1) and outlines them historically as the self-referencing trinity of radicalism, liberalism, and conservatism, where one could not be considered without the two others. Just as for Bourdieu's idées-forces the state was the end result of any struggle, so too for Wallerstein the glue of the three ideologies was their joint promotion of the particular modern state (2011, 11–16; 143–44). For Bourdieu, to vie for symbolic power is to vie for the state; to present idées-forces is to talk about the state; the state's symbolic dimension is an "effect of universality" (Swartz 2013, 130). This modern state emerges from attempts to deal with ambiguities of governance (Swartz 2013, 132), in other words peripheral or autonomous developments and movements delinked from the core and its geoculture.

I propose, therefore, that only by understanding the making of the world-system's geoculture in reference to the alternatives that it appropriated and eviscerated can we make any strides toward "the serious assessment of historical alternatives, the exercise of our judgment as to the substantive rationality of alternative possible historical systems" (Wallerstein 1998, 1). A key example is whether and how we differentiate between antisystemic movements based on and defined by the core's geoculture and those that originated autonomously, not in reference to the core. To do so, we should historically inquire more into how the geoculture "took further form in stimulating the creation, and limiting the impact, of the major kinds of antisystemic movements" (Wallerstein 2011, xvi). I have done so here by considering the alternative spaces and relations in the Ottoman and Russian empires that at times fostered situations and relations ungovernable for the Atlantic empires, or, in effect, challenged the core's geoculture's symbolic power.

5

RECONSTRUCTING COMMODITY CHAIN ANALYSIS AS WORLD-SYSTEMS ANALYSIS

David A. Smith, Paul S. Ciccantell, and Elizabeth A. Sowers

Introduction

Commodity chain analysis emerged as an integral part of world-systems analysis early on (Hopkins and Wallerstein 1986). Commodity chains constitute the building blocks and sinews of the capitalist world-economy. Efforts to create and restructure commodity chains drive the geographic expansion and reorganization of the world-system as core economies and rising challengers seek markets, raw materials, and cheap labor, facilitating capital accumulation on a world-scale (Wallerstein 1974b; Arrighi 1994; Bunker and Ciccantell 2005).

The analytic power of focusing on particular global commodity chains (GCCs) motivated a growing literature in the late twentieth century within this tradition (see, e.g., Gereffi and Korzeniewicz 1994). The empirical insights attracted wide attention and were later rebranded under the label "global value chains" (GVCs) (Bair 2009, Introduction). Over time, much of this work became divorced from the world-systems theoretical framework and its critical emphasis on capitalist power and class relations, the inherent generation of inequalities, and long-term processes of hegemonic competition and economic ascent. Instead, the evaluation of particular production chains increasingly focused on economic efficiency and the potential for "upgrading" to create economic development, particularly in globalized manufacturing industries such as clothing and electronics (see, e.g., Gereffi and Memdovic 2003; O'Riain 2004; Schrank 2004; Gereffi 2018).

Efforts are underway to bring a critical perspective back into commodity chain analysis in a variety of ways (Bair 2005, 2009; Bridge 2008; Ciccantell 2022). In this chapter, we contribute a focus on what we term "raw materialist lengthened global commodity chains" (Sowers, Ciccantell, and Smith

DOI: 10.4324/9781003325109-6

2017, 2018). Our formulation returns to Hopkins and Wallerstein's (1982, 1986) emphases on examining class relations, spatiotemporal relations, capital accumulation, the role of states in the interstate system, and long-term social change. Building on key pioneering insights about the roles of slavery and racism in the construction, development, and long-term change of the modern world-system (Rodney 1982; Bush 1999, 2009; Williams 1944), we integrate our recent work on capital–labor relations, contestation, and resistance at particular nodes in commodity chains (Bair and Werner 2011) and chokepoints that present opportunities/constraints for labor and social movement organizations (Sowers, Ciccantell, and Smith 2014, 2017, 2018). In the following section, we reclaim the original Hopkins/Wallerstein understanding of commodity chains and then present our raw materialist lengthened global commodity chains framework. In the remaining sections, we turn to three themes central to a critical commodity chains approach: contestation, class, and race.

The Original Formulation of Commodity Chains and the Shift to Developmentalism

In their original formulation of commodity chains in the capitalist world-economy, Hopkins and Wallerstein (1982, 1986) sought to systematize the sometimes amorphous understandings of underdevelopment and the relationship between the development of the core and the underdevelopment of the periphery (see, e.g., Frank 1966; Jalee 1968; Cardoso and Faletto 1979). The broad processes of surplus extraction, unequal exchange, and exploitation could be concretely examined by analyzing the material processes in particular industries that extracted raw materials (mineral and biological), labor ("free" or enslaved), agricultural land and its produce, or other forms of wealth from peripheries to enrich core states and firms. From the late 1400s and early 1500s, European states established trade networks and imperial expansion strategies that gained control over raw materials, labor and land, linking cores and peripheries, and built global commodity chains. This shaped the geographic expansion of the capitalist world-economy, the incorporation of lands and peoples as nodes in these chains supported European industrialization, and impoverished peripheries.

Hopkins and Wallerstein (1977) proposed:

> take an ultimate consumable item and trace back the set of inputs that culminated in this item—the prior transformations, the raw materials, the transportation mechanisms, the labor input into each of the material processes, the food inputs into the labor. This linked set of processes we call a commodity chain.

(1977, 128)

56 David A. Smith et al.

Put differently, a global commodity chain (GCC) is a "network of labor and production processes whose end result is finished commodity" (1986, 159). The idea of GCCs explains how local and national economies are integrated by specifying the links among the different processes or segments within the global chain.

One recent analyst (Khalili 2020, 111), quoting Walter Rodney (1982), argues that the emergence of transport networks, such as roads and railways, single-mindedly designed to move African raw material exports to the sea, were crucial "sinews" of the world-economy. While these commodity chains led to underdevelopment and resource drain in Africa, they were critical to facilitate long-term change in the capitalist world-economy over the past five centuries. Economies and states that created the most secure and lowest cost transport networks for their raw materials-based commodity chains gained critical advantages in the process of economic ascent and in challenging other states for hegemonic positions in the capitalist world-economy (Bunker and Ciccantell 2005, 2007).

The Hopkins and Wallerstein formulation of commodity chains took a critical stance toward the workings of core states and firms, whether via direct imperialism or via control over trade networks, investment capital, and markets. As Rodney (1982, 75) puts it,

> development and underdevelopment . . . have a dialectical relationship one to the other: that is to say, the two help produce each other by interaction. Western Europe and Africa had a relationship which insured the transfer of wealth from Africa to Europe.

However, more recently, the critical stance inherent in the world-systems' conceptualization of commodity chains largely disappeared from the now-dominant GCC/GVC literature.

The underlying objective of the shift of GCC analysis away from this original formulation was to understand an increasingly integrated global economy where countries or regions could occupy distinct "export niches" via strategic "industrial upgrading" (Gereffi 1994; Gereffi and Korzeniewicz 1994)—arguably, a product of the time and the rise of a New International Division of Labor (see Frobel, Heinrichs, and Kreye 1980). Gereffi and Korzeniewicz (1994) conceptualize these chains as consisting of a number of "nodes" comprising pivotal points in the production process: Beginning with extraction and supply of raw materials/agricultural products, then moving through stage(s) of industrial transformation, export of goods, and marketing. Each node is itself a network connected to other nodes of related activity; local, regional, and world-economies are ever more intricate web-like structures of these chains. But global commodity chains are more than just sequences of *production*—product *marketing, coordination, and control* of integrated global networks are crucial,

Reconstructing Commodity Chain Analysis **57**

and may be much more lucrative (see Gereffi and Korzeniewicz 1994: Part IV especially).

Gary Gereffi developed his updated GCC framework in the 1980s as the world underwent global economic restructuring, focusing particularly on recent dependent development in Latin America and East Asia (see Gereffi and Wyman 1990). His focus was on the "global shift" (Dicken 1992) of the second half of the twentieth century, linked to rapidly changing communication and transportation technologies, new products and technological innovations, unprecedented powers of multinational firms, and the rise of a "global assembly line" (cf. Ross and Trachte 1990). This approach tended to be rather "presentist": not only jettisoning the historical depth of the original formulation but also foreclosing the possibility that, perhaps, what seemed new/unique was an echo of longer-term processes and cycles. One key aspect of the worldwide production shift was a fundamental change from an industrial capitalist organization form with vertically integrated corporate control over all the backward and forward linkages to a model where "big buyers" shape production networks via outsourcing to other firms—and often globally dispersed production units. To a large degree, this distinction between producer- and buyer-driven chains reflects the type of industry or organization of labor relations. Producer-driven vertically integrated firms also tended to give way to more "flexible" production via a buyer-driven organization—with implications for the relationship between capital and states, business and labor, the "distribution of surplus" along the chain, and the developmental impacts where GCC infrastructure is located (Gereffi 1996).

Gereffi's framing shifted to the language of GVCs, terminology now widely used in geography, business, economics, and even the World Bank, and the potential for commodity chains to foster "development" became the focus of this approach. The enshrinement of this approach in the mainstream analysis of development in the World Bank's *World Development Report 2020: Trading For Development in the Age of Global Value Chains* reveals the widespread acceptance of this terminology, even as trade wars are threatening to disrupt globalization, an acknowledgement made in the World Development Report 2020 itself (World Bank Group 2020). In our view, the shift to GVC terminology marked not just a move toward meso-level analysis and away from long-term, historical processes, but also a move away from the critical stance of world-systems analysis.

Most charitably, the shift to "developmentalism" in commodity chain analysis could be seen as a route to dependent development (Evans 1979), offering some opportunities for upward mobility to some particularly astute and/or fortunate states and economies. But Walter Rodney almost certainly would have used a less charitable term, such as "bourgeois economism," to describe the reformulation of the original concept of commodity chains, as material processes linking the underdevelopment of peripheries to the development and

Raw Materialist Lengthened Global Commodity Chains

The raw materialist lengthened GCCs approach (Ciccantell and Smith 2009) was developed precisely because of the lack of attention to the upstream end of commodity chains, parts of the chain that are profoundly different from "footloose" labor-intensive factories on which the extant literature focused. The raw materialist model (Bunker and Ciccantell 2005, 2007) begins from a focus on the material process of economic ascent in the capitalist world-economy. Over the past five centuries, rapidly growing economies sought to obtain raw materials in large and increasing volumes to supply their continued economic development in the context of economic and geopolitical cooperation/conflict with the existing hegemon and other rising economies. Economies of scale in resource extraction, processing and transport reduce costs and create competitive advantages relative to the existing hegemon and other rising economies. But raw materials depletion and increasing distance create diseconomies of space (increasing costs of raw material transport from distant extractive peripheries) that make finding economic, technological, and sociopolitical fixes to sustaining economic ascent via increasing economies of scale difficult to achieve, maintain, and eventually reconstruct on an even larger scale.

These processes of economic ascent and economic and geopolitical hegemonic competition drove long-term change in the capitalist world-economy over the past five centuries (Bunker and Ciccantell 2005), and the most dramatic and rapid instances restructured national economies and the world-economy in support of national economic ascent. The competitive advantages created by organizational and technological innovations in generative sectors and by subsidies (e.g., low-cost raw materials from peripheries), lead to global trade dominance. The most successful cases of ascent restructure and progressively globalize the world-economy, incorporating and reshaping economies, ecosystems, and space (Bunker and Ciccantell 2005, 2007).

The raw materialist lengthened global commodity chains model (Ciccantell and Smith 2009; Sowers, Ciccantell, and Smith 2014, 2017) begins its analysis of commodity chains by focusing on raw materials extraction and processing, and on transport and communications. These technologies link multiple nodes of commodity chains from raw materials sources through industrial processing, to consumption, and eventually waste disposal. This materially and spatially grounded approach allows analysis of the economic, social, and environmental dimensions of these chains at each node.

Equally important, this approach provides a lens to examine spatially based disarticulations (the marginalization or outright elimination of particular nodes) (Bair and Werner 2011) and contestations over extraction, processing, transport, consumption, and waste disposal across these chains. This grounded analysis can examine development trajectories and the sociopolitical conflicts over the division of costs and benefits in particular nodes and across these commodity chains. This approach highlights the role of contestation and resistance to the construction and reproduction of a particular commodity chain in particular places (Ciccantell and Smith 2009; Sowers, Ciccantell, and Smith 2014, 2017).

To return to the more critical stance advocated by world-systems analysis, we now turn to three areas that are underexplored in the more developmentalist approaches to commodity chains: contestation, class, and race.

Emphasizing the Roles of Labor, Resistance, and Chokepoints

In a recent paper (Sowers, Ciccantell, and Smith 2018), our animating question involved whether labor and social movements can capitalize on interrupting flows of commerce at the points of extraction, processing, or transportation: Are there "chokepoints" that can be exploited to disrupt those chains and possibly either win benefits or force reconfiguration of production networks? Our raw materialist lengthened GCC approach provides a guide for some key factors that might make disruption possible. Our empirical examples provide evidence of both vulnerabilities for labor and social movement organizations to capitalize upon, and challenges that might impede organization (Sowers, Ciccantell, and Smith 2018). In effect, we invert the analytic focus of the GVC approach, seeking not to identify opportunities for states and capital to promote "development" but instead to examine the opportunities for labor unions and social movements to capture benefits from commodity chains or at least ameliorate the potential worst social and environmental impacts of commodity chains via contestation.

Some of the key vulnerabilities stem from the global integration and capital intensiveness of each commodity chain. In terms of global economic integration, the importance of containerized consumer products and oil to the vitality of today's world-economy suggests these chokepoints could be places of power. Increased reliance on "just-in-time" delivery for goods flowing through U.S. ports doubtlessly provides workers at those nodes added leverage. Capital intensiveness and technological sophistication offer challenges and opportunities for labor/SMO interests. Oil pipelines, massive ports, and other large infrastructural investments represent vast "sunk" investments that are much more difficult to relocate than factories or other processing facilities. This offers physically fixed chokepoints in some GCCs that might be eminently vulnerable (for instance, on ports and labor, see Bonacich and Wilson 2008; on the vulnerability of just-in-time production see Herod 2000).

Long commodity chains, however, do present some challenges to insurgents bent on using positional power for disruption. Today's GCCs are complex and far-flung, involving disparate groups of workers in spatially distinct locations, which challenge concerted and coordinated action. Furthermore, the relevant workforces are not evenly organized: Some may be unionized, others subcontractors, or "independent contractors," still other workers contingent or even informal workers. While it is rather easy to see the potential for shared concerns between human rights SMOs and labor, tensions between labor and those who want to defend the environment might be an obstacle to solidarity.

In a related paper (Sowers, Ciccantell, and Smith 2017), we sought to address the following question: Is the contemporary moment one where labor and SMOs can capitalize on interrupting flows of commerce at the points of extraction, processing, or transportation? Our examination highlights opportunities and constraints across three critical commodity chains: containerized manufactured goods, petroleum, and coal, three of the commodity chains that each of us have analyzed extensively—and represent distinct types of GCCs. In terms of challenges to labor organization, the fragmented production of containerized manufactured goods, the separation between the extraction, refining, processing, and consumption of oil, and long distances across which much coal now travels, all constitute significant obstacles to labor organizing, since the span and dispersion of each commodity chain means that multiple groups of spatially distanced and unevenly organized workers would need to be united into a focused labor action across time and space. With many locations that could produce labor-intensive manufactured goods, extract oil, and mine coal and multiple transportation routes for each commodity to consuming nations, this potential for fungibility and restructuring of commodity chains for capital greatly constrains labor and social movements, since there are no single chokepoints available in each commodity chain. This means that coordination of efforts across multiple chokepoints is likely to be needed for success (e.g., coordination between coal mining unions in Australia and Canada, two of the world's largest coal exporters, would likely to be needed to significantly increase wages by leaving coal exporting and importing firms without alternative sources). Tensions between labor and the environment are also relevant here, given that environmental concerns about extraction are often at odds with the priorities of unions and firms. Potential collaboration between human rights SMOs and labor interests based on shared concerns to expand the rights and protections of workers in shipping and mining might prove more promising (Sowers, Ciccantell, and Smith 2017).

One opportunity for labor and SMOs to gain power in GCCs is to create what we term diseconomies of resistance. The liquefied natural gas (LNG) industry began as a means to make use of natural gas resources in socially remote regions. In a fundamental sense, this natural gas was transformed from a waste product of little human use into LNG that could be moved thousands of miles to market. Another redefinition of nature propelled the U.S.'s emergence as the newest large-scale LNG exporter: the extraction of natural gas and oil from shale formations previously economically and technologically inaccessible to humans. Hydraulic fracturing (fracking) and new drilling technologies transformed useless rock into immense reserves of natural gas and oil that drove down prices with excess production and fomented a search for new markets around the world via LNG processing (Ciccantell 2020).

Fracking for natural gas and oil and the need for pipelines to move this oil and gas to U.S. markets and/or LNG export facilities have generated substantial resistance in many parts of the U.S., raising the costs and risks of investments in these industries, particularly in Pennsylvania and New York, a key form of diseconomies of resistance. Much controversy focused on Keystone XL for oil sands oil, but there are a number of natural gas pipelines facing similar resistance, effectively raising the cost of space for some regions' fracked gas, sometimes prohibitively. In a sense, fracking in Pennsylvania and New York ought to suffer the least because of their nearness to huge markets, but serious obstacles to sustained growth exist from the social and political diseconomies of resistance.

While other scholars, such as those working in the supply chain management (SCM) and global value chain (GVC) fields, do attend to issues of labor relations, the critical GCC approach that we use here offers several advantages. By way of a quick summary, labor within the SCM field is typically approached through a lens of efficiency, while GVC scholars often look at how labor is managed and incorporated in GVCs (Taylor, Newsome, Bair, and Rainnie 2015, however recent scholarship works to bring labor "back in" as a central object of GVC analysis, e.g., Newsome, Taylor, Bair, and Rainnie 2015). Our lengthened GCC approach, in contrast, takes labor and labor relations as constitutive elements of global commodity chains and turns other analyses on their heads: While many study how labor is managed within commodity chains with an eye toward efficient operations, we instead investigate how labor-based disruptions can be utilized by strategic actors to improve working conditions. Whether it is through the study of logistics "chokepoints" or LNG diseconomies of resistance, our approach offers the opportunity to view labor in a new light as not just a factor of commodity chains to be managed, but instead as a source of dynamism and change, shaping, and reshaping not only commodity chains but also potentially even the world around them.

Bringing Race Back Into Commodity Chain Analysis

Issues of race, racism, and resistance are at the core of the logistics industry and its operation as a GCC. Alimahomed-Wilson (2020) notes that, in the global picture, logistics networks are run by white men supervising large labor forces of people of color in warehouses and other low-level jobs. This is well illustrated in the US. Research demonstrates that employing vulnerable populations of immigrants in warehouses is a key strategy through which firms successfully provide the logistical support required by flexible, just-in-time production (Ciscel, Smith, and Mendoza 2003); while there may be an uptick of women working in warehouses, recent measures of the warehousing workforce still show that labor force remains predominantly male—66.4% in 2020 (Current Population Survey 2020; Gutelis and Theodore 2019). Port truck driving relies in the U.S. on a low-wage labor force made up of men of color and immigrants, in contrast to the white, native-born workers who were the majority of the trucking workforce earlier in history (Bonacich and Wilson 2008; Reifer 2004). Recent research demonstrates racism and racial violence among West Coast longshore workers, in spite of the antiracist founding commitments of their labor union (Alimahomed-Wilson 2016). Considering these insights together suggests that race and racism are constitutive elements of the logistics commodity chain, just as it is foundational to justify hierarchy and exploitation across the capitalist world-economy (Wallerstein 1990; see also O'Hearn and Ciccantell 2022). This dynamic is key to corporate strategies to divide workers and cut costs, and it makes labor solidarity and cooperation difficult. Just as in Rodney's (1982) analysis of the historical underdevelopment of Africa, racism is embedded in the very sinews of contemporary capitalism even in this era of e-commerce.

The natural gas and oil industries and resistance to pipelines also brings to the forefront the role of race, racism, and resistance in world-systems analysis. Native American resistance to pipelines in the U.S. in recent years evidence the central role of race in analyzing the construction of and resistance to the sinews underlying GCCs (Fenelon 2022).

More generally, Ciccantell and Gellert (2022) demonstrate that race and racism shape resource frontiers and extractive peripheries and constitute a central element of world-systems-based analysis of the upstream end of GCCs. The impacts of resource frontiers and extractive peripheries on existing populations, and especially indigenous populations, are almost universally negative (see, e.g., Hall and Fenelon 2009; Gedicks 2001; Bodley 2014; Mann 2006), engendering often strong and violent opposition from indigenous groups (Ciccantell and Gellert 2022). Overall, as Rodney (1982) argued regarding Africa, racialized indigenous groups are the most frequent victims of severe underdevelopment in resource frontiers and extractive peripheries (Ciccantell and Gellert 2022).

The issue of labor exploitation is of particular theoretical importance. While labor is included in Moore's (2015) model of four "cheap things," labor is often not cheap on a resource frontier. Labor is typically scarce, living conditions are difficult for outsiders, and frontiers are typically socially remote. All these factors lead to (relatively) high wages in resource frontiers, at least those that do not rely on enslaved labor, debt peonage, indentured servitude, exiled criminals, or other forms of coerced labor. A more permanent pool of exploitable (relatively cheap) labor is thus vital to the transition into a more permanent extractive periphery (Ciccantell and Gellert 2022), as Rodney's (1982) analysis of Europe's restructuring of Africa into an extractive periphery demonstrates. In an ironic twist, supplying labor to resource frontiers can be a lucrative industry in and of itself (see, e.g., Williams (1944) on the role of slave trade profits in funding the Industrial Revolution and Haeg (2013), White (2011) and Robbins (1994) on the profits of railroads and shipping firms from European immigrants to the U.S.). This labor influx was typically racialized and carefully managed by firms and states to produce a relatively easily controlled labor force (Ciccantell and Gellert 2022). There are strong parallels between the dynamics of labor and race in Latin American silver mines in the 1500s and in Amazon warehouses in the twenty-first century.

This all requires us to reconsider the essential contributions of earlier work that emphasized the centrality of race and racism in shaping commodity chains. Prefiguring the analysis of dependency and world-systems theory by two decades, Williams (1944) revealed that 10–20% of the capital invested in the British Industrial Revolution derived directly from the slave trade, a global commodity chain that directly supported imperial and trade surplus extraction from Latin America and North America in mining and plantation agricultural production for centuries, simultaneously developing Great Britain and under-developing dozens of peripheral regions.

Walter Rodney (1982, 25) emphasized the role of the slave trade and colonialism in building commodity chains that simultaneously developed Europe and underdeveloped Africa, explaining that

> throughout the period that Africa has participated in the capitalist economy, two factors have brought about underdevelopment. In the first place, the wealth created by African labor and from African resources was grabbed by the capitalist countries of Europe; and in the second place, restrictions were placed upon African capacity to make the maximum use of its economic potential-which is what development is all about.

Just like development and underdevelopment, race and racism were similarly intrinsically and dialectically linked across the regions of the capitalist world-economy. Rodney (1982, 88–89) notes that economic gain motivated the European enslavement of African people, and European racism toward Africans emerged and intensified because

> having become utterly dependent on African labor. Europeans at home and abroad found it necessary to rationalize that exploitation in racist terms as well. Oppression follows logically from exploitation, so as to guarantee the latter. Oppression of African people on purely racial grounds accompanied, strengthened, and became indistinguishable from oppression for economic reasons.

64 David A. Smith et al.

The long-lasting impact on European societies of "the rise of racism as a widespread and deeply rooted element in European thought" was that "by the nineteenth century white racism had become so institutionalized in the capitalist world (and notably in the USA) that it sometimes ranked above the maximization of profit as a motive for oppressing black people . . . but the international proliferation of bigoted and unscientific racist ideas was bound to have its negative consequences in the long run" (Rodney 1982, 88–89), including the Holocaust in Nazi Germany. As Rodney argued decades ago, constructing the commodity chains that supported European hegemonic ascent in the world-economy required racism and racial oppression to supply the labor to enrich Europe and underdevelop its peripheries. The racism that continues to plague the U.S. and Europe built the commodity chains that drove economic ascent and hegemony over the last five centuries.

Bush (1999, 2009) develops an explicitly world-systemic analysis of racism in the capitalist world-economy over the course of the twentieth century, engaging directly with world-systems theory to analyze race and racial formations (Omi and Winant 1994) in an innovative way. His analysis is grounded in the global context of the capitalist world-economy and the roots of racism in European hegemony and is particularly germane for understanding the resurgence of white supremacy in the twenty-first century in the U.S. and globally. The Trump Administration's trade war with China and its racist terminology of the "China virus" are fundamentally a revival of 1800s anti-Chinese racism in the U.S. that destroyed the potential for integrating the Chinese railroad and mine workers into mainstream society, a potential integration that had significant support for a time in the U.S. (Chang 2019). From our perspective, the anti-Asian racism of 2020–21 is rooted in the creation of the western U.S. as an extractive periphery in the mid-1800s. The capitalist world-economy and racism have always been inextricably linked in a profound and exploitative material and ideological relationship over the past five centuries. It rests on a long history of the creation and reproduction of commodity chains connecting extractive peripheries and more powerful core states.

Conclusion

This chapter provides three key conceptual contributions to GCC scholarship. First, we re-establish the origins of GCC analysis firmly in the world-system tradition, demonstrating that, over time, economic efficiency became the animating concern of many GCC analysts, as evidenced in scholarship on industrial upgrading and GVCs. We argue that the original emphasis on capitalist power and class relations, the inherent generation of inequalities, and long-term processes of hegemonic competition and economic ascent from world-systems theory should remain at the core of GCC analysis. Here, we highlight our raw materialist lengthened commodity chain approach as a return to the initial formulation of GCCs by examining critically examining development and underdevelopment.

Our final two contributions come through our use of our raw materialist lengthened commodity chain approach to examine labor and social movement organizing, as well as race and racism, in global commodity chains. We demonstrate the utility of breaking with the efficiency- and upgrading-focused analytic approaches by attending to the underexplored themes of contestation, class, and race in each of these areas. Our examination of labor and social movement organizing highlights "chokepoints" as key sites for potential disruption based on capital intensiveness and integration to the global economy, even as issues of workforce structure and political contestations present challenges.

Finally, drawing on pioneering contributions to the study of race and racism as constitutive elements of global capitalism, we demonstrate the importance of attending to issues of race, racism, and resistance within GCC analysis not simply as factors to be managed or harnessed to increase efficiency. Instead, race and racism centrally influence the structure and operations of commodity chains. Attending to the racialization of commodity chains further unveils the sinews underlying the global economy, illuminates the landscape for resistance, and reveals the long inseparable history of racism and capitalism.

PART II

Continuity and Transformation in World-System Hierarchies

6

THE RISE OF THE GLOBAL SOUTH AND THE REDEFINITION OF WORLD-SYSTEM HIERARCHIES

Víctor Ramiro Fernández, Luciano Moretti, Joel Sidler, and Emilia Ormaechea

Introduction

During the last fifty years, the Global South emerged as the main constructor of a new global order of economic flows and relationships with the potential to transform the global hierarchy of wealth. This process has been marked by the leadership of East Asia, with clear differences in the paths followed by this region and Latin America and Africa. The question addressed in this chapter is whether we are witnessing a perpetuation of the logic of subordination that has characterized the capitalist world-system or if there is now the opportunity to promote a New Bandung.

The structure of the world-system hierarchy has changed in every successive systemic cycle of accumulation and is currently undergoing a process of transformation (Karataşlı 2017). The rise of the Global South signals a new era within the world-system. Nevertheless, the rise of the Global South is not a homogenous process. Instead, the recent trajectories followed by the three main regions of the Global South—Asia, Latin America, and Africa—have diverged. In this respect, the transformations of the last fifty years have involved simultaneously an economic convergence between the Global North and Global South, but also greater inequality within the Global South.

During the post-war period, countries within the Global South promoted developmental strategies based on import substitution industrialization, with heterogeneous outcomes. In the cases of Africa and Latin America, these policies had limited success in promoting sustainable structural transformations (Hirschman 1968). These restrictions were later used by authoritarian regimes supported by the US to dismantle the limited but existing industrialization policies, as part of the neoliberal offensive. In contrast, East Asia is acknowledged

DOI: 10.4324/9781003325109-8

to have followed a successful process of development that, by the 1980s, managed to reduce domestic inequalities and improve its international standing. While some consider this case as an example of virtuous state-led industrialization (Amsden 2004), world-system analysts argue that this success is not merely an outcome of internal processes but results in part from structural systemic logics, represented by "development by invitation" strategies (Arrighi 1990; Wallerstein 1974a). From such a perspective, the presence or absence of monopolistic core-like activities are the main feature to understand the place of each country in the hierarchy of wealth (Korzeniewicz and Payne 2020), and industrialization is considered just one of many possible economic activities that lead to development.

Even though industrialization by itself does not mean development, we argue that it is a key element in order to explain both the rise of the Global South and the greater inequality within this macro-region. In this sense, by combining the analysis of the hegemon's strategies and the internal processes of each region, it is possible to understand the specificities of their industrialization and their different outcomes in terms of development. On the one hand, East Asia's state-led industrialization, supported by US geopolitical permissiveness, allowed this region to develop a more inclusive socio-spatial pattern of capital accumulation, with structural power to resist the speculative and subordinating projects of foreign financial and productive capital by deploying national and regional value chains with local control of strategic functions. It is precisely over this regional dynamic and its revolutionary legacy that the recent Chinese economic boom was framed, and from which growing macro-regional integration is taking place. On the other hand, the absence of these elements in Africa and Latin America could explain the stagnation of those regions and the increasing divergence with East Asia.

To understand these processes, it is necessary to introduce a medium-term view in order to analyze the characteristics of the post-war order and US hegemony in which these different strategies emerged. This implies taking into account the scheme adopted by the hegemonic state regarding each region, and the internal processes that emerged as reactions or responses to those strategies. To do so, we first examine the hegemon's different strategies implemented during the consolidation of the post-war order—and the US' material expansion phase—(1945–1970) to secure its global domain, and the particularities of the strategies adopted in East Asia, Latin America, and Africa. We show how these different strategies and regional processes shaped diverse trajectories of development. Second, we consider how the beginning of the hegemonic crisis, in the 1970s, affected the strategies previously taken by the US. By examining the specificities under which the crisis and the cyclical change took place, we analyze how the increasing financialization and restructuring of production in the Global North progressively relocated the production process to the Global South, with a clear epicenter in East Asia.

The Rise of the Global South **71**

We thus distinguish three moments within the last fifty years of hegemonic crisis (1970–1980; 1980–2000; 2000–2020). While during the first two (1970–1980; 1980–2000), the Global North preserved the hierarchical global structure, the last sub-period (2000–2020) is characterized by a global hierarchical restructuring led by a new material expansion in the Global South. During this process, East Asia became the world's new center of capital accumulation, and today is leading the increasing integration of the Global South through intensifying flows of trade, investment, and capital.

To analyze these three moments, it is necessary to go beyond the GDP per capita approach as the main variable of analysis and consider the qualitative elements of the accumulation process. Studies analyzing the global hierarchies and focusing on GDP per capita distribution accept that the alteration in the distribution of wealth comes from the differentiated positions within global commodity chains. However, they do not consider other factors that also help to explain the mobility of certain countries and regions. Analyses based on the GDP per capita approach are useful for understanding systemic stability, rather than change, and do not account for the regional structural transformations of the world-system, which contributes to understanding the development of some regions within the Global South.

Therefore, it is important to comprehend the key elements that recently contributed to the consolidation of an endogenous structure of capital accumulation in the Global South that is capable of strengthening its internal autonomy. Precisely, the transfer of the core of accumulation from the Global North to the Global South explains the redefinition of the hierarchy of wealth by enabling the Global South to improve its position in the global commodity chains. Hence, it helps explain the emergence of East Asia as the leader of the Global South, and the incapability of "the rest" to improve their positioning in the global commodity chains and in the hierarchy of wealth. In this way, we consider how the specific internal processes and the external relations between each region of the Global South and the hegemon help to explain the different capacities of these peripheral regions to condition internal actors and external capital, and to control their accumulation process.

Post-war Global Order and the Hegemony of the US

After the Second World War, the US became the new global hegemon. As such, it prompted several actions to guarantee its domain and to legitimize the international order both in central and peripheral economies. In the US, an intensive-monopolistic mode of development was configured (Boyer 2016), centered on a "virtuous circle" among corporate capital, organized labor, and the welfare state (Harvey 1998). To some extent, the extraordinary profits of US corporations were redistributed to organized labor in monopolistic sectors and the welfare state played a key role in legitimizing capitalism (O'Connor 1973).

The state-orchestrated post-war economy (Parnreiter 2018) was centered on US vertical-integrated corporations and a geopolitical order that supported the US' interests at the international level. The US configured the Bretton Woods system, created new international organizations, and defined different geopolitical and geo-economic strategies regarding central and peripheral economies, what also implied different strategies within the Global South depending on the regional political and economic conditions.

In the core the US deployed its economic prowess to boost the reconstruction of Europe and Japan through the Marshall Plan and foreign direct investments (FDI) as strategies to contain the "communist threat." At the same time, the auto-centric nature of the US' accumulation pattern (Arrighi 1994) allowed a context of relative autarky in the periphery (Fernández and Ormaechea 2019), within which peripheral countries could undertake some autonomous strategies of state-led industrialization. However, the extent of these autonomies was highly variable (Wallerstein 1995a). The different strategies implemented by the hegemon, together with national and regional historical specificities, produced different outcomes in East Asia, Africa, and Latin America.

On the one hand, a few countries in East Asia developed endogenous and dynamic industrialization processes that resulted, externally, in a successful competitive international insertion in global commodity chains; and, internally, in greater equality. This experience was supported by geopolitical permissiveness to a selected group of countries (Japan, South Korea, Taiwan, Hong Kong, and Singapore). This strategy of "development by invitation" promoted by the US during the Cold War implied an initial boost from US' FDI, and the subsequent incorporation of these countries to global networks of capital (Glassman 2018; Medeiros and Serrano 1999). Internally, strong states had the capacity to manage social conflict between capital and labor, and to rule over relatively weak societies and fragmented local capital (Stubbs 1999; Sugihara 2019). These national trajectories were articulated under the "flying geese" phenomenon characterized by regional integration, trade, and industrialization (Hosono 2017; Sugihara 2019). This strategy allowed a regional endogenous industrialization and the control of core activities based on intensive knowledge.

On the other hand, despite their different history and national trajectories, Latin America and Africa faced similar obstacles in configuring state-led industrialization from which to overcome their peripheral positioning. This was due to the different geopolitical strategy of the US in these regions, external financial restrictions, technological backwardness, the lack of international competitiveness, and historical limitations to develop a regional integration that would be better able to support industrialization. There was also internal socio-political instability, balkanization, and violent conflicts.

In Latin America, despite some tolerance for protectionist trade policies, the US' foreign policy did not allow regional integration and was not willing to tolerate geopolitical threats in its "backyard" (Fiori 2007). In the absence of the direct dangers of the Cold War that were taking place in East Asia, the US did not have incentives to selectively provide the countries of the region with specific permits to deepen state-led industrialization. At the same time, internally, there were increasing conflicts because of the contradictory dynamics deployed by the main economic actors, many of them strengthened by the state (O'Donnell 1996). The patrimonial and rentier practices that prevailed in oscillating demands on the state, coming from both the dominant and subordinated actors, undermined the capabilities of states to coordinate industrialization and set in motion a period of political instability. Progressively, the power correlation within the hegemonic blocs was subverted in favor of the traditionally dominant actors that supported authoritarian experiences as a solution to internal conflicts and social unrest.

Meanwhile, the success of the US' post-war economy resulted in several contradictions that started to undermine US hegemony. First, the over-accumulation crisis and industrial over-capacity became evident in the Global North (Harvey 1998). Second, the world-economy had to face the intensification of interstate competition. The rebuild of the European economy and the rise of their transnational corporations put pressure on the competition for capital resources and market shares. Japan's economy started to expand beyond its borders, opening the path to the East Asian "flying geese" model of development (UNCTAD 2013). Thirdly, the consolidation of the Eurodollar market was a mechanism by which capital flew from the US looking for new investments or seeking the protection of the European banking institutions (Brenner 2009). These contradictions ended up in the signal crisis of US hegemony (Arrighi and Silver 1999). In this framework, the differentiated trajectories between East Asia and Latin America and Africa led to different results when facing the capitalist crisis and cyclical redefinition that took place during the 1970s.

Three Analytical Moments During the Last Fifty Years

1970–1980: Unilateral Response to Multilateral Problems

The 1970s represent the beginning of the US' financial expansion (Arrighi and Silver 1999, 2001). Because of increasing competition, profit rates and investment in fixed capital began to decline, and money capital started to flow toward lower risk and higher reward activities. Capitalists tended to abandon productive activities and began to accumulate capital through financial mechanisms.

This economic downturn combined with the high cost of the US' role as a global military power and capital lender was translated into budget and current account deficits. In addition, the American defeat in the Vietnam War was the demonstration that even the greatest military power that history has ever known can be defeated. A growing tension between democracy and accumulation (Offe 1984) and an increasing offensive against the welfare state were combined. Therefore, when the oil crises erupted, all the conditions for an economic crash and sociopolitical instability were already established.

The US took unilateral steps in response to those events. The Fed announced the end of the gold standard and its replacement by a lax monetary policy. With this action, the monetary world-system was transformed into one based on the US dollar as quasi-world money (Lapavitsas 2013). The Nixon and Carter Administrations decided to advocate for an inflationary solution to the crisis of profitability. The US economy stagnated, and with rising internal prices and money flowing away from its markets, it fell into deficit in the capital account and experienced a deepening state fiscal crisis (Arrighi 2007; Brenner 2009).

These processes took place along with a restructuring of capital accumulation centered on the relocation of productive capital and companies to the Global South (Krippner 2005). This implied a redefinition of the international division of labor in which leading companies relocated their manufacturing activities to the periphery. However, the hegemon's geopolitical actions and global capital's strategies adopted specific characteristics regarding each region of the Global South, depending on their different internal conditions forged during the Golden Age. This accounts for the different productive and financial capital's investments in each of these spaces.

In the case of East Asia, the confluence of the hegemon's geopolitical and geo-economic strategies and the regional historical trajectory allowed those countries to build a business network of coordinated division of labor and strategic specialization. Regional trade was a distinctive characteristic of this strategy (Hosono 2017; Sugihara 2019). By the mid-1970s, and because of the leading role of Japan, this region's GDP grew at high rates and was one of the main receptors of the American delocalization. It was during this period, and because of the Vietnam defeat, that the US recognized the People's Republic of China government, favoring the country's policy of "one China" and allowing China to take a place in the UN Security Council. This event marked the beginning of China's return to the world stage, economic openness, and development. However, it was because of Japan's regional hegemony and the Korean and Taiwan consolidation that East Asia showed an exceptional performance during the global capitalist crisis and the restructuration that were taking place at the center.

Unlike Asia, the strategy of the hegemon toward Latin America was linked to the relocation of financial surpluses that arrived in the region as cheap debt. When the ISI strategy faced economic and social restrictions and several insurrectional movements emerged in the context of the Cold War, the US promoted several coups and supported authoritarian governments that privileged the US' agenda (O'Donnel 1996). In addition to crimes against humanity and political persecution, the response of the military regimes was to conduct pro-financial policies that in many cases deepened the dismantling and transnationalization of local industry.

Africa's development was not successful either. Although initially state-led industrialization was a major consensus, the limited and opportunistic foreign investment, along with the weakness of local economic actors, revealed the structural restrictions to develop an industrial accumulation process (Mkandawire 1988). The internal economic structure was vulnerable to external capture by financial capital. The international financial institutions favored transnational capital's strategy to capture revenues from Africa without any direct investment oriented to sustain real economic growth. These processes sealed off industrialization and strengthened the rentier behavior of the nation-state, weakening its capacity to deploy an alternative economic policy (Ezenwe 1993). Most of the region presented negative growth rates and took increasing debt (Austin and Serra 2015).

1980–2000: The Neoliberal Onslaught and the Illusion of Stability

After the 1970s over-accumulation crisis, productive restructuring and financialization were deepened (Lapavitsas 2013). These processes are relevant to understand the economic and cultural diffusion of neoliberalism and its discourse of self-regulating market and the need to dismantle welfare states. In fact, neoliberalism was the strategy prompted by the GN's concentrated capitals and leading states to overcome the crisis and recuperate profitability.

The underpinning of the last two hegemons (US and UK), through the experiences of Reagan and Thatcher, operated as propellant centers of this neoliberal counterrevolution (Toye 1991). International organizations, such as the World Bank and the International Monetary Fund, became more relevant as mechanisms of capital regulation. Such organizations, controlled by the hegemon (Wade 2011), formed a complex architecture from which this counter-revolution was propagated toward the Global South.

Even though this process also took place in the Global North (Glassman 2006), the periphery was the privileged space in which the neoliberal offensive was fully deployed, particularly Latin America and Africa. During the last two decades of the century, these regions went through combined *roll-back* and *roll-out* neoliberal processes (Peck 2017), mostly designed by international financial organizations (Reinsberg, Stubbs, Kentikelenis, and King 2019). While the *roll-back* was aimed at generating new forms of accumulation by dispossession through privatization and deregulation (Harvey 2003a), the neoliberal *roll-out* promoted new regulatory forms in order to expand the processes of commodification. Therefore, these regions remained subordinated in the global market (Fernández 2014) and socio-spatial inequalities increased (Sassen 2014).

At the end of the century, the neoliberal globalization along with the consolidation of the triad of power (Omahe 1985) supported the illusion of stability regarding world-system hierarchies of wealth and power. The North–South division seemed to be unwavering and "the rest" was invited to emulate the Global North's successful trajectory. Nevertheless, this perspective contrasted with East Asia's actual experience which diverts from the Washington Consensus policies. Far from following an indiscriminate opening of their economies, reducing and manipulating the state and getting into debt, the success of the state-led industrialization in the region allowed a new material expansion centered on the colonization of productive global companies. This process forged the foundations for a transformation in the hierarchy of the world-system.

The different trajectory of East Asia in comparison to Latin America and Africa would allow the former to face the neoliberal onslaught with greater relative success, preserving its state-led industrializing pattern toward sustained growth (Beeson and Islam 2005). It was over East Asia's regional platform that the Chinese reforms of the late 1970s and 1980s took place (Kopf and Lahiri 2018). After these reforms, China opened its markets to FDI but under the rigorous control of the state (Besson 2014) and became the new nodal base of East Asia's regional integration, from which China formed a center of endogenous manufacturing production with increasing technological control of the global commodity chains. This regional dynamism of Asia represents the foundations for the material phase from which structural changes will take place throughout this century.

2000–2020: The China Boom and the Catching Up of the Global South

The new century brought about a new reality in terms of the socio-spatial structure of accumulation and world-system hierarchies. The displacement of the material expansion toward East Asia has consolidated this region as the dynamic center of the new systemic cycle of accumulation. However, the strong interdependence between China and the US shaped a double interrelated pole (Medeiros 2006). In their combination, the regional leadership and global projection of China, and the geopolitical and geo-economic characteristics of US hegemony, help us to understand the scope of the alteration of the world-system hierarchies and the role played by the Global South.

The deepening of the US' financialization process was an expression of its weakening hegemony, notwithstanding its military power and control of the international currency (Arrighi 2007). The preservation of its financial power (Serfati 2008) has run parallel to its loss in the productive, commercial, and investment fields (Guillén 2019). Also, its overwhelming military power has not obtained satisfactory results (Ullman and De Borchgrave 2017), undermining the capability of imposing global dominance when consensus is threatened.

In this complex scenario, the beginning of the new century was shaken by a major event: The resurgence of the Global South. When observed as a whole, the economic convergence between the Global South and the Global North first became visible in the early 1960s, because of East Asia's economic growth and the geopolitical facilitation of its takeoff. However, since the 2000s, it has not only accelerated but, more significantly, also reached the Global North in terms of GDP (measured in PPP). This was accompanied by a reevaluation of the relationships between the structure, dynamics, and hierarchies of the world-system. To understand this, we take into account the economic improvement of this macro-region in its: a) economic dynamic (trade, investment, and manufacturing growth); b) economic dynamism (technological development through R&D investment and patents); and c) the growing control over capital and core activities within the GVC, where there is a greater presence of transnational companies located in the Global South (Fernández and Moretti 2020). As a result, the Global South has become the privileged space of the world-economy in the generation of activities that strengthen the accumulation process and East Asian companies achieved a better positioning in the GVC. Likewise, the growth in trade within the Global South has surpassed the South–North and reached North–North trade at a global level, showing the growing Global South economic integration. This contrasts with the relative retreat of European, North American, and Japanese trade in the regional spaces of the Global South (Horner and Nadvi 2017).

Nonetheless, the same variables that show the increasing relevance of the Global South account for the internal asymmetries in the accumulation and exchange structures. Although there is a strengthening of the South–South economic integration and commercial flows, East Asia is leading this process under the influence of China, which seeks to establish new global institutions—or occupy the already existing—as a strategy to secure its new role in the world-stage. Moreover, regional trajectories also explain how East Asia became a dynamic center, in contrast with Latin America and Africa, and the different patterns of articulation that have been established between the regions. These trajectories present a complex scenario to debate on the scope and forms regarding the hierarchical restructuring of the world-system, and the possibilities that it opens for peripheral spaces to impose their wills in the world-system and forge conditions for development.

In the framework of this process, the consolidation of the Chinese leadership shows particular features. First, China has a distinctive form of accumulation based on the absence of an autonomous capitalist class controlling directly the state (Arrighi 2007). This feature allowed China to control external capital and the financial sector and directed it toward production (Petry 2020). However, this coexists with an increasing presence of enterprise managers that have introduced a capitalist managerial logic, with increasing domain in the mode of economic intervention and planning (Andreas 2008; de Graaff 2020).

Second, China has a long historical non-militarized and non-colonial tradition, which complements the idea of regional leadership that would deactivate the colonial form installed since European capitalism. Nevertheless, China is increasing its military power directed to constrain the US projection in the Western Pacific (Sbragia 2020). And, finally, its external strategy of expansion through FDI has been based on infrastructural investments, constructed around a win–win discursive presentation, mostly directed to the Global South's countries in the framework of the Belt and Road Initiative (Li 2016). This material expansion through growing regional and extra-regional investments is positioning China as the main economic actor within the Global South.

In this context, in Latin America emerged the "pink tide" experience (Chodor 2015) which was composed of administrations that strongly criticized neoliberalism and pushed for regional integration to minimize US interventions. They tried to build an alternative model of development for the region by strengthening MERCOSUR, CELAC, and UNASUR. In general, these experiences implemented policies of income redistribution found on the *commodities boom* of the early 2000s. Precisely, China was one of the main buyers of Latin American exports. While the Global North was sunk under the big 2008 recession, China and the East Asian countries prompted commercial fluxes within the Global South. China became a new source of FDI, competing with Europe as the second source of capital (Nolte 2018). Yet, while the increasing South–South commercial links show up important transformations of the global economy during these twenty years, the new strategies of China and the responses of Latin America (and Africa) give rise to more doubts than certainties about the possibility of establishing more symmetrical relationships.

Debating the Redefinition of World System Hierarchy

The different paths undertaken by the regions of the Global South help to explain the redefinition of world-system hierarchy. This process led not only to the rise of the Global South but also to divergences among East Asia, Africa, and Latin America. The transfer of the center of accumulation from the Global North to the Global South explains this redefinition by the repositioning of the Global South within the global commodity chains. This process took a qualitative leap during the last two decades with the consolidation of East Asia as the economic dynamic center and the incorporation of China as a major player.

This restructuring of the world-system hierarchies can be explained by considering two analytical dimensions: the global-level dynamic and the historical trajectories of the Global South's regions. On the global level, we observe the emergence of the Global South as a macro-space that subverts the hierarchical structure of the world-system. When considered as a whole, the Global South is challenging the traditional domain of the Global North over commodity chains and trade flows. The rise of the Global South as a macro-space is based on a new phase of material accumulation located in the traditional periphery, particularly in East Asia. Firms from Japan, Korea, and China managed to control core activities which allowed them to upgrade in the GVC and promoted increasing trade and capital flows with the rest of the Global South. At the interstate level, China is leading this process based on its geopolitical autonomy. In this framework, China developed an export-oriented economic dynamic supported by foreign direct investment, from which to secure its new leading role within the GVC, reorganize regional integration into a Sino-centric system, and expand its influence to the rest of the Global South.

In contrast, the Global North and particularly the US' financialized pattern of accumulation is dominated by actors and logics oriented to speculative activities in which profit-making occurs increasingly through financial channels rather than through trade and commodity production (Krippner 2005). This affects long-term investment, manufacturing production, and weakens the productive structure, with negative effects on employment rates and income equality (Lin and Tomaskovic-Devey 2013; Lo 2020; Rodrik 2016). Moreover, it does not offer a sustainable pattern of economic growth and development to be emulated.

Seen from this perspective, the rise of Global South implies an alteration in the hierarchies of wealth and power in the world-system. Nevertheless, there are internal economic divergences within the Global South that are visible when considering the second analytical dimension, associated with the regions' historical trajectories. The path followed by Latin America and Africa contrasts with East Asia, mainly because they could not sustain an industrialization pattern of development and build up a state with command capacities. The financial restrictions, the lack of international economic competitiveness, and the overwhelming presence of foreign capital, in alliance with local economic ruling classes, allowed capitalists to capture the accumulation process and the state, undermining its autonomy. When the debt crisis erupted in the mid-1980s, supranational institutions (mainly the International Monetary Fund and World Bank) intervened to restructure the debts of countries in exchange for neoliberal political and economic reforms that promoted different forms of accumulation by dispossession and the re-subordination of local economic structures to globalized and financialized capital.

The new scenario of global geo-economic and geopolitical restructuring, that began this century, allows us to imagine the eventual emergence of a new collaborative structure of power, with a non-subordinating and non-exploitative hierarchy of wealth within the Global South, in which East Asia has the leading economic role and encourages (or at least does not undermine) other regions' development. This could result in a world-system structured around the idea of a "New Bandung" (Arrighi and Zhang 2010). However, the divergent paths followed by each region within the Global South during the post-war period and the last fifty years also open the possibility of new unequal and hierarchical relationships that would challenge the "New Bandung" imaginary. In fact, China's regional hegemony in East Asia tends to recreate a pattern of development in which this region exports manufacturing goods and capital, while importing mainly raw material and food from "the rest," reproducing the historical, unequal, and subordinating logics of capitalism.

Beyond China's objectives for "the rest" of the Global South, the ability to raise a new world order, capable of avoiding the recreation of the subordinating hierarchies prevailing during the *longue durée* of capitalist hegemonies, will be based on the capacities of regional and national spaces within the periphery to create a more autonomous development project. This will demand the rebuilding of weak and captured Latin American and African states, as well as overcoming the failure to achieve a more dynamic and strategic regional integration. This process requires considering industrialization and technological capabilities together with a strong process of social, spatial, and economic redistribution and inclusion.

7

MARXISM AND WORLD-SYSTEMS ANALYSIS IN THE TRANSITION TO THE LONG TWENTY-FIRST CENTURY

Carlos Eduardo Martins

Introduction

This chapter seeks to evaluate Braudelian and Marxist strands of world-systems analysis through a discussion of the world crisis of 2020 and the concept of systemic chaos. Our goal is to establish connections that help pave the way for the development of a Marxist theory of capitalist world-system. We argue that the modern world-system entered a period of transition toward systemic chaos between 2015 and 2020, when the expansive Kondratieff cycle initiated in 1994 came to an end. COVID-19 strikes at an exhausted neoliberal globalization process, highlighting the vulnerability of its main pillars and sources of propulsion: international trade, international flows of capital, political liberalism, and United States hegemony.

The initial section of the chapter discusses the concepts of systemic chaos and the interpretations of the crisis for the long twenty-first century, as formulated by Giovanni Arrighi, Immanuel Wallerstein, and Beverly Silver. The second section of the chapter analyzes the Marxist formulations of Samir Amin and Theotonio dos Santos and advances an original formulation, through a dialogue that also incorporates contributions by Christopher Chase-Dunn and Ruy Mauro Marini.

Braudelian World-Systems Analysis

Some of the most important theorists of world-system have been highlighting the depth of the contemporary crisis and the high probability of rupture and inflection in the structural and organizational patterns of the world-economy in the twenty-first century. This postulation has been based on longue

DOI: 10.4324/9781003325109-9

durée studies in the Braudelian fashion (e.g., Braudel 1995, 1996a, 1996b). Such formulations, despite convergences and complementarities, show significant analytical differences. Assessing the potentialities and limits of these interpretations is of great relevance to advance our understanding of the crisis of the long twentieth century and the perspectives for a transition toward a new era, which must reshape the world power structure, and may even create a new world-system, distinct from the modern world-system. We would argue that this transition puts into question the capitalist world-system itself, and its adequate comprehension demands a broader integration of Marxist apparatus to the analysis that interpretates it.

Immanuel Wallerstein argues that the modern world-system, which is the structure of historical capitalism, will disappear between 2025 and 2050, in a period of systemic chaos when a power bifurcation will take place as antagonist forces struggle to reinvent the world-system under new bases. Wallerstein identifies three potential scenarios for the future: The reestablishment of world-empires by means of global neofascism; the fragmentation of the world-system into regionalized neofascisms; and the affirmation of a socialist world-system, with a high level of equality, freedom, diversity, fraternity, and democracy (Wallerstein 1974b, 1983, 2000; Wallerstein and Cleese 2002).

He bases his proposition on the combination of cycles and secular erosion that determine the terminal crisis of historical capitalism as a system. The modern world-system has presented two big cyclical oscillations (swings) that are logistical, or *trend séculaires*, alongside Kondratieff cycles. By the former, he refers to the slow process of emergence, establishment, erosion, and collapse of a hegemony, which he associates to the 300 hundred years prices fluctuations advocated by François Simiand and Fernand Braudel, divided into phases A and B, of 150 years. Each phase A or B has corresponded, in general, to the slow process of rise, consolidation, and collapse of a hegemony, understood by the author as a quasi-monopolistic economic situation, which relates to the much shorter protagonist periods of 1625–1672, 1815–73, and 1945–67. He claims, therefore, a temporal scheme that was initiated in 1450–1600, when the transition from feudal world-empire to capitalism took place with the consolidation of the modern world-system as its specific institutional architecture. The modern world-system was consolidated in 1600–1750, through the development and eventual depletion of the hegemony of the United Provinces; expanded in 1750–1900, around the emergence, imposition, and erosion of British hegemony; and would conclude in 1900–2050, with the emergence, apogee, and collapse of American hegemony. The decline of American hegemony since 1968 would be hence articulated with a very long B-phase of a Kondratieff cycle, out of a pattern of 25/30 years. Wallerstein (2010a) mentioned at times the possibility of the emergence of a new A-phase, but at least until 2010, considered that the long B-phase was still in force.

These cyclical fluctuations have articulated to an advanced level of structural erosion of historical capitalism, establishing an arrangement that, since 1968, has engendered not only the decline of American power but also of the modern world-system itself. This erosion is the consequence of the high level of development achieved by capitalism and is manifested in the following: the deruralization of the world, restricting the conquest of new frontiers to explore locational advantages of labor costs, due to a depletion of social spaces for expansion on the planet; exponential ecological costs that increase the risks of environmental catastrophes or pandemics, typical of civilizational processes of decay, and generate social pressures for its internalization by capital, decreasing profit rates; a disconnection between liberalism and democracy (as a consequence of the decline of middle classes and an increase of South–North migratory pressures, provoking the agglutination of wide social forces with redistributive demands that surpass the cooptative capacity of the system); and new international rivalries, creating two disputing poles, one that associates the United States, Japan, and China through both cooperation and rivalry, and another that binds Russia and Europe, pressuring profits negatively and elevating social conflicts within states.[1]

Under such conditions, antisystemic movements have assumed a diffuse shape, expressing more the confrontation of the spirit of Porto Alegre's against the spirit of Davos, than revolutionary processes connected with states and world geopolitical disputes. For Wallerstein, the success of the transition toward a more egalitarian new system depends on the capacity of social movements to impose their demands for wage increases, public spending increases, environmental protection, and democratization beyond the limits of liberalism, and also creating a world government to establish new rules and regulations upon the world-economy.

In *Chaos and governance in the modern world system*, Giovanni Arrighi and Beverly Silver (1999) comparatively analyze the systemic chaos of previous hegemonic transitions to build analytical interpretation instruments for the current transition. They begin with the concept of systemic cycle, developed by Arrighi in *The long twentieth century (1994)*. Differently from Immanuel Wallerstein, who restricts hegemony to a short period of almost absolute productive, commercial, and financial dominance of one state over its rivals, Arrighi understands hegemony as a much broader and complex process. Hegemony involves the combination between a state's political and moral leadership in the world-system, anchored, ultimately, in its economic protagonist role. Such hegemony constitutes a historical arrangement, dynamic and multifaceted, with a heterogenic political scope that includes institutional, ideological, and military dimensions; productive, commercial, and financial dimensions in its economic scope; and, in its social scope, the leadership of the bourgeoisie and its more dynamic or stronger fractions over classes and State power.

84 Carlos Eduardo Martins

During a given hegemony, contradictions develop in multiple dimensions, leading to inflection points and its division into two phases: A-phase, of expansion, and B-phase, of crisis. In a B-phase, the productive, commercial, and military strength of hegemonic state tends to deteriorate vis-à-vis emerging powers, but it still supports itself through financial strength to maintain international political leadership. A transition from crisis to systemic chaos is marked by the collapse of its financial and political leadership, by the rupture of international consensus in favor of centrifugal tendencies, and by the development of a bifurcation of power that lasts about thirty years and unfolds into wars to reorganize the world-system. However, Giovanni Arrighi and Beverly Silver don't limit their propositions to a general and abstract model of systemic transition but bind it to the construction of a historical theory of transitions. They polemize with Immanuel Wallerstein, claiming an endogenous model capable of internalizing change, for the properties of the system don't act over actors only in a coercive way, but are modified during their process of affirmation. The theoretical effort must be enriched and amplified by the permanent combination between cyclical patterns of repetition and individualized and singular historical processes, rooted both in structural and irreversible movements of the arrow of time, as well as in the inherent indeterminations of dynamic interactions that involve contingency in many dimensions.

Arrighi points out a tendency to increasing scale combined with a decrease in the number of actors that dispute for power in the modern world-system and indicates, in addition, a pendular oscillation between corporate and cosmopolitan regimes. He describes four hegemonic cycles (Genoese-Iberian, Dutch, British, and American), brought into action, respectively, by city-states, proto-national states, national states, and continental states, and traces their trajectory in between successive hegemonic crises that are marked by the beginning of a hegemonic decline and the rise of new configurations of power. These cyclical periodicities get shorter due to the accelerating interaction among the parts of the system, resulting in the time reduction of subsequent hegemonies. In this account, the North American hegemony lasted approximately 100 years, corresponding to the interval between the British signal crisis in 1870, and the one of the USA in 1970. Arrighi and Silver (1999) affirm that the current transition develops a *sui generis* bifurcation: While economic power is transferred to East Asia, and mainly China, the military power continues concentrated in the United States, establishing an exception vis-à-vis the prevailing patterns of past transition periods.

In *The Long Twentieth Century (1994)*, Arrighi predicted three possible outcomes for the coming systemic bifurcation: The conversion of American power into an Empire that extracts value from the charging of protection costs around the world; the rise of a new pattern, centered in East Asia, based on the disconnection of enterprises in the Braudelian monopoly capitalism; and the entropic acceleration of systemic chaos. In later works, however, Arrighi reworks and

Marxism and World-Systems Analyses **85**

deepens this formulation to include phenomena such as Japan's stagnation and the immense projection of China in the world-economy. In *Adam Smith in Beijing* (2008), China appears as the great state power that challenges American supremacy in the world-system, replacing decentralized network capitalism and an Asia-centered system anchored in Japan. The Chinese challenge is defined by being an articulator of new relations between East and West that displaces the *clash of civilizations* imposed by western colonialism and imperialism against the Americas, Africa, Asia, and Oceania. The mission of this challenge would be to organize a New Bandung spirit and a Global South project that reverse the formula, enunciated by Andre Gunder Frank, of the development of underdevelopment in peripheries in favor of core countries, to the underdevelopment of the later in favor of the development of the former. For that, China should be able to offer an ecological alternative to the development of humanity, replacing the predatory, and devastating western model that it might have sought to imitate during its initial ascent.

Giovanni Arrighi and Beverly Silver (1999) highlight that differently from previous transitions, when interstate and intercapitalist competition shaped social conflicts, in the current transition, the conflicts between capital and labor and between imperialism and national sovereignty tend to assume a protagonist role articulating intrastate and international levels. Arrighi sees the beginning of US hegemonic signal crisis in the combination between the class struggles in United States and the anticolonialist and anti-imperialist struggles in peripheries. The pressures of the working class upon a Fordist–Keynesian regime guided by the military-industrial complex, combined with socialist revolutionary struggles and the assertion of Vietnam's sovereignty, had represented an economic and military defeat against the dominating bourgeois coalition in United States during the second half of the 1960s, leading the most dynamic fractions of its big capital to reinvent the pattern of accumulation and the ways to organize its hegemony internally and worldwide. The authors see in the offensive of social movements around the world, which tend to intensify during systemic chaos, the possibility of making feasible a relatively peaceful transition, limiting the risk of war and catastrophe.

The reinvention of hegemony by the means of neoliberal globalization was an outcome of the incapacity, by expansive monetary policies and a corporate entrepreneur pattern of vertical integration, to contain workers and students' pressures for higher wages, expanded social expenditures, and democratization, as well as the failure of military interventions to dissuade South–North conflicts. These constraints were manifested through capital outflows, rising inflation, dollar devaluation, the rupture of the gold parity, financial capital devaluation, and the strengthening of interstate and geopolitical rivalries. To the defeat in Vietnam was added the Iranian revolution, the Nicaraguan revolution, the role of OPEC in rising oil prices, and modernization projects in Latin America, East Europe, and East Asia that were financed with negative interest rates. A supplier of liquidity to the world-system via its current account surplus, providing reserves for unilateral transfers in support of its hegemony, the United States saw its own international regime entering into crisis by facing a loss of competitiveness in its industrial sector, increasing commercial deficits, and the impossibility to hoard income through a formal empire, as had been the case previously with Great Britain. Confronting such a scenario, they relegated industrial policies to second place, prioritized high finance, and started to capture international liquidity, using dollar overvaluation and indebtedness policies. Through these policies, the USA transformed itself into the epicenter of fictitious capital generation, settling into the B-phase of its hegemony.

Arrighi mentions the historical binds of China with a peaceful order and its old sino-centered system, which had provided a five hundred years *pax*. He points out as its determinant, the fact that this system—balanced through a high level of centralization and low interstate competition—had established an endogenous orientation that promoted a model of accumulation without dispossession, propelled land reform, and used the countryside and infrastructure building to guarantee territorial sovereignty. The China of the twenty-first century sees itself facing a big dilemma: whether to copy the American model, reproducing the oligarchic and unequal wealth pattern of historical capitalism, but subordinating itself politically to the North American exploratory empire; or to articulate a democratic pattern of wealth. Such a democratic wealth alternative would be founded in the presence of the socialist ideology inside the forces that guide the Chinese Communist Party, in the strong regulation and control of the Chinese state over market and capitalist accumulation in its territorial space, in the formation of a giant and predominant urban working class together with a big countryside mass, and in the anti-imperialist struggle against American power, which would pressure toward a great horizontal world orchestration. The increasing inequalities in United States and European countries would fortify the basis of anti-imperialist masses and would prevent any alternative transition toward a world empire power. The contradictions and vulnerabilities unveiled in Iraq's and Afghanistan's invasions would deepen the erosion of North–American imperialism, isolating it worldwide even more by signaling that despite having uncontestable military leadership, American power is insufficient to guarantee the protection costs of the world it intends to control.

In contrast with his general model of systemic transitions and his earlier suggestion of one hundred years for USA hegemony, which taken from its consolidation in 1945/50 would last until 2015/20, if not even longer to include the thirty years systemic chaos, Arrighi affirms in *Adam Smith in Beijing* that since Iraq's intervention the United States hegemony is extinguishing and transforming into pure domination. The author mentions that the gains of dollar seigniorage tend to implode because it is accompanied by high indebtedness, productive decline, limited capacity to offer protection, and the growing economic strength of its competitors. However, he raises a note of caution, recalling the British case, when sterling pound was maintained as an international currency, even decades after the end of its hegemony. The early death of Giovanni Arrighi prevented him to continue his penetrating reflections about the current transition.

Marxism and Capitalism World-System Analyses

Among the authors who have most claimed the approximation of Marxism to world-system analyses are Samir Amin and Theotonio dos Santos; and yet, their differences are substantial.

Samir Amin (1997) denies that a capitalist world-system has existed since the sixteenth century, attributing its emergence since 1800 to the consolidation of the industrial revolution, the spread of waged labor in the United Kingdom, and the leadership of the Britain in international relations. Although he recognizes the existence of inflection points, Amin rejects long cycles, in the name of the autonomy and indetermination of social struggle, and attributes such oscillations to contingent historical factors. For Amin, the existence of cycles would imply a monotonous repetition in social reality. Amin rejects Braudelian longue durée conceptual instruments in his interpretation of the history of capitalism: By doing so, he restricts a lot the power of his theoretical analysis. He also proposes a polemical dual law in capital accumulation: One that acts on an international scale, supported by an interstate system, and that is based on the restriction of the circulation of labor force, propelling world polarization; and another that acts in a national scale and can establish controls for balancing the circulation between capital and labor, expressing the pure dynamic of the capitalist mode of production and limiting polarization through arrangements such as the Keynesian pact.

Theotonio dos Santos is more ambiguous about Immanuel Wallerstein's thesis regarding the existence of a capitalist world-system since the sixteenth century. While dos Santos (2000) has accepted at times the proposition of a modern world-system, he doesn't disavow his original thesis in *Imperialismo y Dependencia* (1978) that what prevailed until the eighteenth century was a regime transitioning toward a capitalist mode of production; such a position is similar to his arguments about socialism, seen as an intermediary formation and not as part of a communist mode of production (Dos Santos 2016). Dos Santos (2016) accepted also the concepts of Kondratieff cycles and systemic cycles formulated by Giovanni Arrighi, but also relied on the concept of scientific-technological revolution. For dos Santos, the scientific-technological revolution, a concept that he incorporates from Radovan Richta (1971 [1969]), represents a new structure of productive forces that opens a new revolutionary era and puts capitalism on the defensive. This scientific-technological revolution began in the post-World War II, in more advanced sectors of world-economy, and reached a second stage in the 1970s with the micro-electronics paradigm, boosting an automation process, increasing the substitution of physical labor for technology applications and of science in production. Although dos Santos proposes a fruitful path of analytical connections between scientific-technological revolution, systemic cycles and the Kondratieffs, the author does not exactly establish them. He analyzes neoliberalism, the ideology of the B-phase of a Kondratieff cycle (1967–94) but continuing after 1994 over a subsequent A-phase, as a result of the ideological terrorism that it has inflicted on social democracy, and not an effect of the distortions produced by systemic cycles or by the scientific-technological revolution of the modern world-system (Dos Santos 1993, 2000 e 2004). The author does acknowledge the expansion of finance capital, affirms that the hesitation of social democracy leaves the way open for a fascist attack, and indicates that US hegemonic crisis, which he points since the 1970s, in *Imperialismo y Dependencia* (1978), would give way to the emergence of continental great powers, with China being the main one. His expectation, however, was that the strength of a new Kondratieff A-phase would make feasible a much-ordered systemic transition through the construction of a period with shared hegemony between declining United States and emerging powers, guaranteeing a global process of management that would impose adjustments in relative powers and limit the risks of conflicts devolving into chaos, and thus open the way for the construction of a post-hegemonic world and a planetary society with a strong democratic character and increasing socialist orientation.

In our book *dependency, neoliberalism, and globalization in Latin America* (Martins 2020), we proposed to push forward in the path opened by Theotonio dos Santos by constructing the bases for a Marxist theory of capitalist world-system.[2] We begin from the concept of the modern world-system of Immanuel Wallerstein, which we consider offers the fundamental elements of the political superstructural architecture of capitalist mode of production. It was due to the strategic control of the State that usurer and commercial capitals created a new capitalist world-economy and initiated the construction of its mode of production. In this period, the imposition of a capitalist mode of production was made without the concomitant creation of capitalist relations of production, by subordinating pre-capitalists forms of production.[3] But it was only with the spread of the industrial revolution and waged labor in the nineteenth and twentieth centuries that the economic pre-capitalist forms were broadly replaced. This happened, however, slowly, long after 1800 (the landmark emphasized by Samir Amin).

We consider, like Marx did in the *Contribution to the Critique of Political Economy*, that in each type of society exists a form of production that is superior and modifies the others, constituting its center of gravity (Marx [1859] 2008). In capitalism, this role has been played by industry, succeeding to its ascent and apogee, the convergence between the capitalist mode of accumulation and capitalist mode of production. Nonetheless, when industry came to be surpassed by the scientific-technological revolution, the divergence reappears in new concrete forms. The scientific-technological revolution only became a dominant reality in world-economy starting in the 1970s, with the emergence of the paradigm of micro-electronics, when a relative decrease of the industrial force inside core countries began to take place. The value of labor force began to connect to the exponential growth of education and knowledge, threatening the rate of surplus value. This led, on the one hand, to the progressive dislocation of capital circulation from the productive sector toward fictitious capital creation by the means of public debt, currency overvaluation, financial assets, and real estate. It also led, on the other hand, to the reallocation of the productive processes to the periphery and semiperiphery in a search for a cheaper labor force, but with similar qualification. This dual tendency amplified inequality inside core countries and led authors, like Ruy Mauro Marini, to defend the notion that the superexploitation of workers, whereby a price below the value of labor (established by average conditions of productivity, intensity, and skill) is paid, has been spreading to core countries; and that these arrangements are increasingly determined by transnational monopoly to the detriment of strictly national bourgeoisies (Marini 1996).[4]

Financialization combines, thus, with two longue durée movements: the emergence of the scientific-technological revolution, driving the decline of the secular tendencies of capitalism, whose epicenter is in its most advanced centers, and the B-phase of the American systemic cycle. Neoliberalism has become the answer for the monopolistic bourgeoisie in imperialist countries to contain wage pressures and the expansion of social expenditure, originated along decades of full employment and along the Fordist transition to a new paradigm of productive forces, information, and knowledge intensive, that brought together students, social movements, and manual workers during the 1968 manifestations. Class struggle in United States and northeast Europe, as indicated by Giovanni Arrighi and Beverly Silver, became critical for the establishment of a neoliberal turn over that would cement the decline of the American protagonist role and of Atlantic axis in world-economy, articulated also to Vietcong resistance to impose a strong defeat to Imperialism.

The strategy of financialization reaches limits, as the capitalist world-system is based on generalized production of commodities and on entrepreneurial and state competition. It was temporarily successful during the Kondratieff B-phase established between 1973 and 1993, but with the outbreak of the A-phase of a new cycle, the buoyance of world-economy moved quickly to China, when rates of growth in the United States and northeast Europe started to lag behind the average of the world-economy. The Kondratieff Cycle that emerged in 1994 didn't have the strength to shift the neoliberal turn back, as Theotonio dos Santos had imagined, because it corresponds to much more profound structural movements. Our hypothesis is that this A-phase is now ending, between 2015 and 2020, and is opening a new period of systemic chaos that coincides with Arrighi's initial measurement of the relevant inflection point. The collapse of the neoliberal consensus under the current environmental crisis, manifested in COVID-19 pandemics, is the detonating force.

Braudel's *trend seculaires* and Wallerstein's logistic cycles with its rigid oscillation of 150 years and measured by price oscillations, don't have enough empirical evidence or theoretical elaboration to be justified. But neither is Samir Amin right in rejecting the concept of cycles when they don't attend to a rigid repetition. The cycles refer to meaningful oscillations that repeat within a complex totality, where other long duration tendencies act and influence their rhythm. They have accelerating factors, like the technological spread and the exponential increase of organization capacity of workers as a result of the development of productive scales that act to restrain their duration (as indicated by Arrighi and Silver 1999). Kondratieff cycles have to be measured by international indicators and must articulate economic phenomena with political inflection points that have a global impact. In the face of the difficulty to measure them through a world profit rate, we must take into consideration world GDP growth per capita oscillations, and the variations and composition of profit rate for the hegemonic country.

The current Kondratieff cycle begun in 1994 and originated from the spurt of US profits and an increase of world's per capita economic growth rates, associated with a set of phenomena that have accompanied neoliberal globalization: the end of the Soviet Union and socialism in East Europe, the Golf War, the imposition of the Washington Consensus, the signature and beginning of NAFTA, and the devaluation of the Remminbi and its peg to the dollar. This phase of expansion has included three crises, 1998–2001, 2008–2009, and, now, 2019 through the present. Its exhaustion is associated with the erosion of neoliberal globalization, manifested through a loss of strength in its main supports (external trade, international flows of capital, political liberalism, rates of economic growth, state and private corporation debt capacity) as well as by the exponential progression of environmental crises (e.g., as expressed by the COVID pandemic). Joe Biden will try to reconstruct the universalist neoliberalism around an Atlantic hegemony, led by the United States, with European Union support, incorporating environmental and social compensatory policies. However, this alternative will seek to reaffirm the underpinning financialization of the United States and the protagonist role of the U.S. Dollar and will be challenged by the emergence of China, by the pressure of social movements against inequality, by popular-national movements in the peripheries and by ecological degradation, all of which will further weaken the neoliberal consensus and its limited formal democracy.

Systemic chaos should put into question not only United States hegemony but also the capitalist system itself. Neofascism and socialism will dispute for the reorganization of world-system with a weakened neoliberalism that will seek to

Marxism and World-Systems Analyses **91**

resume its offensive. Differently from what believed Theotonio dos Santos, the paths toward a planetary civilization will hardly be established by a consensus around US shared hegemony and emerging forces of world-economy, permanently in process of adjustment. We argue, like Giovanni Arrighi and Beverly Silver, that social and political struggles will have a key role in defining the process of systemic reorganization that will follow. Contrasting with Immanuel Wallerstein, we consider that the process of replacement of the modern world-system by another one will involve global projects generated from the articulation of class struggles with interstates and geopolitical disputes. A bifurcation tends to be created, between, on one side, China and its leadership with Russia, propelling global south and Eurasian projects,[5] and on the other side, American imperialism and its leadership articulating a neofascist global project. The first, a project of power involving big continental masses and domestic markets *hinterlands*, the second, a project of maritime powers based on private monopolies and on oligarchic value appropriation. Like Arrighi highlights, the roots of this bifurcation come up during the beginning of signal crisis of hegemony and, in the case of United States, refer to Vietnam defeat, which was much more political than military. Such historical and analytical precedent puts the unity of class struggles of south people and central countries, as key to defeat the imperialist machine and to the transition toward a socialist world-system, taking the defense of peace as a central value.

Notes

1. "Europe (that is, the EC) will constitute a second economic megalithic and a serious competitor to the Japan-United States condominium. The rest of the world will relate to the two zones of this bipolar world in multiple ways . . . The two countries not yet significantly or sufficiently integrated into the networks in creation, but which will be essential to include for all three of above reasons, will be China for the Japan-United States condominium and Russia for the EC. . . . Suppose this picture to be correct: the emergence of a bipolar world economy with China part of the Japan-United States pole and Russia part of the Europe pole" (Wallerstein 2000, p. 442).
2. The English version, published by Brill and Haymarket Books, updates and expands the original version published in Portuguese, in 2011, by Boitempo, reaffirming its fundamental thesis.
3. We consider the mode of accumulation as the central dimension of a mode of production, which may, however, enter in contradiction with its relations of production and productive forces. Typical cases are during the consolidation of a new mode of production, when the later are embryonic and are not yet developed nor generalized/spread or during the decline and terminal phases. On the subject see Marx ([1859]2008) and Chase-Dunn and Thomas D. Hall (1997).
4. Ruy Mauro Marini originally established the concept of superexploitation of labor power to analyze the patterns of accumulation and development in the dependent capitalism, which is based in transfers of surplus value to technological and financial monopolies, leading the fractions of the internal bourgeise that suffers their action to compensate it by the appropriation of part of the value of their workforce. However, Marini sustained that the monopolies impose financial and technological

92 Carlos Eduardo Martins

asymmetries to the centers of the capitalism with neoliberal globalization, spreading the superexploitation of workers to this societies, and generating the dominance of the extraordinary surplus value and fictitious value over the relative surplus value. It manifests itself by the increasing of inequality between 1980 and 2016, the 50% most poor in United States and Canada captured 2% of economic growth and had an income increase of only 5%, and those from Europe had an income increase of 26%, capturing only 13% of total income expansion in this region (World Inequality Report 2018, p. 46). On the debate regarding superexploitation concept and its spread to core countries, see Martins 2018.

5. The hard conflicts against the US and European imperialism, the leadership of the CCP in alternative geopolitical axis, the exhaustion of neoliberal globalization and the long recession that we probably are entering contribute to reinforce the role of the State and the socialist culture in the next future history of China and Russia.

8

ON THE LINEAGES OF WORLD-SYSTEMS ANALYSIS

Sub-imperialism as a Conjunctural Approach

Antônio Brussi

The present chapter argues that the rapid onset of deindustrialization in Brazil since the 1990s challenges the very foundations of Ruy Mauro Marini's concept of sub-imperialism—a major strand of Latin American intellectual production in the twentieth century.[1] Generally, dependency theories understood the process of industrialization as the most effective way for dependent states to break out toward greater economic autonomy. Likewise, as this chapter will show, industrial strength and complexity are also decisive to Marini's definition of sub-imperialism. I will argue that deindustrialization exposes key limits of Marini's theory of sub-imperialism.

This chapter begins by outlining in greater detail the concept of sub-imperialism as developed by Marini, for whom the Brazilian economy represented "the purest expression of sub-imperialism." Next, the chapter reviews some historical economic data that demonstrate the magnitude of deindustrialization in Brazil over the past thirty years and examines how this major transformation affected virtually every dimension of Marini's sub-imperialist "model." Finally, drawing from the experience of Brazil to identify the key empirical difficulties that compromise the intelligibility of sub-imperialism in the current world-economic framework, and arguing that the notion of sub-imperialism captured a phenomenon that was temporarily bound, the chapter concludes with some reflections on how to inscribe shorter-term reflections on the social world within the general framework of a world-system approach.

Dependency and Sub-imperialism: Complementary Perspectives

In 2003, André Gunder Frank invited to participate in a historic meeting of REGGEN in Rio de Janeiro, and feeling the proximity of his death,

DOI: 10.4324/9781003325109-10

insisted on going to Brasilia where he made, at the University of Brasilia (UnB), important statements about the origins of dependency theory.

In 1962, invited by Darcy Ribeiro to teach at the newly created UnB, Frank established contact with Vânia Bambirra, Ruy Mauro Marini and me, an encounter that profoundly marked our lives. Once there, he offered a seminar on "structural functionalism," a methodological thought that dominated the social sciences of the time and that he was very close to it as an outstanding student at the University of Chicago, the headquarters of that line of thought. In that historic conference that unfortunately was not recorded, he said that it was in that period the "dependency theory" was forged when, in our debates, we deepened the criticism on the dominant development theory, expressed in classics such as Rostow (by the way, his colleague at the University of Chicago.

(Dos Santos 2000, 159. Author's translation)

Summarizing his historical findings on sub-imperialism, Marini stated that:

[T]he expansion and acceleration of both the circulation of productive capital and the circulation of money capital configured a new world capitalist economy, resting on an international division of labor that was different from the one before the world crisis [1929] . . . The simple center-periphery model, characterized by the exchange of manufactures for food and raw materials, was over. We face a new economic reality in which the industry assumes an increasingly decisive role. This is true even if the industrial capital expands and strengthens in extractive and agricultural areas, and even more so when we consider the worldwide extension and diversification of manufacturing. The result has been a reordering, a hierarchy of capitalist countries in a pyramid form and, consequently, the emergence of middle centers of accumulation—that also are middle capitalist powers—which has led us to speak of the emergence of sub-imperialism.

(Marini 2012, 43. Author's translation)

By his turn, Theotônio dos Santos (2000, 111) has presented "the law of dependent development" as follows:

There is nothing to indicate . . . that our growth as industrial exporters will reverse this trend towards underemployment, marginality and social exclusion. Data have confirmed the deepening of these trends. Thus, we can conclude that: The development of dependent capitalism, particularly our conversion into large industrial exporters, does not ensure greater absorption of labor than in the past. On the contrary, everything seems to indicate that the masses of unemployed, underemployed and marginalized people will increase in our economies, in absolute and relative terms.

(Author's translation)

Marini would certainly endorse these claims without repair. In fact, his most important intellectual objective was to identify the open perspectives for the condition of dependency and to present the differences that marked possible or probable the trajectories of dependent states.[2]

However, among all *dependentistas* of his time, Marini was perhaps the first scholar to elaborate an interpretation of the development process of dependent societies extracted from what he understood to be the structural transformations that occurred in the capitalist mode of production. Based on a solid knowledge of Marx's *The Capital*, his central thesis associated the transformations that took place at the center of world capitalism, when a competitive world economy turned into an economy predominantly oligopolized, in which multinational industrial and world-financing companies, headquartered in the systemic center of the world-economy, controlled the process of subordination of the peripheries.

Marini stated that such control was no longer exerted through the exchange of industrialized products for raw materials, through the control of international transportation and/or through the financing of peripheral production, as had usually been the case throughout the nineteenth century and in the first decades of the 20th. Instead, this exchange now took place within dependent countries, giving a new meaning to the idea of imperialism of the time. Within a small number of dependent States, and especially since the end of World War II, the same tendency process of concentration and centralization of capital—the generator of monopoly capitalism—also acted to accelerate a process of industrialization. But such industrialization took place in a context of relatively low labor absorption and operated for a very restricted domestic market (due to an extremely concentrated income distribution), limiting the potential volume of production that this type of industrialization could reach. Interacting with a high concentration of capital, industrialization in such a context led to the elimination and/or denationalization of smaller national companies and pushed large domestic capital to seek, in order to avoid their own demise, a closer association with big finance and/or with large multinational companies newly installed in these host countries.

With this association, oligopoly capitals and the domestic bourgeoisies of dependent countries (with their respective States) cooperate to overexploit the local labor force. Moreover, within such dependent environments, a second source of surplus extraction emerges: the one taken from the surpluses of the more fragile dependent States located in the political/geographical surroundings of the stronger associated dependent States. Marini identifies this exploitative association as the geo-economic environment of sub-imperialism.

96 Antônio Brussi

However, Marini insists not to leave aside another peculiarity. Only a few states have reached the point where their objective economic conditions are sufficiently "mature" to integrate themselves as sub-imperialists in the global restructuring of capitalism. First, it is essential that the organic composition of capital in these prospective sub-imperialist countries stay at an intermediate level between the center and the systemic periphery. According to Marini (2013, 40), such a level would involve an industrial gross domestic product (GDP) around one-third (1/3) of the national product, a threshold that during the 1970s in Latin America was met only by Argentina, Brazil, and Mexico. The second indispensable characteristic for these economies to leverage their States to the sub-imperialist stage, according to Marini (2013, 41), is "the arrival (of these dependent economies) to the monopoly and financial capital phase." Combining both criteria, Marini concludes: "in our day, Brazil identifies itself as the purest expression of sub-imperialism" (2013, 41).

Summing up, Marini (2013 [1976], 40) presented sub-imperialism in its strictly economic dimension

> defined as: a) from the restructuring of the world capitalist system that derives from the new international division of labor; and b) from the laws of the dependent economy, essentially: overexploitation of work; the divorce between the phases of the capital cycle; extreme monopolization in favor of the consumer goods industry; the integration of national capital with foreign capital or, what is the same, the integration of production systems (and not simply the internationalization of the domestic market, as some authors say.
>
> *(Author's translation)*

In the detailed preface to the fifth edition of *Subdesarrollo y Revolución* (1974), Marini emphasized that his definition of sub-imperialism revolved exclusively around the economic dimension of the concept, as he recognized that State policies were indispensable for attaining hegemonic purposes domestically and some independence in the international political environment.

Regarding the international dimension, he made use of the concept of autonomy, a notion that, in the Latin America of the 1960s, approximately meant independent foreign policy.[3] However, a "certain degree of autonomy" is not enough to trigger sub-imperialist projects if the stimulating motivation underlying the process does not include the project of a progressively stronger state, with an unequivocal aspiration for power. In this case, the objectives of the State and its political institutions go beyond the strict economic limits of facilitating business, guaranteeing labor overexploitation, and supplying demand for domestically produced goods and services. Here, it is necessary to build and consolidate chains of interests between networks of production and consumption in order to strengthen the political nexus between the "sub-power" and the dominant interests of its client States. Therefore, for Marini the political key to sub-imperialism is the association of some autonomy together with sub-power projects, maintaining notwithstanding some subordination within the limits established by the hegemonic imperialist State.

Nevertheless, the growing trajectory of neoliberal ideology in Brazil since the end of the military cycle in 1985 paradoxically set a limit to the autonomist project. The civil governments of President José Sarney (1985–1990), Fernando Collor-Itamar Franco terms (1990–1994), and, to some extent, the presidency of Fernando H. Cardoso (1995–2002) corresponded to periods of transition, of affirmation of democratic principles in foreign policy, of overcoming tensions with Amazonian neighbors, of building Mercosul, for example, without, however, stopping waving between more autonomist and universalist tendencies and more liberal and lined up orientations. For the purposes that guide these comments, therefore, the confluence of the end of the industrialization cycle and of the autonomy projects of the Brazilian State—the foundations of sub-imperialist perspective—became clearly perceptible after democratization, with the exception perhaps of the government of President Lula da Silva (2003–2010). Even so, it is noticeable that the foreign policy implemented by the Workers Party, the search for autonomous leadership within the Third World environment, took place more in the field of international politics than in the field of economics, as shown by the cases of Venezuela and Iran.[4]

The (Not So) Recent Deindustrialization of the Brazilian Economy

Much of the industrialization of the peripheries of the world-economy occurred in the context of rising American hegemony, after the Second World War. A similar trajectory can be observed in Brazil. Here, some industrial capacity had begun to be built in the last years of the nineteenth century, particularly in the more populated areas, but focusing primarily in operating within merely adjacent, local or, at most, regional circuits of production and trade. In these early phases of growth, in a world dominated by the principle of comparative advantages, industrial activity was able to survive without institutional support from the Brazilian State, following the stimuli given to the maintenance of coffee's price in the world market. Such policy ended up boosting industrial growth in those niches unwanted by foreign competition (like simple textiles, for instance).

It was only during the 1930s crisis, shaped by concerns to stop the evasion of scarce strong currencies, that a new development policy was implemented in Brazil: import substitution industrialization (ISI).[5] Differently from the up to then prevailing pattern of economic growth, driven by world demand for exportable goods, ISI intended to stimulate growth from within national borders, through a whole set of state policies based on two interconnected premises: the importance of industrialization to overcome underdevelopment and the growth and strengthening of the domestic market to improve social well-being. In order to attain such goals, State actions were indispensable to provide an attractive environment for private investments—domestic and foreign—mainly through the protection of the national market via high import tariffs and exchange rates controls favorable to domestic industrial production. Additionally, States were supposed to direct investments into those sectors where private capital was not attracted either because the investment required longer maturation or because they were too costly to implement.

Figure 8.1 shows the success of ISI policies from the late 1940 to 1985. In the case of industry, its relative weight grew from the early 1950 until 1985, when it reached 39.59%, the maximum percentage industrial activities would reach in the national GDP. After 1985, the long retreat of industrialization in the Euro-American section of the world-economy finally reached Brazil. This contraction, initially taking place in the industrial world, was first identified as a "persistent reduction of industrial workers participation in the total employment of a country or region"—the original meaning of deindustrialization, a concept created by Rowthorn and Ramaswany (1999). The reduction started in the core of the world-economy during the 1970s and hit Brazil by the 1990s. Subsequently, the concept was expanded to comprise also a relative diminishing of the value added to the national product (Oreiro and Feijó 2010, 220–21).

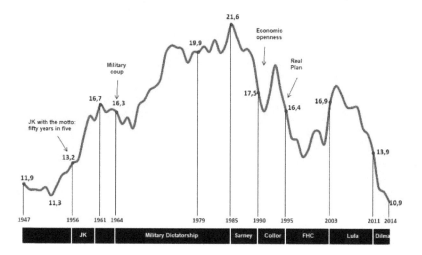

FIGURE 8.1 Crisis in Brazilian Industry—Participation of Industry in GDP

Source: In: FIESP (2015)—Participação da Indústria de Transformação no PIB 1947–2014. www.fiesp.com.br. Accessed: 21/01/2020.

The Brazilian case fits in both dimensions of the concept. In the case of industrial workers participation in the total employment of Brazil, data from the Federação das Indústrias do Estado de São Paulo (FIESP) and from the DIEESE (Departamento Intersindical de Estudos Sócio-Econômicos) show that industrial workers participation fell 28% between 1985 and 2010, decreasing from a participation of 25.4% to 18.3% during those years (DIEESE 2010, 10). Data from the FIESP (2019, 13) show that in 2016, the percentage of industrial workers in the total of employed people had fallen to 14.6%. Figure 8.1 shows the variation of the value transformation industry added to the national product.

The data clearly show that the industrialization boom ended with at the conclusion of the military cycle in Brazil in 1985. They also show that, after redemocratization, there were two small manufacturing booms, one during the period of President Itamar Franco (1992–1994) and the other in the early years of President Lula da Silva first government (2003–2006). As highlighted by these two cases, the rhythms of the country's deindustrialization were not merely a product of specific political orientations, as small booms happened in a more centrist government and in a more reformist one. But the overall tendency became increasingly clear and unambiguous. The dismantling of the transformation industry was so dramatic that, by 2018, the share of manufacturing in Brazil's GDP was lower than in 1947, when the country began the import substitution of durable consumer goods (e.g., such as refrigerators and sewing machines).

So would it be correct to argue that the Brazilian state further pursued its sub-imperial ascendancy over the most fragile economies of Latin America and some African States to compensate for its meager industrial performance (visibly shrinking since the 1980s)? Perhaps, but in an environment of intense and continuous decline of industrial activity, as the one just described, the external scenario also proved to be quite difficult for the Brazilian industry. Table 8.1 presents an aggregated data of Brazil's total exports to South America, Central America, the Caribbean, and Africa—most of the peripheries of the world-economy—in the period 1997–2019 and the total export data of Brazil during those years. Data do not show the destination and the kind of product exported, indicating only the variation of the importance of these regions for the Brazilian foreign trade.

Although the figures show a waving performance until 2008, from that year on these regions (South America, Central America, the Caribbean, and Africa) have shrunk their participation in Brazilian trade. Such relative decrease of these closer peripheries to Brazil—South, Central America, and Africa—in acquiring Brazilian products, is once more not connected to political-ideological positions, presenting a similar and irregular performance during more conservative governments and more progressive ones. Second, it is visible how big the fall of exports to those regions, whose quantum in 2019 had reverted

100 Antônio Brussi

Table 8.1 Brazil: Exports to Central and South America, the Caribbean, and Africa (1997–2019) (US$)

Year	Total Exports (A)	Exports to Central, South, Caribbean, and Africa (B)	B/A %
1997	52,947,495,532	15,529,600,919	29.33
1998	51,076,603,549	15,122,128,530	29.60
1999	47,945,909,310	11,939,482,871	24.90
2000	55,018,346,483	13,730,284,222	24.95
2001	58,128,223,219	13,816,479,106	23.76
2002	60,290,491,129	11,699,529,658	19.40
2003	72,975,027,454	15,180,935,570	20.80
2004	96,332,184,410	23,375,642,408	24.26
2005	118,692,856,544	32,552,117,612	27.42
2006	137,708,096,759	39,743,827,531	28.80
2007	160,521,882,755	46,412,266,840	28.91
2008	197,778,858,085	57,335,717,220	28.98
2009	152,910,580,383	41,840,753,967	27.36
2010	201,788,337,035	53,773,779,750	26.64
2011	255,936,306,857	65,635,994,566	25.64
2012	242,277,307,190	58,736,776,491	24.24
2013	241,967,561,759	60,696,530,125	25.08
2014	224,974,401,228	52,190,316,429	23.19
2015	190,971,087,339	43,870,152,152	22.97
2016	185,232,116,301	41,536,134,950	22.42
2017	217,739,218,466	48,881,829,055	22.44
2018	239,263,992,681	48,931,647,853	20.45
2019	223,998,669,052	39,874,970,907	17.80

Source: Ministério da Economia, Indústria, Comércio Exterior e Serviços

Comércio Exterior, estatísticas de comércio exterior, Séries Históricas. Accessed: 22/01/2020.

to the same current value of 2006. It is also important to consider that such a retraction raises questions regarding the strength of connections the Brazilian companies developed with their customers of South and Central America and, to a lesser extent, to the African States. Thus, in view of such a setback, are we not again facing evidence enough that these numbers indicate the conjunctural character of those sub-imperialists links during the last decades of the twentieth century?

However, the decline in the participation of Latin America and Africa in the export basket of Brazil may raise doubts about the general decline in the industrial production for exports because it might have been redirected to other markets. Data presented in Table 8.2 confirm, beyond any reasonable doubt, the size of the drop of the value of industrial exports of Brazilian industry.

On the Lineages of World-Systems Analysis **101**

Table 8.2 Brazil: Percentage of values of total exports (US$) according to product type (2001–2019)

Year	Basic Items (commodities)	Semi-manufactured	Manufactured goods	Special Operation*
2001	21	16	58	5
2005	24	15	59	2
2006	27	14	57	2
2007	29	14	55	2
2008	30	14	53	3
2009	37	14	47	2
2010	39	14	44	3
2011	45	14	39	2
2012	45	14	39	3
2013	44	14	39	2
2014	47	13	37	3
2015	43	16	38	3
2016	43	15	40	2
2017	48	14	35	2
2018	44	14	39	3
2019	50	13	37	0

Source: Correio Braziliense, Brasília, 26/04/2020, p. 08.

*Special Operations—Drawback.

Table 8.2 shows in detail the values of total Brazilian exports in the period 2001–2019. Basic items (grains, low-processing agricultural products such as juices, extractive products such as minerals, oil, and wood) jumped from just over a fifth of exports in 2001 to half of the total in the period. Meanwhile, semi-manufactured and manufactured goods showed a very substantial drop, especially manufactured products whose position fell by more than a third during that period (36%). These data reinforce the importance of the loss of competitiveness the deindustrialization of the Brazilian economy has caused to the manufacturing activities of the country in the last decades and the resultant shrinking of the conditions to export. Therefore, the capacity to extract surplus from its surrounding peripheries, another component of Marini's sub-imperialist argument, waned together with deindustrialization.

In fact, loss of competitiveness and the decreasing in exports to the world peripheries are strong evidence that industrial innovation also retracted in Brazil.[6] The result of all these losses could very well be that there is no other option but to move away from thinking on industrial extroversion, and to put into jeopardy what once was thought to host the country sub-imperial vocation.

In a context where the "structural" supports of sub-imperialism's theses are no longer present—like the advance of industrialization and the solidification

102 Antônio Brussi

of autonomy in the interstate system—a new path was opened to strengthen the sub-imperialist arguments. The policies of a State development bank, the National Bank for Economic and Social Development (BNDES), were then seen as the latest symptom of Brazilian State sub-imperial practices.

The emergence of BNDES as an auxiliary financial tool to help the Brazilian commercial expansion toward South America followed the creation of the Aliança de Livre Comércio Sul Americana, ALCSA (Free Commerce Area of South America) in 1993. The idea of that new economic organization composed by a new set of States and with a new denomination (South America instead of Latin America) answered to the Mexican decision to become part of the NAFTA (North America Free Trade Association). ALCSA also intended to develop connection between Mercosul and the Community of Andean Nations (CAN), thus reinforcing the links among all South American nations (Luce 2007).

In August 2000, in order to develop an infrastructure of transportation, energy, and telecommunications that would reinforce the integration of South American countries, policy makers created the *Iniciativa para a Integração da Estrutura Regional Sul Americana, IIRSA* (Initiative for the Integration of Regional Infrastructure in South America). Together with ALCSA, they became the main BNDES stimulator in providing the required financing to build the aforementioned infrastructure (Luce 2007; Costa and Gonzalez 2014). However, by 2015 a period of political and economic disarticulation hit South American States, disorganizing and discontinuing those projects of regional integration proposed by the ALCSA/IIRSA and the importance of BNDES as its strategic financial stimulator.[7]

It was in that political environment that BNDES, the financing arm of the Brazilian State, allegedly favored Brazilian companies at the expenses of other South American States that called the attention of sections of Latin American *dependentistas* researchers to what was then called the new phase of sub-imperialism in South America.

Relevant to my point here was the bank's financial arm to stimulate exports of goods and industrial services to countries of South America and Africa that would be in Brazil's sub-imperialist orbit. In this regard, Adrian Sotelo Valencia (2018, 502) emphasizing the contemporary nature of sub-imperialism based on the BNDES behavior, among other things, states:

> In . . . regard, [to the importance of expansion abroad] Marini was aware—but he did not measure its magnitude neither its strategic importance simply because the phenomenon was not unfold in full at that time—that who now controls the sub regional expansion is the Brazilian State through the National Bank for Economic and Social Development (BNDES) to countries, for example, like Bolivia and Paraguay . . . and to others located on continents like the African.

> *(Author's translation)*

In order to test the relevance of the main Latin American development bank as an inducer of sub-imperialist ties based on the destinations of engineering services and commodity exports financing, I present the data in Tables 8.3 and 8.4.

Table 8.3 shows that 74% (US$ 7,748 billion) of a total of 10.5 billion dollars went to countries of Africa and Latin America, excluding Argentina, Cuba, and Mexico. Another significant evidence is how important were Angola and Mozambique, especially the first, in receiving the financing of engineering services in the period, as well as the resources involved.

However, in order to have a better view, it is necessary to complement those figures with those in Table 8.4, listing the whole set of States that had received financing from the BNDES during the period covered by Table 8.3, except for the year 2019. The list presents 47 countries, core, and not core, without specifying the purpose of the financing, including the aforementioned engineering services. The value of Table 8.3 is equivalent to 27.5% of the total financing granted by BNDES in the period (US$ 38,084.60) (Table 8.4). In addition, the financing granted to the United States alone exceeded by 70% all that was granted for engineering services to all the States supposedly in the orbit of Brazilian sub-imperialism, even considering Argentina and Mexico, countries that certainly are outside the Brazilian sub-imperial connection.

Table 8.3 Engineering Services BNDS—Main-financing destination 1998–2019—US$ millions

Country	Project	Values
Angola	86	3,273
Argentina	3	2,006
Venezuela	9	1,507
Dominican R.	23	1,215
Ecuador	5	685
Cuba	7	656
Peru	2	348
Mozambique	36	188
Guatemala	1	168
Ghana	2	154
Mexico	1	90
Paraguay	1	77
Honduras	1	59
Costa Rica	1	43
Uruguay	1	31
Total	179	10,500

Source: Gazeta do Povo, Porto Alegre, 02/07/2019.

Accessed: 20/05/2020.

104 Antônio Brussi

Table 8.4 Values and countries that have received financing from BNDES 1998–2018 (US$ millions)

Central Countries	US$ Millions	Not Central Countries	US$ Millions
United States	17,784.7	Argentina	3,490.1
Holland	1,468.4	Angola	3,397.6
United Kingdom	644.7	Venezuela	2,223.3
Spain	388.1	Dominican Rep.	1,443.3
France	331.9	Ecuador	914.3
Italy	256.1	Cuba	882.8
Canada	254.5	Peru	645.4
Ireland	205.4	Poland	548.8
China	106.5	Chile	479.9
Norway	90.0	México	456.8
Japan	80.8	Cayman Islands	243.4
Switzerland	39.1	Paraguay	211.7
Arab Emirates	36.0	Mozambique	188.3
Sweden	6.0	Guatemala	167.9
Germany	0.5	Ghana	153.6
Bahamas	0.2	Bolivia	153.4
		El Salvador	152.1
		Uruguay	109.1
		Belarus	72.1
		Colombia	68.6
		Honduras	59.4
		Panamá	55.0
		South Africa	52.6
		Kazakhstan	50.6
		Costa Rica	48.3
		Portugal	32.9
		Montenegro	32.4
		Jamaica	23.9
		Niger	16.4
		Equatorial Guinea	11.1
		Nicaragua	5.3
		Zimbabwe	1.3
Total	21,692.90	Total	16,391.70

Source: Gazeta do Povo, Porto Alegre, 02/07/2019. Accessed 05/20/2019

Furthermore, if one excludes from the group of non-central states those unquestionably outside the circle of influence of the Brazilian State,[8] a little less than one billion dollars went in addition to the amount allocated to engineering projects. These numbers demonstrate how small has been the amount of resources loaned to the peripheries.

From the preceding, it is possible to consider that the worldwide expansion and affirmation of Brazilian engineering constitutes an emblematic example of the weight that political—thus conjunctural—dimension has had in the process. Recent examples of corruption in Brazilian politics and society, together with the dismantling of the country's main construction companies, are eloquent enough to illustrate how restricted were whatever sub-imperial project associated to them.

In short: The political and economic trajectory of Brazil during and after the military dictatorship (1964–1985), the very trajectory that came to be understood by Marini as sub-imperialist, was not the outcome of strategic design. Instead, it was the expression of the anti-systemic reaction of the State and economic interests as they confronted very specific limits to economic growth. Facing a limited domestic market, resulting from a very unequal distribution (and concentration) of income, successive governments under the military had no option but to seek alternative markets abroad (such as, at first, the Latin American periphery). The alternative would have been to significantly change income distribution, a path foreclosed by the nature of the political base of that military regime.

Likewise with the new iteration of "sub-imperialism," the growing importance of finance capital in Brazil continued to represent a reactive answer to a reoccurring crisis of capital realization (the transformation of production into an increased surplus value and in an even greater amount of invested capital). Capitalist elites and states in dependent countries such as Brazil continue to face obstacles to growth as before, manifested in limited domestic markets for both consumer and capital goods, as well as by limited state capacity to collect taxes and stimulate the economy. From this point of view, what some interpret as a new financial phase of a "sub-imperialist solution," might involve instead significant continuity with Brazil's recent past, as State and economic elites continue to pursue ad hoc policies (all avoiding to alter a highly unequal income distribution) to temporally and very partially overcome what are in fact structural limitations to economic growth.

Sub-imperialism: A Middle Range Theory or a Scrutiny of a Conjuncture?

In the late 1940s, Robert K. Merton (1949) coined the term "medium-range theories" as intermediate guides to more empirical works addressing more specific aspects of the social universe. Although aware of the peculiarity—and usefulness—of this methodological resource for the consolidation of social macro-theories and on the distance that such more limited studies keep from the notion of sub-imperialism or dependency, it is opportune to verify if more bounded theoretical and empirical objects can be helpful to the deepening of a world-system perspective.[9]

106 Antônio Brussi

First of all, in order to put Marini's conception and the medium range studies side by side, it is necessary to bring to the analysis the notion of time, which is virtually absent on both sides of the equation. In the case of Marini, it is essential to remember that the foundations of the restructuring at the core of world capitalism were what according to him generated what he called sub-imperialism. But by bringing a world-system temporality to the process, a capitalist restructuring becomes the result of innovative waves that periodically disorganize important parts of the regular flow of economic life while inaugurating new directions of accumulation, new products, processes and centers of productive activities, redefining the position and participation of each component in the system's dynamics. In addition, a systemic restructuring as such, which causes simultaneous effects of creation and destruction in the world-economy and in the interstate system as a whole, does not evolve as a linear movement or a continuous progression. It fluctuates, sometimes like a pendulum, as when it alternatively expands or contracts opportunities for the political strength of a working class, or when, in an undulating manner, it raises or limits the predominance of production or of finance in the world-economy, as in the course of systemic cycles of accumulation. Summing up, the idea of an evolving pendulum movement, which continually recognizes the role of time as a substantive variable, is quite distant from the notion of stage or phase of capitalist progressive path.

Using such an approach one could argue, for example, that the most recent period of restructuring of the capitalist world-economy, with its predominance of high finance and neo-liberalism, interrupted what Marini considered a new stage of the imperialist movement, and ended up downgrading Brazil to a more conventional position of dependence (in fact, as mentioned earlier, while the economic indicators characteristic of sub-imperialism in Brazil have declined, changes in the world-economy also have increased the Brazilian production of primary products quite strongly—thereby entailing the maintenance of an overexploitation of the labor force, the most important aspect of dependency).

Moreover, it is not clear that politics consistently gained relative autonomy from economic interests following the end of the civil-military dictatorship in 1985. Political administrations shifted irregularly to the right or to the left but by the end of the Workers Party rule (2003–2016), had all converged toward reactive responses to economic decline. Thus, although politics waved intensely during that period, they reinforce the conclusion that what the theory of sub-imperialism really emphasized fit better what happened during the civil/military dictatorship in Brazil, not before or later. Taken together, these changes demonstrate the temporally limited dimension of the notion of sub-imperialism.

However, a similar limitation is also present—albeit for different reasons—in the "Mertonian" construction of a middle-range theory. The relevance of temporal delimitation is absent from this mid-range theoretical proposal because, according to the author's own advice, such propositions have to be conceived as an integral part of the social structure. Thus, when addressing permanent aspects of the social structure, mid-range theories limit themselves to interpreting their structurally significant and consolidated manifestations, leaving aside inconclusive, conjunctural occurrences, and processes. In this sense, the manifestations identified by middle-range theories do not include social occurrences that stimulate significant structural effects while in motion, in process. By subordinating the understanding and prediction of inconclusive social processes to grand theories,[10] conjunctural occurrences are not part of the interpretative claim of mid-range approaches, for they do not allow consideration of the relevance of these processes to social life before their solid structural insertion.

True, theorization can anticipate possible new socially relevant occurrences; but Merton (1949, 452) states that:

> middle-range theory is not concerned with the historical generalization that a degree of social order or conflict prevails in society but with the analytical problem of identifying the social mechanisms which produce a greater degree of order or less conflict than would obtain if these mechanisms were not called into play.

Thus, the usefulness of the methodological content of Merton's medium-range theories for rethinking a world-systems approach is limited for at least two reasons. First, because it does not include, in its structural foundations, the time dimension. It does not allow us to conceive of the particular development of a given State vis-à-vis other ones as historical or as part of a single system in process. Such a view has serious theoretical/interpretive consequences, for it is not conducive to the dissolution of distinctions between ideographic and nomothetic studies into a single multidimensional system of historical sciences. Such dissolution can only take place if it promotes the understanding of a world-system as unique, thus making it possible to historicize it in its distinct dynamics, in a single systemic history. Second, such timelessness prevents mid-range theories from being able to address systemic restructuring that affects places, processes, sectors, or even activities so intensively as to dissolve prevailing interpretations of the world (e.g., such as the theory of imperialism or its younger sibling, sub-imperialism theory).

If timelessness and a-historicity of medium-range theories are of little use for reviving efforts like those of the notion of sub-imperialism, then what sense can this recollection have for a so needed shorter time approach regarding the perspective of the world-system?

In a tentative way to search for directions for the world-system perspective regarding shorter approaches in a more conjunctural time span, it might be useful to reorient the focus of medium-range studies. Thus, instead of trying to build theories with more topical objectives to deal with empirical aspects

108 Antônio Brussi

of social reality irrespective of its time/space dimensions, the objective should be to bring space/time as independent variables, overdetermining those more restricted empirical processes of the economy and of world politics. With this move, it would be possible to transpose the medium-range studies to the scope of the effects that the systemic restructuring eventually cause to processes, sectors, activities, or even places; but allow for the assumption, however, that they compose a clearly defined spatial and temporal dimensions.

In other words, such changes would allow medium-range analytical perspectives to deal with analyses and interpretations of conjunctural nature, consequently with historicity and spatiality systemically delimited. Thus, interpretations of macro-structural scopes, such as those of hegemony and rivalry in Wallerstein or the Arrighi systemic cycles of accumulation could welcome efforts more temporally and spatially localized, that would seek to scrutinize how the systoles and diastoles of the capitalist world-system reorganize and redirect the regular flows of economic and political life in a given state or region.

Conclusion

To the extent that sub-imperialism can be defined as a conjunctural consequence of one dependent pattern that emerged to face the downturn movement of an early industrializing country, so can its later features be interpreted as an ensuing political and economic adaptation of Brazilian import substitution industrialization when it faced its first retraction in the 1960s. Consequently, when these promoting policies reached their limits, due to the changes taking place in the world-economy and world-politics, Brazilian sub-imperialism also had to become part of the past.

Thus, political proposals or plans to reindustrialize the country have to consider quite carefully the constraints that eventually may come into play, especially if such projects are conceived without special concerns over strong domestic income redistribution, or relying mostly on stimuli other than domestic demand.

Nothing prevents, however, national States from temporarily assuming positions of ascendancy over other States, particularly in the context of favorable restructuring of the world-economy and of the world-politics (similar to what happened to Brazil during the decades of 1960 to 1980). In view of what has occurred years later with that particular trajectory, however, the probability of setbacks is also high, along the lines described here. In situations like these, historical experience and good science recommend care to avoid taking the cloud for Juno, that is, taking conjunctural expansion or retraction as something structural, permanent.

Notes

1. I would like to thank Patricio Korzeniewicz for his helpful comments on an earlier version of this work.
2. Even while highlighting the proximity between the concepts/theories of dependency and sub-imperialism, as both concepts came from a similar/theoretical matrix and from the same Latin American political/economic space/time of the 1960s/1970s, this chapter does not deal in any detail with dependency studies. Industrialization—or even industrial activities—is not as indispensable to the notion of dependency as they are (I hope to show) to Marini's concept of sub-imperialism.
3. For detailed discussions regarding the concept of autonomy, see Ruiz and Simonoff (2015, 9).
4. In the last month of Cardoso presidency (2002/12) and the beginning of Lula's (2003) Brazil lead the international support of Chaves government against a coup that was soon aborted. In the case of Iran, Brazil, and Turkey proposed a plan of nuclear agreement that Iran was willing to accept but United States rejected.
5. The Brazilian State conceived its first intervention in the economy in 1906 to defend coffee prices that lasted with changes until 1930.
6. For a detailed account of the loss of productivity of Brazilian industry, see Tomás Amaral Torezani (2019, 18).
7. "20 anos de IIRSA na América do Sul: quem está comemorando agora?". Le Monde Diplomatique, 4/9/2020.
8. Countries of Table 4 that are outside the circuit of economic influence of the Brazilian State and economy are Argentina, Poland, Mexico, Cayman Islands, Belarus, South Africa, Kazakhstan, Portugal, and Montenegro.
9. The difference is due to Merton's concern to offer to sociological investigations a set of theoretical and conceptual tools that would free them from the limitations caused by the great theories, with levels of abstraction that prevented measurable manipulations of more empirical aspects of reality. In the case of Marini, his concern was to pave the way to investigate the peculiarity that the most recent stage in the history of capitalism, the era of globalization of finance capital and multinationals, manifested in some special places of the peripheries. We can see, therefore, the theoretical–political distance of these propositions: on the one hand, to reduce the focus to enlarge the details and, on the other hand, to detail new developments—in fact, advances—of the Marxist theory of imperialism in the circuit of peripheral states.
10. "We focus on what I have called theories of the middle range: theories that lie between the minor but necessary working hypotheses that evolve in abundance during day-to-day research and the all-inclusive systematic efforts to develop a unified theory that will explain all the observed uniformities of social behavior, social organization, and social change" (MERTON 1949: 448).

9
THE DIALECTICS OF TIME AND VALUE ACCUMULATION

Alienation on a World-Scale Dimension

Ísis Campos Camarinha

Introduction

World-systems analysis and Marxist dependency theory have many convergent points to explore. One of these points regards a center-periphery approach, the International Division of Labor as a starting assumption to interpret the capitalist world-economy. An underlying characteristic of this asymmetric division is *value transfer*, the transfer of value created by peripheral to core countries, as a way of overcoming contradictions inside core countries as strategies of capital export, making it possible to continue the process of accumulation. This transfer has a long-term perspective duration, a historic sum, reproducing itself over and in time, as accumulation on a world-scale dimension. However, it is not only a transfer of monetary value but also, essentially, a transfer of time worked—as the substance of value is labor time. We should try to view value transfer as a tool of interpretation to provide a grasp on the process of alienation on a world-scale.

This chapter aims to address both theoretical and empirical analysis of this hypothesis: the transfer of value and time. Our theoretical analysis is divided in two sections, the first where we explore the concept of *timespace*, launched by Immanuel Wallerstein and inspired by the Braudelian tripartite perspective of time, adding space as a fusion to enhance it. We explain the centrality of this conceptual tool to world-systems analysis. Wallerstein proposed five *timespaces*: episodic, cyclico-ideological, structural, eternal, and transformational. We propose to add another: the *historical-category timespace*. This refers to the categories of Marxist political economy, its historical determinations and dialectical articulation according to modes of production and socioeconomic formations. It is through this *timespace* that we access the explanation for the transfer of

DOI: 10.4324/9781003325109-11

value, how it is put in motion within the capitalist logic of reproduction. The second section explores this *historical-category timespace* making use of Marini's theoretical explanation of dependency, unequal exchange, and superexploitation. This explanation serves as a bridge to connect the centrality of *timespace* to world-systems analysis and Marxist dependency approach. Marini uses Marxist categories, value, price, labor time, surplus, profit, cycle of capital, division of labor, productive forces, exploitation, etc. He dialectically articulates them to explain how the law of value operates in conditions of dependency. Core and periphery are two types of spaces in the international division of labor. Their socioeconomic formations have been historically determined encompassing all other *timespaces* of capitalist world-system. Despite the fact that political economy categories are present in both spaces (as predominates capitalist mode of production), however, as they are different socioeconomic formation, core and periphery spaces present specificities related to the reproduction of capitalist accumulation. They are under the same laws, but there are some specific tendencies and characteristics for periphery that have long-term implications, reproducing dependency. These tendencies are, for example, trade terms deterioration, value transfer, and external vulnerability. Together with other characteristics, it produces a cumulative effect of contradictions that persists and marks the impossibility of overcoming underdevelopment and dependency.

Last, the third section is dedicated to an empirical analysis of the transfer of value hypothesis on a world-scale dimension. We depart from Giovanni Arrighi's country classification by GDP *per capita* to investigate specific tendencies related to the structure of international division of labor. He identifies organic core, organic semiperiphery, and organic periphery countries using GDP *per capita* data. So, using World Bank data, we compare his findings according to these zones on how those mentioned tendencies appear by using a time cumulative analysis for each balance of payments account. We conclude that there is a strong time cumulative concentration of value transfer on a world-scale, there is a strong tendency of transfer through primary income account, trade deterioration, and thus, external vulnerability. These tendencies are also convergent with data on working time, so we may be able to reveal another characteristic of dependency and its coexistence with these other tendencies, superexploitation.

The argument of the chapter is as follows: The historical-category *timespace* is the level of analysis that makes possible to unveil the underlying process of accumulation on a world-scale through the mechanism of transfer of value so well explained by Marxist dependency theory. It deals with political economy categories according to how they articulate in each socioeconomic formation (abstractly speaking, modes of production) and how these socioeconomic formations articulate with each other and determine the space direction of accumulation process and capital flows. It unveils the categorial or, we could say, the categorial microscopic process of accumulation of one of the elements of its superstructure, the core–periphery space zones. The central concept is dependency and this concept is explained by making use of Marxist political economy categories, how they are dialectically articulated in periphery to reproduce dependency as an economic inherent process. The underlying tendency of value transfer is identified through an empirical time cumulative perspective, or, in other words, it can be identified as a *longue durée* structural characteristic of the process of accumulation on a world-scale dimension as we analyze balance of payments account, expressed in structural concentration, and accumulation of international capital flows in the form of primary income, for example. This contribution, thus, is also a contribution for the understanding of *longue durée* process, another point of convergence of world-system analysis and Marxist dependency theory. Another argument, which is perhaps more controversial is that the transfer of value also represents a transfer of time because it extracts part of the effort for development, part of the time spent in the past by working groups and by capital resources. World-scale law of value operates transferring value and time.

The Centrality of *Timespace* to World-System Analysis

Fernand Braudel's critique on history, and, of course, on how history uses *time*, advocates that there are three dimensions of time: one related to short-term events (descriptive in time and space), another related to conjunctural movements such as cycles, rhythms, and tendencies ruled by specific inner logics, repeating in time in phases, patterns, and, another, the structural dimension which "dominates the problem" of *longue durée* (Braudel 1970). Short-term history, events, helps to microscopically examine real-time manifestations of changes, episodes, and societies historical facts on particular space and time. It is a moment of comparison and analysis that is necessary to the analysis of continuity and transformational aspects, which leads us to the second dimension where tendencies, cycles, and rhythms are presented as manifestation of specific logics. The third dimension, structural, is the dimension where specific ontological characteristic dominates, but it cannot be fully understood without finite fragments of time in its totality, neither without those other time dimensions. These three dimensions are epistemologically used to understand determinations, concepts, logics, laws, and characteristics of civilizations. All these dimensions overlap each other creating *total* history (Braudel 1970).

Wallerstein (1988, 1996e, 1997) expands this original tripartite division proposing the "non-cleavage" concept of *timespace*. He argues that there are five *timespace*s: episodic-geopolitical, transformational, structural, cyclico-ideological, and eternal. Episodic-geopolitical *timespace* is related to short-term events, Braudel's short-term dimension; cyclico-ideological *timespace* is related to conjunctural time, cycles, and tendencies expressed in the interaction of powerful forces, which could be economic, political, or ideological, usually emphasizing "*a longer run of time, that involves some definition of the situation deriving from an evaluation of the meaning of location in time and space of particular groups*" (Wallerstein 1996e, 2), or, even, deriving from reversible process underlying forces according to how they interact with each other. Structural *timespace* is the dimension where systemic comparisons are made to study historical systems. It is the dimension of Braudelian *longue durée*. Social and power relations of production, juridical-political superstructure, international division of labor, Empires, and hegemonies can all be analyzed within these *timespaces*. For example, the concept of word-economy, the concept of capitalist world-system, and world-empire.

Eternal *timespace* relates to extremely long-term, persistent phenomena such as climate, geography, and inherent power relations within societies. "*The defining characteristic here is an assumption of timeless and spaceless, in effect, of the irrelevance of time and space to the analysis*" (Wallerstein 1996e, 2). Transformational *timespace* relates to a particular time and space where some crisis, change, or event happens and transforms qualitatively the system. There is rupture.

Additionally, to these five *timespace*, we would like to propose another, which we call the *historical-category timespace* (Camarinha 2020). The idea is to internalize Marx's political economy contribution. Economic categories, such as value, price, commercial capital, industrial capital, financial capital, division of labor, abstract labor, concrete labor, profit, money, money capital, surplus value, exchange, commodity, interest, use value, exchange value (and so on) are historically determined, therefore, *timespace* determined. Time here is a methodological movement to identify abstract similarities and transformations in historical processes, and capable of revealing ontological aspects of modes of production. The idea is to internalize the abstract concept of mode of production and of socioeconomic formations. This is the dimension, for example, of some capitalist development laws like the tendency of the rate of profit to fall (intertwined with the cyclico-ideological *timespace* manifested in Kondratieff cycles) and the process of value transfer within core–periphery international division of labor, or, in other words, the dimension where we are able to understand the category of *dependency*. It is not only a linear succession of categories, but also a complex totality articulated in time and space according to social relations of production and previous historic cumulative process articulated by those other *timespaces*. All these *timespaces* overlap each other and the intersection between them is the nuclear methodology of totality. All *timespaces* interact to create *tendencies* and *ontological characteristics* while developing core–semiperiphery–periphery structure as a superstructure of states system. *Dependency, superexploitation,* and *transfer of value* are important categories to understand how it is sustained.

Eternal *timespace* is related to geographic realities and particularities such as natural resources, localization, and maritime access and other physical aspects that were used by primitive accumulation but still have intrinsic importance, geopolitical, and environmental implications, for example—space in this global sense is timeless; structural *timespace* created initial political power relations developing mercantile-capitalist international division of labor among a system of states with different power concentrations; cyclical ideological *timespace* is a heuristic tool for hegemonic transitions and economic cycles analysis as well as transformational *timespace*, both mediated by contradiction, crisis, secular trends, and, ideologically, by a particular path toward "capitalist geoculture," named *"centrist liberalism"* by Wallerstein (2011). These *timespaces* overlap, but we only understand historical system by a systematic study of each one in their mutual interactions. Time as epistemological category involves change (episodic, transformation), continuity (structure, eternal), mutability in continuity and continuity in mutability (tendencies and cycles), and logical determined concurrences (dialectics, categories mutual determination). Therefore, *timespace* is a central analytical tool for world-system analysis, it has an undoubtful centrality because is capable of capturing the totality of capitalist world-system and at the same time permits to capture the relevance of each time and space.

Marini: A Theoretical Bridge to Connect *Timespace* and Dependency

To build from Marx, if the substance of value is labor and its measurement labor time, therefore, essentially, the transfer of value is a transfer of time. It is expressed in differences between value and price; and, concretely, due to the nature of money as the "universal form of wealth" (Belluzzo 2013), money is the commander and buyer of real wealth, commodities that are, in turn, the products of labor time.

In the capitalist system, money allows a split in time and value. The development of money as a general equivalent (in capitalist relations of property) makes possible the effective separation and represents the abstraction of labor in its magnitude in time and value. Although time in itself, as particular and individual, is impossible to be transferred due to its inherent concrete character in the act of production ("in the past"), on the other hand, "in the future," when in monetary/value form and abstract future, it can be alienated, creating an asymmetric command of time and wealth accumulation. The temporal link is money and market prices. The development of money as a form of value is a "crystallization" of time. Price and value, wages and labor time, are unequal, and money is the "embodied" form of this separation in the moments of capitalist reproduction. Money commands general time of labor in the form of price. Precisely, the independence that money achieves within capitalist structure of property relations allows the transfer of wealth (created in the past), particular time, as quality, mediated by quantity under the form of money and price. When money turns into capital, its more developed form, this process generates cumulative effects of wealth concentration, an unequal wealth accumulation, which is, also, time cumulative. Money is able to serve as a "time capsule." Our task now is to understand how this qualitative and quantitative process might be seen from an international point of view by making use of *historical-category timespace.*

In Marini's work "Dialectic of Dependency," dialect is revealed as a *law of value relationship which is negatively and time cumulative determined.*[1] As explored also by Samir Amin, Marini explains that the law of value operates on a *world-scale dimension.*[2] The universal law of value appears negatively determined or transgressed between core–periphery relationships: At the same time ("dynamic of concurrences"), this relationship overcomes capitalist contradiction inside core countries, while simultaneously generating an intensifying process of *superexploitation* within the periphery. Marini (2011a, 151) argues that capitalist "superiority" means that it alienates, not the entire time of worker's existence (like slavery), but the share of worker's time existence that can be used in production without the need to sustain labors reproduction costs. Time is one of the most important mediations of value and accumulation.

As we know, Latin America and, in general, peripheral countries, once part of International Division of Labor in the 16th allowed capitalism to arrange several types of modes of exploitation (Wallerstein 1979). The transfer of value and the transfer of time between core and periphery happened trough extra-economic mechanisms and helped to structurally configurate the seeds toward its economic reproduction in the nineteenth and twentieth century. Once law of value generalizes within the system, the transfer of value keeps its flux, but mainly and also supported by economic relations that are, obviously, inseparable from historical facts. These historical facts are that peripheral countries began to export natural resources (metals and food) to core countries (metropole) which started what we could call *primitive dependency* and configurates the starting point of our internal socioeconomic formation: economic activities dependent of external demand. But later, development and generalization of the law of value in the British and North American systemic hegemonic cycles, especially the latter, dependency achieves another status and flows mediated trough relative autonomous economic relations that reproduce itself—Marini (2011b, 143–44), imperialism and dependency. He uses the term *spiral* in the last section of his article, and the term *new spiral* to represent metaphorically this transition from primitive dependency to modern dependency.

Trade terms deterioration has to be seen as a global concomitant relationship in which the existence of monopoly (historically created and then economically reproduced), or, increased differences in productivity and industrial stages, both, allows core countries to sell its products above its intrinsic value, while at the same time ("dynamic of concurrences"), periphery sends

116 Ísis Campos Camarinha

its products bellow its intrinsic value (whether as an absolute or relative movement). This operates a transfer of value expressed in monetary forms according to market prices. This unequal exchange, in the eyes of periphery capitalists, must be somehow compensated with *superexploitation* to increase the quantity of products offered to world-economy, or, also, compensated, macro-economically, by more specialization. The result, of course, produces an opposite effect: a chronical cyclical process of relative price reduction of exported periphery products, and, like a *spiral* deepens unequal exchange and superexploitation. At the same time, this process unfolds because of a primary division inside dependent countries between production and circulation, or labor as producer and labor as consumer, a split within the cycle of capital (Marini 2011b). These parallel processes affect concrete conditions of work and, then, these conditions go back as problems of circulation and reinforce the *spiral*.

The same laws generate opposite and contradictory effects in different social spaces. In time, these cumulative and concomitant processes suffer qualitative changes when capitalist world-economy generalizes industrial revolution to peripheral social spaces. Terms of trade deterioration, the unequal exchange, are defined by the realization, monetarily in price, of periphery products bellow its intrinsic value in terms of time, when exchanged by other products. It has to be balanced with external debit (financing) when the demand of manufacture products exceeds periphery capacity to export. This doesn't happen as a frozen episode, but as a process in time. This particularity is also accompanied by another concomitant separation between spheres of consumption as industrialization takes place—high income x low income—in periphery countries (Marini 2011b).

Internationalization of production resulted in the use of foreign technology by periphery, which added another "*ring* to the *dependency spiral*." The *spiral* refers to the reproduction of dependency on the basis of dependency categorial abstractions, but as well, concomitant, on the basis of categorial abstractions of "pure" capitalist mode of production mediated and determined by concrete process and historical facts. A global and total perspective which makes general law of value even more contradictory worldwide—surplus value (relative and absolute), dual character of labor embodied in commodity, and of labor itself (producer and consumer),[3] exploitation, superexploitation, value transference, productivity, international division of labor, moments of capitalist cycle (production and circulation), realization, value, price, unequal exchange, monopoly, market, profit, etc., all of these categories articulated in Marini's "Dialectics of Dependency."

Accumulation in dependent economies is attached to an external logic, subordinated, and anchored on property relations that allows modern dependency, allows the transfer of value/time. "foreign capital" could be interpretated as a specific form of capital for peripheries' cycle of reproduction. In this sense, the monetary dimension of *current account transactions and balance of payments accounts* reveals the transfer of value, accumulation on a world-scale dimension, consolidated by specific relations of juridical-property rights, whether on the form of profit, dividends, rent, royalties, trade terms deterioration, etc.

Assessing Empiric Trajectories for Transfer of Value

The method we used to assess empiric trajectories consists of analyzing balance of payments data from 1960 to 2019. The classification of countries as organic core, semiperiphery, and periphery was based on Arrighi's (1998) findings and may be understood as a "snapshot" in time where obviously countries may move from one zone to the other in time. But one important methodological consideration is that Arrighi (1998) considered as "organic" those countries that did present the same position in the period covered by his data and methodological assessment in this particular chapter of "Illusion of Development," chapter which was also written with Jessica Drangel. Later Karatasli (2017) updates this work covering a larger period in time and identifies a fourth zone emerging in the twenty-first century. Unfortunately, we have acknowledgement of this updated work only after the conclusion of our own empirical assessment, but in the near future, we intend to update our own work.

Our assessment consists of using Arrighi (1998) organic countries findings in each zone and analyze if (i) *current account transactions*; (ii) *external trade balance*; (iii) *net primary income*; (iv) *net financial account* and; (v) *net capital account* exhibits time/historic cumulative value concentrations according to each zone. By time cumulative value concentration, we mean if and with what magnitude, core countries have received a greater share of world-economy surplus by assessing each of balance of payments account.

According to Arrighi (1998), per capita GDP, in some way, express the aggregate return by each specific country participation in international division of labor. This assessment allows us to analyze transfer of value/time hypothesis on a world-scale dimension and as a *longue durée* process.[4] The results reveal a clear concentration of value accumulation which reflects the transfer of value from organic periphery/semiperiphery to organic core.

Organic core countries have accumulated for them 53% of current account positive results of the total current account surplus in the years available with data. This is significative since it shows a structural basis for the transfer of value. The periphery accumulated 32% and the semiperiphery 15%. When working time[5] is incorporated, we are able to see Marini's point on superexploitation. In the case of organic core, weekly hours usually worked varies from 34 to 37, for the semiperiphery from 36 to 47, and for the periphery from 40[6] to 53.

The IMF manual on Balance of Payments (BPM6)[7] brings an emphasis under the notion of "economic value," its "functional categories," nature

118 Ísis Campos Camarinha

Table 9.1 Accumulation by type of balance of payments account, organic zones, and working time, 1960–2019

Current Account	Core	Semiperiphery	Periphery
Historical Surplus Accumulated	53%	15%	32%
Working Time	34–37 hours	36.6–47.4 hours	40.4–59.5 hours
Net Primary Income			
Historical Surplus Accumulated	83%	2%	15%
External Trade Balance			
Historical Surplus Accumulated	44%	24%	32%
Net Financial Account			
Historical Surplus Accumulated	60%	16%	24%

Source: Percentage numbers calculated by the author from the original data of balance of payments account available on World Development Indicators of The World Bank. Access: https://data. worldbank.org/indicator. ILO weekly hours usually worked and refer to the year 2019 or the most recent year available. Data were not available for most of the countries from 1960 to 1980, so it covers better the 1990s, 2000s, and 2010s. see Appendix 1.

and correlations as a system of economic relations while interactions between residents and non-residents. An economic value created, acquired, transformed, etc., and its accounting system in monetary form according to what they represent for the totality of economic system. *"Transaction is an interaction between two institutional units that occurs by mutual agreement or through the operation of the law and involves an exchange of value or a transfer"* (IMF Balance of payments and international position manual, p. 29). The accounting principle is the double entry, meaning that for each transaction corresponds two moves regarding economic value, for example, if a resident of a country exports for a non-resident, this transaction is account by the "provision of physical resources" and a "receipt of financial resources" (currency) from non-residents. The same happens with the sale of shares, bonds, flows of direct investment and so on, every transaction is marked with a credit and a debit.

"*The different accounts within the balance of payments are distinguished according to the nature of the economic resources provided and received*" (IMF Balance of payments and international position manual, p. 9). If the resident provides it receives, an exchange, for example, in the case of receiving currency and deposits for the provision of physical goods (export), there is a specific "functional category" in the financial account named "reserve assets" and a subitem "currency and deposits": *"Entries in the financial account can be corresponding entries to goods, services, income, capital account, or other financial account entries"* (IMF Balance of payments and international position manual, p. 133). "Currency and deposits" are economic assets, financial instruments with extreme liquidity therefor.

Financial account has other "functional categories," direct investment, portfolio investment, financial derivatives, and employee stock options and other investments. There may be an asset acquisition or a liability incurrence, each one has a type of financial instrument corresponding "claim," whether interest, dividend, rent, etc., whose flows are registered in the primary income account, meaning that this account refers to income generated by "economic values" in those other "initial" forms (financial account or capital account), this last one related to "nonproduced nonfinancial," such as exploitation of natural resources, corresponding to royalties, rents, for example. There are balances for each account, and because of this logic of accounting economic values, with its transaction corresponding entries, according to its nature, it results in some important global correlations. The balance of current account (trade, primary, and secondary income) and the balance of capital account is equal to the balance of financial account. So, a country may be net lending or net borrowing revealing its position in the world:

> The overall balance on the financial account is called net lending/net borrowing. Net lending means that, in net terms, the economy supplies funds to the rest of the world, taking into account acquisition and disposal of financial assets and incurrence and repayment of liabilities (net borrowing means the opposite) . . . Net lending/net borrowing can be derived from either the sum of the balance on the current and capital account or from the balance on the financial account. In concept, the values should be equal.
>
> *(IMF Balance of Payments and International Position Manual 2009, 133)*

Net primary income is the expression of capital juridical–property relations of assets or the expression of capital-income related to rate of returns on production and financial instruments who owns what and has rights on what. It expresses the inflow and outflow of income due to investment, financial acquisitions of assets, or natural resources exploitation. The results show that organic core accumulated 82% of the total primary income surplus by zone in the period covered by the data available for all countries—interest, dividends, profit, reinvested earnings, rent, etc. The results from *net financial account* reveal magnitudes of 60% for organic core. Therefore, core countries tend to be net lending, while semiperiphery and periphery net borrowing. Core countries tend to have more assets than liabilities, which generates them a constant inflow in the primary income account. The "money" that enters in periphery and semiperiphery may be speculative or not, in the second case, of course, it generates economic multipliers for those economies, but part of the value created is also sent, in the future, abroad. The main question to be answered is: Is this transfer of value higher than the original amount of money/investment received?

External trade balance results express the tendency to trade terms deterioration related to the increase of imports relatively to exports due to peripheral/ semiperipheral industrial stage of economic activities. Considering historical accumulated surplus external trade balance has better results for organic periphery/semiperiphery because the share retained by organic core reduces to 44%.

Conclusion

Dependency happens as a process in time, and this process generates a transfer of value/time, as argued by Marini, so time/value are real aspects of capitalist accumulation. We tried to demonstrate this insight by analyzing the monetary aspect of value transfer of current account transactions, as well as other accounts, where we could find strong tendencies of concentration of accumulation from a historical-time perspective regarding core–semiperiphery–periphery structure. These results provide significant empirical evidence of the value transfer expressed by these concentrations. The results show important correlations and characteristics that help to understand the meaning of dependency and superexploitation over time as alienation and accumulation on a world-scale dimension. The most important tendency in historical accumulation by organic zone is in net primary account.

The process of deindustrialization explored by Brussi in this volume enhances these tendencies, but, on the other hand, deindustrialization doesn't mean that sub-imperialism is a phenomenon of the past. In fact, this "unequal exchange" reflected by all these tendencies is "compensated" with superexploitation and sub-imperialist strategies allied to foreign capital. What might be change is the strategy itself, not the phenomenon. These tendencies express the transfer of value and mean a "spiral" of economic reproduction of dependence, as explained by Marini in his Dialectics of Dependency. It is an indispensable analytical tool to understand international division of labor as asymmetric zones, one aspect of *structural timespace* overlapped by *historical-category timespace* dimensional logic. In short: We argued that for world-system analysis, the concept of *timespace* is central to understand the proper ontological dimensions of the capitalist world-system, and that one ontological dimension of capitalist world-system accumulation is the underlying process of dependency reproduction as transfer of value on a world-scale dimension.

Dialectics of Time and Value Accumulation 121

Table 9.2 Period covered by country and type of balance of payments account

	Current Account	Net Primary Account	Net External Balance	Net Financial Account
Core				
Australia	1989–2019	1960–2019	1960–2019	1989–2019
Canada	1960–2019	1970–2019	1961–2019	1960–2019
Denmark	1975–2019	1966–2018	1966–2019	1975–2019
New Zealand	2000–2019	1971–2018	1970–2019	2000–2019
Norway	1975–2019	1978–2019	1970–2019	1975–2019
Sweden	1970–2019	1970–2019	1960–2019	1970–2019
Switzerland	1977–2019	1970–1994	1970–2019	1977–2019
United Kingdom	1970–2019	1970–2018	1970–2019	1970–2019
Unites States	1970–2019	1970–2018	1970–2018	1970–2019
Germany	1971–2019	1970–2018	1970–2019	1971–2019
Semiperiphery				
Argentina	1976–2019	1962–2019	1962–2019	1976–2019
Chile	1975–2018	1960–2019	1960–2019	1975–2018
Costa Rica	1977–2019	1960–2019	1960–2019	1977–2019
Greece	1976–2019	1960–2018	1960–2019	1976–2019
China (Hong Kong)	1998–2019	1960–2019	1960–2019	1998–2019
Hungary	1982–2019	1993–1998; 2004–2018	1991–2019	1982–2019
Ireland	2005–2019	1995–2018	1970–2019	2005–2019
Israel	1960–1961; 1965–2019	1970–2018	1970–2019	1960–1961; 1964–2019
Jamaica	1976–2019	1960–2018	1960–2019	1976–2018
México	1979–2019	1960–2019	1960–2019	1979–2019
Panama	1977–2019	1960–2019	1960–2018	1977–2019
Portugal	1975–2019	1970–2019	1970–2019	1975–2019
Romania	1971–2019	1989–2019	1990–2019	1971–2019
South Africa	1960–2019	1960–2019	1960–2019	1960–2019
Spain	1975–2019	1970–2018	1970–2019	1975–2019
Turkey	1974–2019	1967–2019	1960–2019	1974–2019
Uruguay	1978–2019	1960–2018	1960–2019	1978–2019
Russian Federation	1994–2019	1980–2019	1989–2019	1994–2019
Venezuela	1970–2016	1960–2014	1960–2014	1970–2016
Periphery				
Afghanistan	1979–1989; 2008–2019	1960–1981; 2009–2019	1960–1978; 2009–2019	1979–1989; 2008–2019
Angola	1985–2019	1985–2019	2000–2018	1985–2019
Bangladesh	1976–2019	1973–2019	1960–2019	1976–2019
Bolivia	1976–2019	1976–2019	1960–2019	1976–2019
Burundi	1985–2018	1960–2019	1960–2019	1985–2018
Camerron	1977–2018	1967–2019	1965–2019	1977–2018

(Continued)

122 Ísis Campos Camarinha

Table 9.2 Continued

	Current Account	Net Primary Account	Net External Balance	Net Financial Account
Central African Republic	1977–1994;	1960–2017	1960–2019	1977–1994
Chad	1977–1994	1960–2019	1960–2019	1977–1994
China (Mainland)	1982–2019	1981–2019	1960–2019	1982–2019
Egypt	1977–2019	1965–2019	1965–2018	1977–2019
El salvador	1976–2019	1965–2019	1965–2019	1976–2019
Ethiopia	1977–2018	1981–2019	2011–2019	1977–2018
Guinea	1986–2018	1986–2019	1986–2019	1986–2018
Haiti	1971–2018	1980–2019	1988–2019	1971–2018
Honduras	1974–2019	1960–2019	1960–2019	1974–2019
India	1975–2019	1960–2019	1960–2019	1975–2019
Indonesia	1981–2019	2010–2019	1967–2019	1981–2019
Kenya	1975–2017	1960–2019	1960–2019	1975–2017
Liberia	1979–1987; 2004–2018	2000–2019	2000–2019	1979–1987; 2004–2018
Madagascar	1974–2018	1960–2019	1960–2019	1974–2018
Malawi	1977–2018	1960–2019	1960–2019	1977–2018
Mali	1975–2018	1967–2019	1967–2019	1975–2018
Mauritania	1975–1998; 2012–2018	1968–2019	1961–2019	1975–1998; 2012–2018
Mozambique	2005–2018	1991–2019	1991–2019	2005–2018
Nepal	1976–2018	1960–2019	1965–2019	1976–2018
Niger	1974–2018	1960–2019	1960–2019	1974–2018
Nigeria	1977–2018	1960–2018	1960–2019	1977–2018
Pakistan	1976–2019	1960–2019	1960–2019	1976–2018
Papua New Guinea	1976–2018	1960–2019	1961–2004	1976–2018
The Philippines	1977–2019	1960–2019	1960–2019	1977–2019
Rwanda	2010–2018	1970–2019	1960–2019	2010–2018
Senegal	1974–2018	1968–2019	1960–2019	1974–2018
Sri Lanka	1975–2018	1960–2019	1960–2019	1975–2018
Sudan	1978–2018	1960–2019	1960–2019	1977–2018
Tanzania	1976–2018	1988–2019	1990–2019	1976–2018
Thailand	1975–2019	1960–2019	1960–2019	1975–2019
Togo	1974–2018	1960–2019	1960–2019	1974–2018
Uganda	1980–2019	1960–2019	1960–2019	1980–2019
Zambia	1978–1991; 1997–2019	1960–2019	1994–2019	1978–1991; 1997–2019
Zimbabwe	1977–1994; 2009–2017	1960–2019	1975–2018	1977–1994; 2009–2017

Notes

1. Mathias Luce (2018) has a brilliant work, which, in fact, was our main reference of dependency and unequal exchange as a negatively determined process of law of

value and also "the category of dependence" and "unequal exchange as transfer of value." Another crucial reference for this understanding is Samir Amin (1975), he defines what is "accumulation on a world scale," how countries exchange unequally, for example, how 1 hour is not changed for one hour of work.

2. Justifying the title of the chapter.
3. "Initially the commodity appeared to us as an object with a dual character, possessing both use-value and exchange-value. Later on it was seen that labour, too, has a dual character: in so far as it finds its expression in value, it no longer possesses the same characteristics as when it is the creator of use-values. I was the first to point out and examine critically this twofold nature of the labor contained in commodities. As this point is crucial to an understanding of political economy, it requires further elucidation" (Marx 1990 [1867] v.1: 131–132).
4. The data are not fully complete. We accessed World Development Indicators, but most of the countries don't have data since 1960, only a few of them. The data get more complete as we get to the 1980, 1990, 2000, and 2010. Although this is not the ideal, we think that for a preliminary study the findings are consistent with the hypothesis. We decided to keep the cover 1960–2019 because the original data from World Development Indicators are organized for that period. See Appendix 1.
5. The data are from ILO (International Labor Organization): weekly hours usually worked and refer to the year 2019 or the most recent year available by country. Data were not available for some countries.
6. Two periphery countries are bellow this 40 hours, Rwanda and Malawi.
7. Usually what literature calls "capital account" refers to what in this last manual of IMF is called "financial account." This "capital account" (non-produced non-financial) distinguishes from what is "financial."

PART III

Social Contradictions of Capitalism in the Twenty-first Century

10

"PRIMITIVE" ACCUMULATION UNDER HISTORICAL CAPITALISM AND THE UNEQUAL SOCIAL REGULATION OF THE GLOBAL LABOR FORCE

Kelvin A. Santiago-Valles

This chapter considers the role of "primitive" accumulation in socially generating (i.e., regulating) and reproducing the global labor force as sharply differentiated and heterogeneous in conflicting ways. In the following, I briefly illustrate some of the characteristics specific to certain cycles of "primitive" accumulation via a few examples from the mid-1700s to the present. The chapter focuses primarily on the institutional sites and dimensions of these social regulatory mechanisms, rather than on their inherently linked structures of knowledge, which I have examined elsewhere.[1] Though I do not directly consider contemporary debates on "primitive" accumulation (e.g., Perelman 2000; Harvey 2003a, 137–82; Federici 2004, 133–65; Bonefeld 2008, 13–96; Negi, Auerbach, Büscher et al. 2009; Patnaik and Moyo 2011; Brass 2011; Sanyal 2013; Neocleous 2014, 48–87), I indirectly take them into account to the extent that they are germane to my reinterpretation of Marx's analysis of coercion within "primitive" accumulation (primarily in *Capital, vol. I*).

Capital Accumulation and the Relational Asymmetries of the Global Labor Force: À Propos Terence K. Hopkins

Any examination of so-called primitive accumulation needs to begin by focusing on labor. Within capitalism as a historical system, labor is an inherently contested and asymmetrical social relation, linked to, yet necessarily entailing, its opposite (i.e., capital), thereby involving wage-based work, albeit going beyond it. Labor under capitalism needs to be created and continually reproduced as separated/dispossessed from its means of subsistence, as both processes (dispossession and reproduction) mutually (re)shape each other (Marx 1977, 716, 724). In this sense, capital as a social relation—what Marx calls "the

DOI: 10.4324/9781003325109-13

capital-relation itself" (ibid.)—is conceptually and historically commensurate with separation/dispossession inasmuch as Marx, "not only conceives of capital as separation but also sees [separation] as the constitutive force of capital" (Bonefeld 2008, 80).

One of the earliest reflections on "primitive" accumulation within world-systems analysis, particularly, vis-à-vis labor, was provided by Terence K. Hopkins in a brief but important section of his conceptual-methodological essay "The Study of Capitalist World-Economy: Some Introductory Considerations." There he insists (1982a, 15, 16), with Marx, that one of the areas "where further theoretical work is needed" is on the question of capitalist accumulation and the place it "occupies in the world-historical or world-systemic accumulation of capital." For Hopkins, this immediately leads to an examination of so-called primitive accumulation, initially as this process is commonly understood, that is, as a "residual" category specifically related to "the 'transition' from feudalism to capitalism in northwestern Europe" (ibid., 16). However, he then points out that "the concept may also be interpreted as referring to . . . the continuing creation (extension) of the conditions for the 'capitalistic' development of capital to all branches of production (old and new) in every nook and cranny of the globe outside of the geopolitical area of their initial world-historical creation" (ibid.). For Hopkins, Marx's assumptions in *Capital, vol. I* leave open the specificities of how capitalists procure and accrue surpluses from the various labor forms outside the wage relation—for example, "slaves, serfs, indebted tenants," "family farmers and other small producers"—(ibid.), likewise passing over how such non-wage labor forms are socially (re)produced. Yet what is implicit in this formulation is that the "continuing creation (extension) of the conditions for the 'capitalistic' development of capital" globally necessarily involves "the continuing creation (extension)" of the differences between wage labor and non-wage labor under capital—including the geohistorical distribution of those labor forms—as one of those key "conditions for the 'capitalistic' development of capital."

From there Hopkins moves to the other area "where further theoretical work is needed," that is, to say the question of how labor is socioeconomically replenished, in this case regarding the asymmetrically distributed wage levels across the axial division and integration of regions within the world-economy (ibid., 18–21). The broader context in this regard, for him, is imperialism, colonialism, and unequal exchange. And that inevitably leads him to the intrinsic relationship between historical capitalism's structural inequalities and their impact on laboring populations—"the processes of systems of relational rank in the modern world (what is conventionally called stratification)"—*in relation to* the social (re)production of those inequalities. For Hopkins, in this context, social (re)production refers to "the political processes that give shape and substance to systems of relational and, thus relative, social rank (processes such as enactment and enforcement of laws supporting or preventing relations of personal bondage, civil liberties and civil rights, progressive or regressive taxation, open or closed or discriminating immigration)" (ibid., 21–22). As I argue in the following, one of the characteristics of those "systems of relational rank" is the polarization of the global labor force, while so-called primitive accumulation plays a significant role in some of the "processes that give shape and substance to systems of relational and, thus relative, social rank," specifically as regards to certain sectors of that global labor force. All of which brings us back to how the asymmetrical formation of world labor is made and maintained.

During the different phases of historical capitalism, the global labor force always has been polarized and unevenly fashioned. The systemic heterogeneity of the laboring population across the planet partly is exemplified by the substandard social conditions of the majority of the world's working classes. Conversely, the most coercively regulated forms of dispossession, exploitation, and domination play a key role in fashioning and replicating such heterogeneity, above all by way of the mechanisms of "primitive" accumulation throughout its various cycles, along with the corresponding forms and patterns of knowledge. What Marx (1977, 916) characterized as the more prevalent use of violent force, "itself an economic power," lies in marked contrast to the less brutally regulated segments of a sexually racialized global labor force,[2] based on the latter social fraction's extremely relative advantages (Aglietta 1979, 80–81, 170–74; Mies 1986). As I also explain later, ongoing "primitive" accumulation plays a structurally decisive role in defining that relational polarization within the world's labor force. In the same way, this divergence is ethno-racialized[3] insofar as the world's laboring-poor majorities are located disproportionately in, or originate from, the socioeconomic peripheries of the world-economy (a.k.a., peoples in and from the "Third World"). More specifically, such polarization has a relatively greater and more detrimental impact on laboring sectors sexually racialized as subordinate, to wit, the peripheral-feminized and/or dispossessed female sectors of the population (Mies, Bennholdt-Thomsen, and von Werlhof 1988; Manning 2015).[4]

Although in a different context, Marx seemed to reference the ethno-racialized aspects of this relational polarization within the world's labor force when he described how chattel slavery and industrial child labor became "systematically combined." For him, these were unevenly interdependent yet divergent forms of mid-nineteenth century capitalist dispossession and destitution during the British imperial era. "While the cotton industry introduced child slavery into England, in the United States, it gave impulse for the transformation of the earlier, more or less patriarchal slavery into a system of commercial exploitation. In fact, the veiled slavery of the wage laborers in Europe needed the unqualified slavery of the New World as its pedestal" (Marx 1977, 925; see also Marx 1963, 111–12).

The overwhelming majority of the global labor force historically has become the target of multiple waves of the harshest social (re)production/

130 Kelvin A. Santiago-Valles

regulation, which in turn has precipitated protracted waves of social resistance to capitalist dispossession, as I briefly illustrate in the following. Each long-term era transforms the historical specificity of certain populations in order to create and maintain the kind of labor subject to the greatest degradation, making those populations more profitably exploitable at a given moment. This is labor whose structurally deficient social reproduction falls short of providing for their physical and mental sustenance and everyday life (Emmanuel 1972, 122–29, 161–92; Aglietta 1979, 170–74; Braudel 1992, 197–98, 266–72 and passim; Amin and van der Linden 1997; Linebaugh and Redicker 2000). Which now brings us to *Capital, vol. I*'s account of the harshest methods of social regulation, namely those corresponding to "primitive" accumulation.

Conceptual Logic and Mode of Exposition: "Primitive" Accumulation in *Capital, vol. I*

As I have elaborated at much greater length elsewhere,[5] Marx's exposition in Part Eight of *Capital, vol. I* follows an implicit conceptual-methodological progression in how he defined "primitive" accumulation and in how such processes came into being. Initially—in chapter 26—Marx (1977, 874–76) presents capitalism taken as a whole and more generally, glossing over the particular aspects of the ways laborers are divorced from their means of subsistence. In that opening chapter of Part Eight, "primitive" accumulation mainly appears as unfolding *previous* to "the mode of production corresponding to capital" (Marx 1977, 875). But when his inquiry shifts—in chapters 27 to 31—to discussing capitalism much more historically and focusing on the specificities and development of the mechanisms of dispossession (ibid., 877–926), then so-called primitive accumulation comes into view as happening *during* the era of capitalism, albeit at a time in which "the mode of production itself had as yet no specifically capitalist character" (ibid., 900).

Finally—in chapters 32 and 33—his analysis approaches the question from the vantage point of advanced capitalism (ibid., 927–40). It is then, that is, once socioeconomic transformations have "sufficiently decomposed the old society" and "the capitalist mode of production stands on its own feet" (ibid., 928), that the "merciless . . . methods of the primitive accumulation of capital" reveal themselves to be untenable and redundant insofar as they "form the pre-history of capital" (ibid.). In this third moment of Marx's exposition (i.e., after advanced capitalism comes into view as true, genuine capitalism), the preceding era at last shows itself to be capitalist only in the most superficial, incomplete, and simplified terms. The latter conceptual-methodological approach is partly analogous to his distinction between formal and real subsumption of labor to capital (ibid., 1019–34). This analytical movement illustrates how, within Marx's argument, "the previous mode of presentation must, itself, be subjected to research and

"Primitive" Accumulation **131**

must constitute in turn the material of a new presentation" (Negri 1984, 13; see also, Mezzadra 2011, 304–05, 307).

One common denominator in Marx's overall argument is that "primitive" accumulation usually not only involves the most brutal and/or extremely penetrating processes for separating laborers from their means of subsistence but also tends to entail the most violent and cruel methods for continually guaranteeing (i.e., reproducing) such dispossession. We should bear in mind that he defined the accumulation of capital in general as "how capital arises from surplus value," meaning "The employment of surplus value as capital or its reconversion into capital" through continuous and incremental reinvestment (Marx 1977, 725). It also is important to remember the fundamentals of capitalist social reproduction whereby the laborer, "separated from its means of objectification and realization," "constantly produces objective wealth in the form of capital, an alien power that dominates and exploits him" (ibid., 716). All of which brings to mind his passing remark (1981, 354–55) in *Capital, vol. III* (concerning the tendency toward the falling rate of profit) that the dispossession he described in Part Eight of volume I (on "primitive" accumulation) was simply the historical origin of practices "subsequently appearing as a constant process in the accumulation and concentration of capital" (see also, De Angelis 2008, 33). By the same token, if capitalist accumulation is understood as the endless creation of capital by surplus value and if surplus value can only be generated via the dispossession of labor from its means of subsistence, then it becomes difficult not to see that the very existence of capitalist accumulation must inherently necessitate the uninterrupted dispossession of labor. That particular conclusion runs contrary to David Harvey's (2003a, 137–82) well-known formulation about "accumulation by dispossession," a critique already proposed by Massimo De Angelis (2007, 231).[6]

Moreover for Marx, "primitive" accumulation likewise includes equally harsh non-wage procedures—"Colonial system, public debts, heavy taxes, protection, commercial wars, etc." (Marx 1977, 922)—for obtaining complementary volumes of wealth, together with what he called "extra-economic" methods of destitution, in order to reinvest in wage-based capitalist production. Capital's need for such techniques was driven by the limitations of capitalist production, first and foremost during its pre-industrial phase (ibid., 914–16). However, he additionally describes how no less brutal wage-focused pauperizing methods operated to maximize capitalist earnings throughout the industrial era. For instance, chapter 28 depicts governments in late-eighteenth- to mid-nineteenth century Western Europe continually imposing "barbarous laws" on a general scale (not merely "in exceptional cases") in order to discipline and unrelentingly punish labor: for example, restricting trade-union activity and legally limiting wage levels (ibid., 902–04).

Marx's argument here calls to mind the relationship between "primitive" accumulation and capitalist accumulation in general. Yet it also suggests some

132 Kelvin A. Santiago-Valles

of the implications and contradictions concerning how he saw the prospects and trends of capitalism historically in light of how the systemically polarized and hierarchically located fractions of the global labor force are socially (re) produced. For Marx, the general law of capitalist accumulation requires certain levels of structural coercion for the active segment of labor and especially for those reduced to penury, which already presupposes that dispossession has been initiated: Capitalist accumulation is about the torture, oblivion, bondage, and deprivation of labor (ibid., 799) meted out in order to continue *an existing* process of dispossession.

Yet from the perspective of the historical long term, the relatively disparate expressions of capitalist violence—particularly via "the concentrated organized force of society" (ibid., 915) across the different cycles of so-called primitive accumulation—involve a more concrete and heightened level of capitalist coercion (ibid., 875, 885–92, 896–99, 915–25). In other words, *whenever and wherever these harsher and more intense mechanisms are deployed as part of capitalist production and reproduction, that is precisely when and where "primitive" accumulation is at work.* Such historically specific brutality is excessive and disproportionate only as compared to the regular levels of coercion fitting the formal-abstract logic of capital accumulation. Nonetheless, this level of ferocity and penetration would be *not only* indispensable (from the point of view of capital) *for originating* the torment and degradation akin to the general law of capitalist accumulation. From capital's perspective, the higher level of violence and assault intrinsic to "primitive" accumulation would in the same way be necessary *to organize and maintain* certain types of labor formation, thereby guaranteeing the perpetuation of historically specific modes of augmented—albeit, relative—misery, impoverishment, insecurity, and devastation. Ergo, all capitalist accumulation necessarily functions across a whole spectrum of coercion, with "primitive" accumulation unfolding at the most barbaric and terroristic end of that spectrum (Corrigan 1977). Of course, the exact methods and configurations of such violence, the degrees of ruthlessness involved, and the proportions of the given populations being thus devastated, are all historically and geographically contingent.

Marx seems to have inferred a number of trends in the exposition within Part Eight of *Capital, vol. I.* For one thing, he apparently assumed the general course of capitalist accumulation would transform all labor into wage work—and that such accumulation, at its most advanced stage, would be generated and propagated through strictly economic mechanisms. Then again, it looks as if he expected that capitalist development eventually would eliminate the need for "extra-economic" force, when the "worker can be left to the natural laws of [capitalist] production" (ibid., 899). The problem, of course, is Marx apparently took for granted that the fundamental socioeconomic imbalances he described within the global labor force under capitalism—along with the sexually ethno-racial inequalities mentioned in passing and the requisite "most merciless barbarism" regulating/reproducing this variegated congregation of labor—would all be transcended when capitalism fully reached that "certain [advanced] stage of development." This is to say, he seems to have envisaged those populations (to be exact, the ones impacted by the future increase in the "mass of misery, oppression, slavery, degradation, and exploitation") becoming a socioeconomically uniform and waged majority of labor under world capitalism (ibid., 929). Alas and if my reading is accurate, such assumptions are not only questionable in relation to Marx's own era (Davidoff 1974; Steinfeld 2001; Piqueras 2009): They are even more debatable relative to historical capitalism today, once again illustrating the persistent differentiation (however uneven) and continuing polarization within the contemporary labor force globally.

"Primitive" Accumulation Under Economic Neoliberalism

The protracted and fluctuating modalities of so-called primitive accumulation over the past century and a quarter clearly illustrate how the most ruthless means of capitalist accumulation have persisted in some mutated form or another. Such mechanisms have undergone yet another cyclical resurgence with the rise of contemporary globalization since the 1970s. The advent of the long-term phase of economic decline worldwide, in turn, launched the current neoliberal/neo-positivist methods of social regulation and discourse. The more brutal measures were a response to the gains made by the global upsurge in labor resistance and poor people's movements (along with their middle-class collaborators) during the late-1950s to early-1970s, many of them of anti-capitalist and anti-imperialist inflection (Arrighi, Hopkins, and Wallerstein 1989, 98–112; Jian, Klimke, Krirasirova et al. 2018). That wave of resistance raised the costs of reproducing global labor at the time, including increases in the costs of managing such labor and of handling the concomitant revolts negatively impacting corporate profits (Wallerstein 1995b).

Beginning in the mid- to late-1970s global capital reacted to this labor revolt and broad social unrest with a shift toward more coercive forms of control . through the spread of flexible production, financialization, degraded manufacturing, the expansion of personal and business services, and the informalization of the world-economy, accompanied by massive population displacements. Those modes for disciplining the world's laboring majorities were in line with the diktats of the World Bank and the IMF who went about imposing governmental austerity programs, the privatization of state industries and services, downgraded labor rights, sharply reduced subsidies to the urban poor and rural populations, augmented state security and surveillance, and/or currency devaluations. The Global South has been the principal target of the latter measures, in this manner catalyzing civil wars and interstate rivalries, in conjunction with even larger mass migrations and streams of refugees. This expanding spectrum of coercive methods overlaps with the further industrialization of war, the globalization of local armed conflicts, militarized policing, and securitized social reproduction (Arrighi, Hui, Ray, and Reifer 1999, 88–95; Bhattacharyya, Gabriel, and Small 2002, 28–57; Harvey 2003a; Gregory and Pred 2006; Federici 2008; Santiago-Valles 2012, 186–87; Sassen 2014).

This most recent wave of "primitive" accumulation has taken the form of highly coerced non-wage precarious labor (chattel slavery, debt bondage, sharecropping, contractual servitude), the generalized expropriation of vulnerable populations (involving "[degraded] women and children," indigent refugees, "lesser peoples," and dislocated aboriginal communities), together with formally "waged" compulsory labor, as well as casualized and depreciated wage work. In the past three decades especially, this cycle of "primitive" accumulation has encompassed a wide range of forms, for example, gem cutting in rural India (Kapadia 1995), New York City's garment sweatshops and retail-food services (Kwong 2001), land grabs in Africa (Allen 2011), the privatization of water in Bolivia (Swyngedouw 2005), the timber industry and oil pipeline construction in Myanmar (Johansen 2000), global sex trafficking (Jeffreys 2008), service subcontracting in U.S. military bases in Iraq and Afghanistan (Ross 2011), and the expanded dispossession of Arab lands by Israel (Hever 2013). The fact that these and other related instances comprise populations in and from the global periphery is not fortuitous, insofar as they are the direct result of "the colonial division of labor . . . on a world scale" (McMichael 2012, 31–32), given that "colonialism racialized international inequality" (ibid., 4). Even official data which very narrowly defines (and grossly undercounts) highly coerced labor—as in the reports issued by the International Labor Organization—is wont to indicate that "Modern slavery[7] was most prevalent in Africa (7.6 per 1,000 people), followed by Asia and the Pacific (6.1 per 1,000 people), then Europe and Central Asia (3.9 per 1,000 people)" (ILO 2017, 10).

The Corollary Global Waves of Resistance

As we have seen, the procedures of "primitive" accumulation have been foisted more on certain populations than on others, demarcating the former as the most sexually racialized segments of the global labor force. This heightened level of brutality has generated groundswells of revolt that have also tended to be cyclical and aimed against the exploitation and/or domination of these same populations by global capital and the corresponding state institutions. Simultaneously, the ruptures within existing forms of rule and the clashes between rival fractions of global capital similarly have surfaced like clockwork. And such fissures and strife usually involve no less cyclical crises within the social-regulatory mechanisms and dominant knowledges: Here the prevailing techniques are competing with emergent—and eventually ascendant—instances of leading knowledge and social regulation that materialize to better dissect and manage wayward subaltern populations.

"Primitive" Accumulation **135**

Yet the mechanisms of "primitive" accumulation by the same token have played a key role during watershed periods in both how the predominant structures of social regulation and knowledge and their competing counterpart structures are producing and reproducing the majority of world's labor force. That is what transpired, for instance: throughout the 1760s–1810s (uneven decay of the spectacular institutional violence typical of the Linnean Great Confinements and rise of the utilitarian/Lamarckian Second Servitudes), the 1850s–1880s (asymmetrical deterioration of classical-liberal forms and the transformation of the Second Servitudes along positivist/Social Darwinist lines), the 1910s–1940s (crisis and protracted waning of the Social Darwinist/eugenicist Second Servitudes and rise of rehabilitationist/Fordist forms), and from the 1970s to the present (crisis and uneven decline of rehabilitationist/Fordism and rise of neo-liberal/neopositivist modalities) (Cohen 1985; Adas 1989; Garland 2001; Holt 2000). These shifts partly overlap with—but are not reduced to—the extended periods of decline within long-term, global economic cycles: for example, during 1720–1772, 1864–1896, 1920–1949, and 1973 up to today (Braudel 1992, 72–86; Arrighi 1994, 7–9). The ensuing transformations to some extent moreover have been known to in the same way coincide with the prolonged crises and subsequent breakdown of globally hegemonic states within the capitalist world-system, as was the case of 1680–1743 for Holland vis-à-vis the hegemonic interregnum of 1743–1815, then 1875–1914 for the United Kingdom vis-à-vis the hegemonic interregnum of 1914–1945, followed by 1973 to the present for the United States (Silver and Slater 1999).

Thus we have one important way in which waves of social resistance have reacted to the larger-scale, longer-term capitalist accumulation of wealth and misery—especially its harshest and most brutal expressions (i.e., the cycles of "primitive" accumulation)—that have in turn inadvertently influenced shifts in global hegemony. For example, the increasing devastation, brutality, and military discipline of eighteenth century chattel slavery led to the 1720s–1770s and 1790–1815 waves of slave rebellions and anti-slavery conspiracies that shook the Americas, the Caribbean, and Western Africa. This tide of anti-slavery insurgency resulted in the short-term disruption of the Atlantic slave trade precisely when this trade was a leading source of "primitive" capitalist accumulation on a world-scale—especially for Great Britain. The insurgent wave also struck when the United Kingdom and France were jockeying for domination and leadership within the capitalist world-system after the collapse of Dutch global hegemony in the mid-1700s, leaving no immediate successor. In the medium term, the same slave rebellions culminated in the Haitian Revolution, depriving France of its most profitable overseas possession (St. Domingue), then the most important and lucrative colony in the entire world. The serious erosion of this key source of revenue hampered France in conducting its worldwide war against Great Britain, enabling the British colony of Jamaica to briefly regain first place in global sugar exports during 1810–1820. All of this contributed decisively (albeit,

136 Kelvin A. Santiago-Valles

fortuitously) to the rise of British hegemony within the world-economy and to the spread of industrial slavery and other globalized forms of extremely coercive labor: that is to say, the Second Slavery or, alternatively, the [Social Darwinist] Second Servitudes (Tomich 2003, 56–73; Santiago-Valles 2005, 57, 63, 65–68).

These waves of social unrest epitomize how insubordination among the laboring-poor and subaltern majorities often spreads more rapidly in response to the degradation of mass social conditions wrought by the machineries of so-called primitive accumulation. Such challenges usually take advantage of fault lines internal to existing forms of rule and of rising inter- and intra-capitalist conflicts over control of the world-economy. But further research on these recurrent struggles against the shifting cycles of "primitive" accumulation could benefit from in-depth studies of the racialized differentiation and polarization within an unevenly coerced global labor force. The latter illustrates why much more conceptual work and empirical research is needed on how such cycles of so-called primitive accumulation are inherently racial, not only in their institutional dimensions but also in their epistemic aspects as well. This chapter has attempted to demonstrate how rethinking the complex relationship between historical capitalism, highly coerced labor, and heterogeneous labor formation offers a window into the operations and specificities of "primitive" accumulation even as reexamining so-called primitive accumulation helps us uncover the framework of those very same complexities—which perforce leads to a reconsideration of Marx's analysis of the subject, particularly in *Capital, vol. I*.

Notes

1. As I explain in chapter 1 of a book manuscript under revision and tentatively titled *Rethinking "Race," Labor, and Empire: Global-Racial Regimes and "Primitive" Accumulation in the Historical Long-Term*, the sequentially arranged architecture of dominant knowledges cannot exist nor operate outside of—nor ultimately be distinct from—the otherwise contested institutional sites corresponding to different epistemic cycles where, among other things, scientific discoveries are made and structurally intended to be accepted, nor separate from the institutional forms these discoveries assume; more generally, such recurring knowledges are not external to the places where information is processed and normalised, nor apart from how this information crystalizes; the successive structures of knowledge do not come into being as extraneous to where techniques are learned and distributed, nor can they be differentiated from the ways in which these techniques are represented and charted.
2. As I also clarify in chapters 1 through 3 of *Rethinking "Race," Labor, and Empire*, historicizing the overlaps between "race" and labor in this manner does not presuppose a "social class" to which one adds, or intersects with, "race" and "sex/gender", as multiple categories or not. Rather, I am arguing that the ethno-racial differentiated composition of global labor entails aspects of social polarization involving gendered/sexualized characteristics that socially construct—*and depreciate*—broad swaths of laboring populations worldwide as "subservient," "pliant," "guileless," and yet "unpredictable," "emotional," "in need of supervision," etc., to wit as "naturally" subordinate for these reasons too (Manning 2015; see also, endnote no. 4). This is particularly the case for those toilers within colonial/(neo)colonial spaces and/

"Primitive" Accumulation **137**

or among peripheral-feminized and/or dispossessed female laborers (Fanon 1967, 177–90; Said 1979, 38, 40–41, 207; Scott 1989, 98–99; Riley 1988; Nandy 1989, 11, 32–33). Yet such an inquiry does not get us very far without acknowledging other populations (laboring and elite) sexually racialized as more dominant (masculinized and/or male) by existing social apparatuses. The entire process unfolds relative to the broader hierarchical polarization of all populations across the different periods of capitalist accumulation. The issue is critically important insofar as, for the majority of the global labor force, those sexually racialized aspects of labor are associated with higher levels of coercion. Not coincidentally, these last levels of coercion are precisely what characterize the mechanisms that epitomize "primitive" accumulation.

3. As I further spell out in chapter 1 of *Rethinking "Race," Labor, and Empire*, distinct cultural differences and traits among peoples are the "material bearers (*Träger*) of" certain broad social hierarchies (racial subjects, individual, and collective) in the capacity of specific physiognomized social inequalities (Wynter 1990, 358–59): that is what makes such traits indispensable to the historically specific aspects of labor under capitalism. But what does the term "physiognomized inequalities" refer to here? By that I mean that it is only "in certain relations" that such human differences and attributes become racial subjects—individual and collective (Coronil 1996, 57). It is only then that human differences and attributes are diminished, accumulated, and transformed into socio-historically contingent and hierarchically organized corporeal features and bodily conduct among peoples (their physiognomization). It is precisely under these circumstances that "race" emerges as such, that is to say, as a quantum. Within the structural context of historical capitalism, this is precisely how social differences otherwise identified and lived as "cultural," "national," "religious," "linguistic," etc.—in a word, "ethnic"—can and do become embodied inequalities. To be exact, they become racial: "ethnicity" is transformed into "race," hence the term *ethno-racial*.

4. Yet this sexualized over-exploitation via "primitive" accumulation is hardly limited to laboring populations ethno-racialized as socially inferior within historical capitalism. For example, and during Europe's Industrial Revolution, liberal-economic forms of social regulation and ways of knowing made adult-female wage labor and child wage labor directly homologous—and, ergo, *cheaper* than adult-male labor. Within this same mental landscape and reorganized labor process, those populations were socially produced as inferior in income and working conditions compared to adult-male wage labor across nineteenth century Great Britain (Marx 1977, 367–411, 513–527; Davidoff 1974). As features of "primitive" accumulation and by shrinking the costs of the variegated and differentiated work force being exploited by global capital, such mechanisms involved the feminization and infantilization of broad sectors of wage labor (and/or of colonized peoples) at that time and thus helped accelerate the pace of industrialization in the United Kingdom during the height of British global hegemony.

5. This is the focus of chapters 4 and 5 of *Rethinking "Race," Labor, and Empire*.

6. I have provided my own extensive critique of Harvey's related line of reasoning in chapter 6 of *Rethinking "Race," Labor, and Empire*.

7. However, this report warns that "These results should be interpreted cautiously due to lack of available data in some regions, notably the Arab states and the Americas" (ibid.). The ILO defines "modern slavery" as encompassing bonded labor, forced domestic work, debt bondage, and serfdom, as well as the work performed by the victims of human trafficking. Among the latter, women and girls are disproportionately represented and includes those living in forced marriage and those subject to commercial sexual exploitation (ILO, 9–10, 17, 18).

11

"PRIMITIVE" ACCUMULATION IN URBAN SEMIPERIPHERY

Ethno-racial Elites, Rezoning, and Displacement in Manhattan, New York City

Kai Wen Yang

Introduction

This chapter investigates an enclave path to "primitive" accumulation in New York City's semiperipheral ethno-racial enclaves.[1] It will illustrate this path through a case study on the rezoning in and around Chinatown and the Lower East Side (LES), two working-class neighborhoods in the Borough of Manhattan. It argues that semiperipheral social relations, exhibited among the enclave elites, provide the conditions to materialize the violent extra-economic means of "primitive" accumulation. One of which is rezoning, a crucial urban planning instrument that unlocks economic developmental potentials at a micro-level. The chapter rescales the concept of semiperiphery from world-system analysis, which typically refers to a polarization between the two segments of the "indigenous bourgeoisie" ("national" and the "external bourgeoisie") along with a semi-proletarianized sector of the working class, at the nation-state level, to analyze the rival fractions of the ethno-racial elites and their class alignments at the enclave level. The Chinatown/LES case demonstrates that an inter-enclave segment of the ethno-racial elites is instrumental in shaping, supporting, and/or implementing the extra-economic means of "primitive" accumulation, such as the East Village/Lower East Side (EVLES) rezoning plan and the Rebuild Chinatown Initiative (RCI) plan, in order to reproduce an urban economy, which centers on the finance, insurance, and real estate (FIRE) sectors.

The two neighborhoods of Chinatown and the LES are examples of enclave urbanism "whereby metropolitan regions are becoming agglomerations of unequal urban districts, sharply divided by race, class, and other social distinguishers, and often physically separated" (Angotti 2012, 113–14). There are

DOI: 10.4324/9781003325109-14

two types of enclaves: The gated/securitized capital-intensive enclaves that are driving the FIRE economy (Marcuse 2009), and the ethno-racial enclaves that are sites of class conflicts and are targets of neoliberal development policies and triage policies of "planned shrinkage" and "benign neglects" (Angotti 2012, 118–20; Kwong 1999; Lin 1995; Wallace and Wallace 1998). Chinatown and the LES are ethno-racial enclaves, and within which, there are further divisions of "ethnic catchment areas," sought after by enclave elites for privatization and real estate development (Sites 2003). Ethno-racial enclaves have cultivated collaborations between local "ethnic growth machines" and "transnational growth coalitions" (Lin 2008; Hum 2021), which have both sustained an informal economy (Kwong 1999, 2009), planting new semiperipheral class relations inside the declining core city (Taylor 2003).

There are three observations regarding the status of ethno-racial enclaves. First, securitized capital enclaves like Wall Street or the Hudson Yard, on the one hand, and the ethno-racial enclaves like Chinatown and the LES, on the other hand, are spatial units of a single unified process of "primitive" accumulation. Second, they exist in an interdependent manner; hence, it is a hierarchized and differentiated *enclave relationality*, which connects the core and the semiperiphery, at the urban level and inside the core itself. Third, the urban semiperipheral elites polarize toward the enclaves' reproduction or gentrification/displacement (Boyd 2005; Kwong 1979, 1996). These observations are interconnected and point to an enclave path to "primitive" accumulation. To better understand the connections between ethno-racial enclaves and "primitive" accumulation, the chapter will interrogate "primitive" accumulation and semiperipheralization as two intertwined processes. After explaining such connections, the chapter will turn to the Chinatown/LES case study to demonstrate the enclave path.

Urban Semiperiphery and "Primitive" Accumulation

In *Capital: Volume One*, Marx's (1990 [1867], 873–76) discussion on the so-called "primitive" accumulation centers on the separation process that divorces labor from the means of production and subsistence. The history of such separation was "conquest, enslavement, robbery, murder, in short, force" (Marx 1990 [1867], 874). "Primitive" accumulation embodies the plural spatiotemporality of the capitalist world-economy (CWE). Marx (1990 [1867], 876) wrote, "the history of this expropriation assumes different aspects in different countries and runs through its various phases in different orders of succession, and at different historical epoch." Hence, "primitive" has been written with quotation marks for the reason that it is not a "pre-history" matter. The process is historically specific (Perelman 2000) *and* it serves as a constitutive presupposition (Bonefeld 2001) to (re)produce capital accumulation on an expanding scale across the world.

World-system analysts have provided studies on the diverse paths to "primitive" accumulation (Arrighi, Aschoff, and Scully 2010) and on the temporal specificities of the process (Frank 1977; Hopkins, Wallerstein, Kasaba, Martin, and Phillips 1987), which shapes the cyclical patterns and the spatial configurations of historical capitalism. Recent studies have focused on the semiperipheral context, for instance, Turkey and China (Karatasil and Kumral 2019; Zhan 2019a). In the case of Turkey, multiple paths to "primitive" accumulation (i.e., the "Castilian/Spanish road," the "Junker/Prussian road," and the "farmers/ American road") appeared within and across "hostile conjunctures" (i.e., the crisis of British world hegemony and the US world hegemony), whereby the outcomes of each path (class formation, dispossession, etc.) occupied specific spatial locations. In the case of China, the process of *accumulation without dispossession* (AWD) is at work in the semiperipheral country (Zhan 2019a). AWD distinguishes land expropriation from dispossession, which is often collapsed in the "accumulation by dispossession" (ABD) framework. For instance, in the process of rural industrialization, "land was expropriated to create collective enterprises, but in exchange, peasants were given enterprise-based assets, including secure jobs" (Zhan 2019a, 460). Likewise, in Turkey, small landowners (via the "farmer/American road" in the Anatolia) had also retained their unproductive land but sought employments in the cities. The result was a semi-proletarianization that gradually led to a full scale of proletarianization in the cities (Karatasil and Kumral 2019, 544).

However, "primitive" accumulation is not exhausted at the nation-state level. The process is present in the urban semiperiphery, which is spatial category resulting from the disintegration of the CWE's core zone. As Peter Taylor (2003) observes, the expression of such disintegration is "the *creation of a new semiperiphery* at the *very heart* of the world-economy" (Taylor 2003, 137; added emphasis). As a result, the core city is compartmentalized into different categories of land parcels. Some are more "core-like" than the others, and some are "semiperiphery-like," or "periphery-like," hence, the point on enclave urbanism (Angotti 2012). Likewise, NYC as a "center of gravity" of the CWE has become difficult to discern (Slater 2004, 603), and within which, the "backward zones" and the non-core parcels of the city (Braudel 1979 [1992], 42; Midnight) become up for grab in a new round of "primitive" accumulation (Midnight Notes Collective 1990). Robert Fitch (1993) argued that real estate and financial interests banded together to form an "urban land cartel." This "growth coalition" aimed to valorize the portions of the city that they owned (Fitch 1994, 42). For instance, David Rockefeller's planning group, Downtown Lower Manhattan Association, replaced factories and blue-collar workers with office towers, luxury residences, and department stores to cultivate a Lower Manhattan FIRE economy (Fitch 1993).

Karatasil and Kumral (2019) suggest that the era of US hegemonic decline presents a new "hostile conjuncture." New and rival fraction of the bourgeoisie

Displacement in Urban Semiperiphery **141**

and new rounds of expropriation have emerged in the semiperiphery context. In NYC, a new and rival fraction of the bourgeoisie (i.e., the FIRE sectors; specifically, real estate development corporations that are publicly traded, for example, Vornado Realty Trust and SL Green Realty Corporation) has also emerged. Its "crack cocaine" financing sources (i.e., corporate bonds and the EB-5 investment program) are threatening a relatively older cohort of landowning elites, such as the Trump family.[2] New methods and instruments of expropriation have also been developed in order to enclose and rearrange the compartmentalized spaces of the declining core city. The rival fraction is actively seeking the city's "soft sites," which have generally retained a large quantity of undeveloped floor area within an existing allowable floor area ratio (FAR). When the existing zoning district restricts or prohibits capital-intensive developments, the rival fraction has lobbied City Hall to *upzone* such parcels, blocks, and/or the entire neighborhood. The mission is to expand capital enclaves into ethno-racial enclaves through maximizing the density (the FAR) of the latter's developable "soft sites" for future developments. This new rival fraction has particularly joined forces with a segment of the ethno-racial elites from inside the *urban* semiperiphery in order to redevelop the urban semiperiphery's "soft sites."

When "ethnic" capital "strikes back" from abroad, for instance, from Hong Kong and Taiwan and settled in core cities, such as London and NYC (King 1990; Kwong 1996; Lin 1995; Sassen 1988), this migration of capital created a

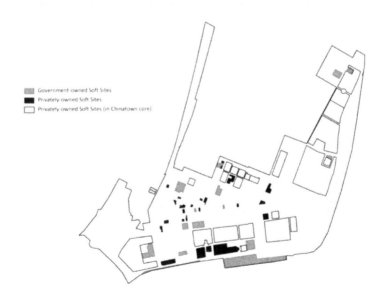

FIGURE 11.1 Chinatown and the Lower East Side Soft Site Map

network of ethno-racial enclaves. The enclaves were divided into an "upper circuit" of ethno-racial elites whose survival depended on the exploitation of a "lower circuit" of cheap/bonded labor, which were waged/semi-waged/non-waged, and un/documented (Kwong 1979, 1996, 1999, 2009; Lin 1995). This "lower circuit" constituted an "ethnic strata" of the working class and resembled class dynamics from the semiperipheral nation-state. Like the "indigenous bourgeoisies" from the semiperiphery, the enclave elites also fostered diverging class alignments in relations to the rival fraction of the bourgeoisie and its expansion of capital enclaves. In the semiperipheral nation-state, the "indigenous bourgeoisies" are divided between the domestically oriented segment and the internationally oriented segment, through which popular mobilizations and policies for development diverge (Gates 2009, 82–86; Wallerstein 1976). The urban counterpart of the internationally oriented segment of the "indigenous bourgeoisies" is the inter-enclave ethno-racial elites who are in growth coalitions with the rival fraction of the bourgeoisie. The inter-enclave elites are tasked to transform the ethno-racial enclaves, plug them into the wheels of capital enclaves, and/or directly replicate developments from the latter in the former.

On the other hand, the growth coalitions may not share the interest of a domestically oriented segment of the enclave elites who are small proprietors and business owners and whose survival depends on preserving the enclave. In order to capture the tension between the two segments, the space of ethno-racial enclaves can be better grasped as a semiperipheral urban corridor region (Figure 11.2), whereby the local center of the enclave is polarized by developments from adjacent cores (Terlouw 2002, 18–19). Likewise, Chinatown and the LES can be visualized as a corridor hanging between Lower and Midtown

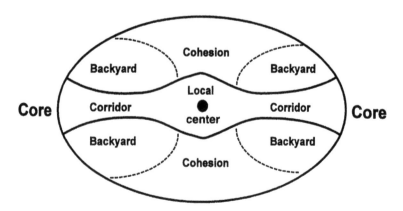

FIGURE 11.2 External Cores and the Division of the Corridor Region

Displacement in Urban Semiperiphery **143**

FIGURE 11.3 Chinatown and the Lower East Side Zoning Districts

Manhattan's core commercial/residential zoning districts (Figure 11.3). These high-density districts are capital enclaves and are themselves the results of enclosures and redevelopments from earlier decades, starting with the Rockefellers' deindustrialization of Lower Manhattan in the 1950s (Fitch 1993), the gentrification of East Village/LES in the 1980s (Abu-Lughod 1994; Mele 2000; Midnight Notes Collective 1990; Patterson 2006; Smith 2005), the post-9/11 redevelopment of the Financial District in Lower Manhattan (Angotti 2011; Gotham and Greenberg 2014), and most recently, adding Bloomberg's Hudson Yard in Mid-Manhattan.

The spatial cleavages that the enclave faces are internal to the enclave and external in relation to its context. In short, Terlouw (2002, 19) wrote "the polarization between the corridor region and the adjacent cores is a semiperipheral spatial force from a higher scale that tears the region apart." In opposition to the inhabitants who remain committed to the old region, the role of the inter-enclave elites is to graft the "upper circuit" of enclave developments into the polarizing corridor, connecting a seemingly isolated ethno-racial enclave to the surrounding capital enclaves. When the domestically oriented segment of the enclave elites fail to control the local center, the local enclave center is subsequently carved up by the adjacent cores. As development begins, the enclave's distinction becomes less obvious and "all become part of a larger integrated polynuclear regional system" (Terlouw 2002, 20). It becomes possible for enclave developments to directly replicate FIRE developments from the adjacent cores or to support them.

Actions to "tear" and "carve" the corridor region are alluding to a question on how the extra-economic forces of "primitive" accumulation have been inserted into the semiperipheral enclave space and cut it apart for integration. The answer is embedded in the complex process of rezoning. In NYC, the main instrument for land-use planning and regulation is the Zoning Resolution, which broadly controls (1) how land may be used, (2) how much can be built (via a formula that sets a maximum floor area ratio [FAR]), built floor area divided by total land area), and (3) how much land must remain unbuilt (Angotti 2016, 19). The Zoning Resolution includes the *"Zoning Text*, which defines the permitted uses, maximum building sizes, and open space requirements, and the *Zoning Maps*, which indicate where the text is to be applied" (Angotti 2016, 19). Rezoning is a systemic and meticulous area-by-area reclassification through zoning amendments. Rezoning is a major tool to "unlock development potential in once-unprofitable working-class and ex-manufacturing districts across the five borough" (Busà 2017, 56). Anyone can apply for a Zoning Map change and a Zoning Text Amendment change. However, the applicants are often NYC's Department of City Planning (DCP), Community Boards (CBs), and real estate developers.

The trajectory in rezoning the semiperipheral ethno-racial enclave is what this chapter has called an enclave path to "primitive" accumulation. This path entails an enclave relationality that occupies the interstitial corridor space between capital enclaves and ethno-racial enclaves, enabling an encounter between the inter-enclave elites and the rival fraction of the FIRE bourgeoisie. The formation of a coalitional network between the two provides the social and material conditions to meticulously articulate zoning amendments, which unlock economic developmental potentials in ethno-racial enclaves. An interesting feature of the enclave path is the inter-enclave segment of the ethno-racial elites who have collaborated with the state (i.e., via critical zoning institutions such as DCP) and moved the tentacles of the "FIREmen" into immigrant and working-class neighborhoods, and have often done so in negotiations for community amenities such as mix-income "affordable" housing units (Abu-Lughod 1994; Angotti 2011; Midnight Notes Collective 1990, 64–76; Patterson 2006). Real estate developers, Mayor Bloomberg, and subsequently Mayor de Blasio, have regularly mobilized and utilized the existing social network of the ethno-racial elites and their co-optations (i.e., via community benefits agreements) to rezone NYC, explicitly targeting low-income and ethno-racialized neighborhoods (Angotti and Morse 2016; Busà 2017).

Rezoning and Displacement in Manhattan's Chinatown and the Lower East Side

The literature on the process of gentrification in Manhattan's Chinatown focused on real estate capital and Chinese foreign investments, highlighting how housing/tenant organizations have fought eviction (Hum 2021; Hum and Stein 2017). The urban planning literature revealed the racial specificity of rezoning and how such rezoning has caused displacement (Angotti and Morse 2016; Stein 2016). Works on the politics of gentrification discussed how Chinatown business spaces could provide the foundation for activist actions and political possibilities for women (Wong 2019). The focus on a single fraction of capital overlooks the CWE's spatial divisions at a micro-level, its periodic rearrangement of such divisions, and its articulation of new urban spaces within a rearranged declining core city. Local networks of class alignments thus shift accordingly, which incubates but also defines the limits of new political possibilities. In other words, the elites' class alignment with the city's governing and growth coalitions define their politics in ordinary neighborhood spaces.

In order to better understand the internal class dynamics of Chinatown/the LES and how enclave elites' class alignments have facilitated rezoning and connected the two neighborhoods to Manhattan's capital enclaves, the chapter will now turn to the two neighborhoods' enclave path to "primitive" accumulation. We will begin by considering the spatial structure of Chinatown and the LES as a semiperipheral corridor that is linked to the Financial District and to East Village, from its southern and northern limits, respectively.

The 9/11 attacks briefly paralyzed the Lower Manhattan economy. The Bush government chose the Community Development Block Grants and tax-exempt Private Activity Bonds (renamed as "Liberty Bonds") as two funding mechanisms for redevelopment projects. Lower Manhattan Development Corporation (LMDC), a subsidiary of Empire State Development Corporation (ESDC), was created to oversee the distribution of block grants and direct the revitalization of Lower Manhattan after 9/11. LMDC's board members are representatives from the FIRE economy (Gotham and Greenberg 2008, 1045). LMDC helped finance the largest luxury-housing boom in NYC history (Gotham and Greenberg 2008, 1050). LMDC selected Asian American for Equality (AAFE) as its redevelopment partner.[3] AAFE has worked exclusively with Enterprise Foundation and helped to privatize public assets in Chinatown and the LES (Abu-Lughod 1994, 318–20). With LMDC's and Enterprise's backing, AAFE created the Rebuild Chinatown Initiative (RCI).[4] RCI formed a coalition between elites from ethno-racial enclaves and capital enclaves. Its steering committee and the national advisory board included representatives from real estate corporations, banks, community development corporations, nonprofit housing developers/services providers, higher educational institutions, traditional family associations, and representatives from other typical

146 Kai Wen Yang

neoliberal growth coalitions, such as the New York City Partnership (NYCP) (Asian Americans for Equality 2004, iv–v).

In 2002, AAFE's RCI received a $250,000 grant from Freddie Mac for a three-month study on post-9/11 Chinatown. In 2003, RCI received an additional $1.5 million from Freddie Mac.[5] In 2004, AAFE's RCI created Chinatown Partnership Local Development Corporation (CPLDC). In 2008, CPLDC's Board of Directors consisted of David Cheng, Co-Treasurer and Executive Director of Chinese-American Planning Council (CPC), Jimmy Cheng, Vice President of United Fujianese American Association, Bill Lam, President of Longines Realty, Justin Yu, President of Chinese Consolidated Benevolent Association (CCBA), Pin Tai, Co-Vice Chair/Executive Vice President and General Manager at the East and Midwest Region of Cathay Bank, June Lee, Direct of External Affairs at Verizon, and Charles Lai, the Co-founder and Executive Director of Museum of Chinese in America (MoCA). As of 2019, the board included Robin Mui, the CEO of *Sing Tao Daily*. AAFE's creation of CPLDC in 2004 congealed with the creation of LMDC in 2001. The inter-enclave elites of RCI and CPLDC were then linked with the "FIREmen" of LMDC.

The inter-enclave elites from CPLDC, AAFE, and RCI polarized the semi-peripheral corridor of Chinatown/the LES toward the Financial District. This polarization is best illustrated in RCI's *America's Chinatown: A Community Plan*

> the plan *is about linking: resources, issues, vision and short-term implementation*. It directly corresponds to the Mayor's plan for Lower Manhattan, which emphasizes connectivity, cultural magnets, anchor office development, waterfront access, parks, housing, neighborhood amenities, and improved shopping. It would revitalize Chinatown, to make it an essential component of the Mayor and Governor's vision of Lower Manhattan as a global office hub, creative center and liveable neighborhood.
>
> *(Asian Americans for Equality 2004, 2–3; original emphasis)*

This inter-enclave elites selected Canal Street as the corridor to connect the ethno-racial enclave of Chinatown/the LES with the capital enclave of the Financial District (Figure 11.4). The Canal corridor cut through the local enclave center of Chinatown, opening up two entrances at Broadway and Water/Bowery Streets. Both were connected to the Financial District. The west entrance was through Broadway and the east through Water/Bowery Streets.

The opening of the corridor aimed to create a "Pacific Rim Office District" and provide "job mobility and training" for the emerging service sectors. Such new developments were crucial for the inter-enclave ethno-racial elites who wished to replace the declining garment sector with new health care, hospitality, and construction sectors. Two decades later, Chinese-American Planning

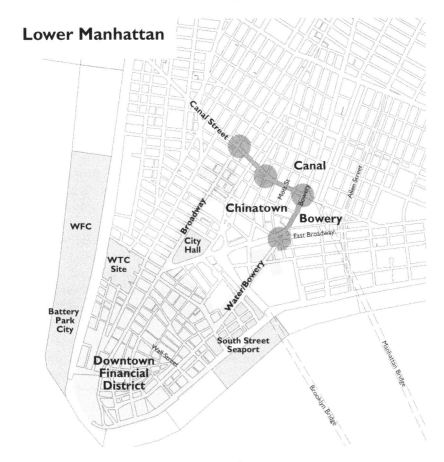

FIGURE 11.4 Canal Street Connective Corridor

Council (CPC), one of RCI's steering committee members, eventually became one of the largest nonprofit employers in the homecare industry, which exploits predominantly immigrant women of color in 24-hour workdays.[6] The corridor was also crucial for forging a joint venture between some of Chinatown's elites and the Alliance for Downtown (AFD) (Asian Americans for Equality 2004, 18–20). The latter's board included publicly traded real estate investment trusts (REITs), such as SL Green Realty. The access to a diverse pool of financing sources, domestic and foreign, made them competitive in the real estate sector and threatening to the older cohort of real estate families, for instance, the Rudins, Dursts, Speyers, and Malkins.[7]

Canal Street corridor (between Broadway and Water/Bowery Streets) falls into M1–5B, C6–2G, and C6–1G zoning districts. M1–5B zoning district has a manufacturing FAR of 5.0. C6–1 and C6–2 zoning districts have the same FAR of 6.0. The "G" suffix indicates strict regulations governing the conversion of non-residential into residential use. All three existing zoning districts have a range of medium to high density. There have been three attempts to make zoning text and zoning map amendments for the Canal corridor. The first attempt was AAFE's RCI proposal (Asian Americans for Equality 2004), which only provided a map (Figure 11.5). This was so because RCI could act as a 197-a plan,[8] which provides the "statements of general planning principles and land use policy direction."[9] A general upzoning principle was enough to guide the City Planning Commission's (CPC) evaluation on future zoning actions (see Asian Americans for Equality 2004, 18). The overall goal of RCI was to stimulate housing and office developments and lift the existing restrictions to promote homeownership.

The second attempt came in 2010. The city created the Chinatown Working Group (CWG) in 2008. It was tasked to rezone Chinatown. Chinatown Business and Property Owners Group (CBPOG), a coalition of real estate developers, aimed to persuade CWG into upzoning the Canal corridor (Figure 11.6). Keith Lipstein of ABS Partners, a CBPOG member, said, "I'm a big proponent, at least from a commercial standpoint, of that [Canal] area being rezoned to the highest possible density."[10] The examples of this recommendation are C6–4 through C6–9 districts. These districts are inside major business districts, with a maximum FAR of 10.0 or 15.0. Edison Properties, also a CBPOG member, own a parking lot on 174 Centre Street. In 2005, it acquired 126–128 Baxter Street (behind the parking lot) and a $37 million loan to redevelop the two buildings. Joining the two parcels, on Centre and Baxter Streets, could enable larger constructions. However, the two buildings on Baxter were rent-stabilized with mostly Chinese immigrant seniors. In 2007, the company refused to renew the leases and attempted to buy out the tenants in order to demolish the two buildings.[11]

The latest attempt came during the COVID-19 pandemic in September 2020. DCP's SoHo/NoHo rezoning covers a section of the Canal corridor between Broadway and Baxter Street. DCP renamed it "SoHo East."[12] The rezoning aims to convert the existing M1–5B, C6–2G, and C6–1G zoning districts into M1–5/R9X and M1–6/R10 zoning districts (Figure 11.7). The M1–5/R9X zoning district has a 5.0 FAR for commercial/manufacturing, 9.7 FAR for residential with mandatory inclusionary housing (MIH), and 6.5 FAR for community facility. The M1–6/R10 zoning district has a 10 FAR for commercial/manufacturing, 12 FAR for residential with MIH, and 10 FAR for community facility. Inclusionary zoning provides a 20 percent bonus in floor area to developers who provide 20 percent of units as "affordable" housing (with HUD's AMI; see Angotti and Morse 2016). Under Mayor de Blasio, inclusionary housing becomes mandatory in all upzoning. Parallel to the AWD framework, inclusionary zoning, and the MIH program do not thoroughly

Displacement in Urban Semiperiphery **149**

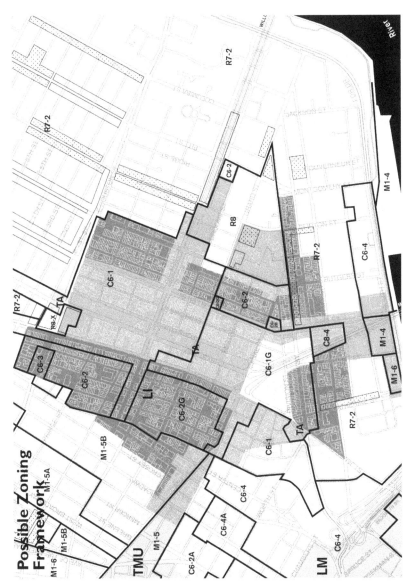

FIGURE 11.5 Rebuilding Chinatown Initiative's 2004 Upzoning Framework

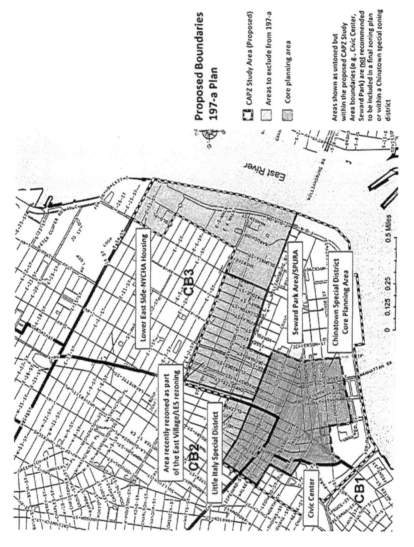

FIGURE 11.6 Proposal for Chinatown Special District

Displacement in Urban Semiperiphery 151

remove low-income tenants. In fact, they retain a small portion of low-income units, but such quantity could not offset displacement.

The polarization of the semiperipheral corridor is also indicated by the East Village/LES (EVLES) rezoning plan, which was passed in 2008. The rezoning targeted East Village and a section of the LES south of E Houston Street. The area had a R7–2 and a C6–1 zoning district. Then, the R7–2 zone had a maximum residential FAR of 3.44, a maximum community facility FAR of 6.5, and no height limits. In the EVLES rezoning (Figure 11.8), DCP divided the R7–2 zoning district (along with a strip of C6–1 district) into a number of R7A, R7B, and R8B zones. These new zones covered most of the whiter and

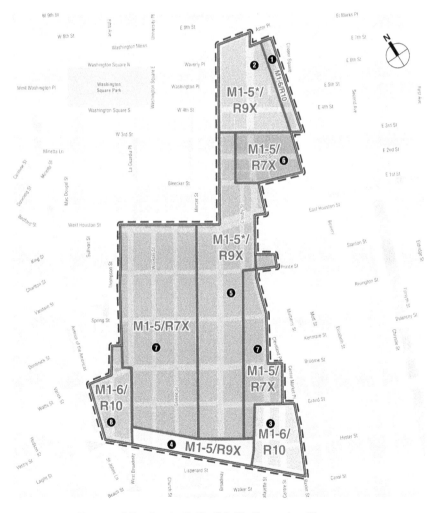

FIGURE 11.7 Proposed Zoning in SoHo/NoHo Rezoning Plan

wealthier area of East Village (above E Houston Street). The R7A zone had a residential FAR of 4.0, a community facility FAR of 4.0, and a height limit of 80 feet. The R7B zone had a residential FAR of 3.0, a community facility FAR of 3.0, and a height limit of 75 feet. The R8B zone had a residential FAR of 4.0, a community facility FAR of 4.0, and a height limit of 75 feet.

This contextual zoning of East Village was offset by an upzoning on Chrystie Street, E Houston Street, Delancey Street, and Avenue D. These streets and avenue in fact marked the boundaries between East Village, the poor sections of the LES (a.k.a Alphabet City), and Chinatown. The city changed the C6–1

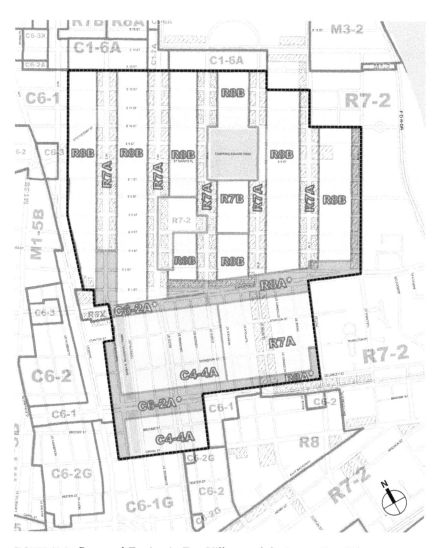

FIGURE 11.8 Proposed Zoning in East Village and the Lower East Side

FIGURE 11.9 Extell Tower and Proposed Towers at Two Bridges, Lower East Side

zone to C6–2A, C4–4A, and R8A zones. The new C4–4A zone has a FAR of 4.0 for residential, community facility, and commercial lots. The new R8A and C6–2A zones have FARs of 7.2. The heights were set at 120 feet for inclusionary housing purposes. There are no height caps outside the EVLES zoning boundaries, including LES' Two Bridges waterfronts. While East Village, Chinatown, and the LES all belong to Community Board 3 (CB3), the city only contextually zoned the whiter and wealthier East Village. These racially exclusive zoning amendments pushed capital-intensive developments into Chinatown and the LES. When the EVLES rezoning was going through the ULURP process in 2008, AAFE and other inter-enclave elites ignored local protests and gave testimonies and public statements in support of the rezoning.

Without height caps, real estate developers have replicated "the billionaire's row" from Central Park inside the two neighborhoods, particularly along LES's Two Bridges waterfront. In 2013, Extell Development Corporation, a competitive NYC real estate company, acquired 227 Cherry Street at the Two Bridges waterfront. Subsequently, Extell displaced the then existing one-story supermarket and redeveloped the site into an 80-story luxury condominium tower, which was named One Manhattan Square (OMS). The list price starts at $1.3 million. Next to Extell's OMS, Mayor de Blasio approved four more out-of-scale luxury mega-towers on Two Bridges' Large-Scale Residential Development (LSRD) area (Figure 11.9). The city and the developers have again found supports from inter-enclave elites for such developments.

Conclusion

The present case study demonstrates an enclave path to "primitive" accumulation. This path is shaped by an enclave relationality that produces a growth coalition between the inter-enclave elites and the rival fraction of the FIRE bourgeoisie. A rescaled concept of semiperiphery helps to capture this coalition. Here, the semiperiphery is understood as the spatial structure of an urban corridor. An ethno-racial enclave sits at the center of the local center of the corridor and it is polarized toward the surrounding capital enclaves. Such polarization is "tearing" and "carving" the ethno-racial enclave apart for redevelopment, creating new urban spaces inside a declining core city. Rezoning or amendments to the existing zoning text and zoning map have materialized this semiperipheral spatial force. An interesting feature of the enclave path is the inter-enclave segment of the ethno-racial elites who have collaborated with city agencies and moved the tentacles of the "FIREmen" into immigrant and working-class neighborhoods through rezoning. In Chinatown/the LES, the inter-enclave elites have helped to meticulously orchestrate rezonings, aiming to connect the two neighborhoods with Midtown Manhattan or the Financial District. The instrumentality of rezoning is central in the enclave path to "primitive" accumulation. However, without an existing semiperipheral corridor, the inter-enclave segment of the ethno-racial elites, and the internal/external coalitional forces that links the inter-enclave elites to the new and rival fraction of the FIRE bourgeoisie, rezoning could lose its sense of direction in the making of new urban spaces (or the "new enclosures") to prolong the FIRE economy inside a declining core city.

Chinatown/the LES is not the only ethno-racial enclave in NYC, and ethno-racial elites are more than an embodiment of a logic of collaboration and co-optation. Future research is needed to identify the class composition of a given ethno-racial enclave and how different segments of the ethno-racial elite have related to the surrounding capital enclaves. In addition, the present case study has only focused on the inter-enclave segment of the ethno-racial elites. Not all enclave elites are pulled toward zoning-induced real estate developments. There are segments of the enclave elite who oppose upzoning and have formed temporary alliances with the semiproletariat, the ethnic strata of the working class, or the working class overall. Future research is needed to identify how the enclave elites have mobilized popular support from different segments of the working class to support or oppose the state in real estate developments or in zoning/land use matters. The concept of enclave path could help indicate different class alignments that lead to different types of zoning amendments in the production of new urban spaces.

Notes

1. I thank Beverly Silver, Corey Payne, and Kelvin Santiago-Valles for their comments on this chapter.
2. Gabriel Sherman. "The Anti-Trump." *NY Magazine* September 22, 2010. Retrieved August 29, 2021 (https://nymag.com/news/features/establishments/68503/)

Displacement in Urban Semiperiphery **155**

3. *Philanthropy News Digest.* "Chris Kui, Executive Director, Asian Americans for Equality: September 11 and the Economic Impact on Chinatown." August 13, 2002. Retrieved on September 27, 2017 (http://philanthropynewsdigest.org/newsmakers/chris-kui-asian-americans-for-equality)
4. Alembic Community Development. Rebuild Chinatown Initiative: The Community Speaks. Retrieved July 16, 2021 (https://alembiccommunity.com/rebuild-chinatown-initiative-the-community-speaks/)
5. Albert Amateau. 2003. "Freddie Mac Kicks in $1.5 Million for Chinatown Housing." *The Villager* June 3, 2003. Retrieved on July 16, 2021 (www.amny.com/news/freddie-mac-kicks-in-1-5-million-for-chinatown-housing/)
6. E. Tammy Kim. "Opinion: When You Are Paid 13 Hours for a 24-Hour Shift" *New York Times* June 30, 2020.
7. Konrad Putzier. "For Family Dynasties: Adapt or Die" *The Real Deal* August 1, 2015.
8. The 197-a section of the City Charter allows Community Boards, Borough Boards, CPC, DCP, the Borough Presidents, and the Mayor to sponsor plans for development. 197-a plans can also be sponsored by neighborhood and civic organizations. 197-a needs not be detailed but it should provide the general guiding principles for development, growth, and improvement within the city. This is so because anyone can be an applicant for zoning map and text changes where all the details are required. DCP, Community Boards, and private developers are often the applicants. As long as the zoning amendments are guided by zoning principles, the aforementioned entities' intended actions could in theory be guided.
9. New York City Department of City Planning. *197-a Plan Technical Guide*, p. 21
10. Anton Troianovski. "Groups Push Competing Plans for Chinatown," New York Times June 14, 2010.
11. Julie Shapiro. "Tenants hope win won't be demolished on appeal." *Downtown Express* May 1, 2008.
12. *Department of City Planning.* "SoHo/NoHo Neighborhood Plan Draft Scope of Work for an Environmental Impact Statement CEQR No. 21DCP059M ULURP Nos. Pending October 28, 2020," p. 10

12

GLOBAL CRISIS AND MILITARIZED MIGRATION MANAGEMENT

A World-Historic Perspective

David B. Feldman

On December 19, 2018, 152 representatives of the United Nations (UN) General Assembly signed the Global Compact for Safe, Orderly, and Regular Migration in New York. The non-binding document is "the first inter-governmentally negotiated agreement . . . covering all dimensions of international migration in a holistic and comprehensive manner" and had been agreed upon by 165 members of the assembly at a meeting in Marrakesh earlier in the month.[1] In his remarks on the achievement, UN Secretary General Antonio Gutierres explicitly located the Compact within the broader fight to "counter the current groundswell of racism and xenophobia," as manifested in the proliferation of border walls and migrant detention centers around the world. Several countries ruled by right-wing governments—such as Israel, Hungary, and Brazil—followed the lead of the Trump administration in the United States and refused to ratify the accord. A closer inspection of the Compact, however, reveals that it is far from a "pro-migrant" document. While the authors avoid the inflammatory rhetoric associated with the attacks on undocumented immigrants by demagogues such as Donald Trump, they explicitly call for a reduction of "the incidence and negative impact of irregular migration," and the construction of a system of "orderly" migration. In effect, the UN accord is part and parcel of a "global tendency towards formally regulated, so-called 'managed migration'" (Schierup, Likić-Brborić, Delgado Wise, and Toksöz 2018, 737), and the logical outcome of fora such as the International Dialogue on Migration and the United Nations High-Level Dialogue on International Migration and Development.

Many scholars have already critiqued the UN's promotion of managed migration (or migration management) for substantively excluding representatives of civil society and labor unions from the deliberative process, and for

DOI: 10.4324/9781003325109-15

generally depoliticizing the phenomenon of migration (*Globalizations* 2018). Some have gone even further, noting how recent transformations in global political economy have fundamentally transformed migration patterns across the globe, and drawing links between migration management and ongoing crackdowns on unauthorized migration (Delgado Wise 2018). This chapter takes these insights one step further and introduces the concept of *militarized migration management* to describe a nascent world-historic project for controlling and disciplining migrant populations. I begin with a brief review of some of the existing world systems-inspired literature on migration, and then move to a schematic presentation of militarized migration management.

A World-Systems Approach to Migration

Nearly forty years ago, Portes and Walton (1981, 14) asserted that world-systems theory was unable to account for "the massive displacements of peripheral labor toward the centers" of the world-economy following the Second World War because the "theory of unequal exchange assumed perfect mobility of capital and relative immobility of labor as the key to the process of surplus extraction." The main target of Portes and Walton's critique was undoubtedly the early writings of Immanuel Wallerstein, which did in fact minimize the importance of labor mobility in the capitalist world-system. Wallerstein (1991, 2010b) eventually relaxed these assumptions, noting that the flow of labor across national borders is linked to Kondratieff cycles of growth, and that this migration has important ramifications for the ideological legitimization of capitalism. And yet, he broached the subject from an extremely high level of abstraction that, simply put, does not shed much light on contemporary dynamics. Many of the contributors to the 2010 PEWS annual conference dedicated to "mass migration in the world-system" adopted a similarly abstract approach, with some even using millennia as their temporal unit of analysis. Others took off in the opposite direction, carrying out case studies of the causes and effects of migration in specific locations and time periods, but saying relatively little about the development of the world-system as a whole (Jones and Mielants 2010).

The present chapter seeks to avoid the extremes of too much and too little abstraction. I hope to paint a picture with strokes that are broad enough to tell us something meaningful about migration at a global scale, but that contain enough detail to capture the unique nature of the current historical conjuncture.

This type of analysis is not unprecedented in the world-system perspective. In their groundbreaking analysis of working-class formation, class struggle, and capitalist development in nineteenth and twentieth century Calabria, Giovanni Arrighi and Fortunata Piselli (1987) provide a textured and detailed account of the dialectical relationship between migration patterns and a constantly evolving social structure. Without losing sight of the historical specificities of various localities, the authors demonstrate that micro-level developments are inextricably bound up with macro-level changes in the world capitalist economy, and they show how intraregional heterogeneity eventually gave way to a single homogeneous pattern of migration after the Second World War. Although the article has far-reaching theoretical and methodological implications, its empirical data are drawn from a rather small region in a single country.

Closer to my approach are those efforts to explicitly integrate migration into a periodization of the capitalist world-system, such as Lydia Potts' (1990) *The World Labour Market*. Potts argues that the birth of the capitalist world-economy several hundred years ago coincided with the emergence of a world market for labor power. She is most interested in flows of labor from the periphery to the core and shows how certain mechanisms for mobilizing and disciplining workers tend to predominate during particular stages in capitalist development. Her analysis of migration during the mercantile colonial era up to the early development of industrialization proper is particularly useful. Focusing largely on the plantation economy in North America and the British empire, she details how Indian slavery and forced Indian labor from the Americas were largely replaced by African slavery and then "coolie migration" from south Asia.[2] For their part, Portes and Walton (1981) place more importance on "colonizing" migration, or the "geographic displacement to areas where appropriate natural resources and labor were more readily available,"[3] during the expansion of the European-based mercantilist economy. In their view, the emergence of "labor migration" from the periphery to new industrial centers during the twentieth century marks an epochal shift. They are most interested in studying the "massive displacements of peripheral labor toward the centers" after the Second World War, including the specific ways migrant labor was mobilized, transported, and utilized.[4]

During the 1980s, several observers began to take note of contemporary changes in global political economy and the role of migrant and immigrant labor within it (Cohen 1987). In her highly influential study, Saskia Sassen (1988) shows how the globalization of production and capital promotes outmigration from rapidly industrializing countries in the periphery to "global cities" in need of low-wage migrant and immigrant workers for their increasingly services-based economies. She points out that migrants often travel to their former colonizers as a result of pre-existing economic, political, and cultural ties; the erection of legal and physical barriers to their cross-border movement only serves to illegalize them, ensuring they remain politically vulnerable and tractable workers (see also Portes and Walton 1981, ch. 2). By 2007, the unauthorized population of the United States had reached roughly twelve million. In 2016, there were just under five million undocumented immigrants living in the European Union (EU). In short, the highly exploitable labor of undocumented workers has constituted a "fundamental structural componen[t]"

(Baldwin-Edwards 2008, 1457) of the capitalist system since the 1980s and 1990s. But global capitalism is clearly undergoing a process of restructuring, and there is no reason to assume the de facto regime of regulation via illegalization will remain unchanged. Even before the onset of the COVID-19 pandemic, the unauthorized populations in the US and the EU had been slowly but surely declining from these peak levels. I contend that it is already possible to discern the contours of a nascent and qualitatively distinct system of militarized migration management.

My analysis of global capitalism and its crisis draws heavily on William I. Robinson's (2004, 2014, 2020) theory of capitalist globalization as a qualitatively new epoch in the open-ended development of world capitalism marked by the transnationalization of production and class relations. As capital responded to the crisis of the 1970s by breaking free from the fetters to accumulation that popular classes had managed to impose on it at the level of the nation-state, a heterogeneous but increasingly self-conscious transnational capitalist class began to congeal. The expansion of transnational capital into the former Second and Third Worlds involved a new round of primitive accumulation that threw hundreds of millions of small-scale producers onto an emergent global but highly segmented labor market in which "surplus labor in any part of the world is now recruited and redeployed through numerous mechanisms to where capital is in need of it" (Robinson 2006, 81; see also Golash-Boza 2015). At the same time, widespread dispossession and extreme wealth polarization has rendered large swathes of the world's population superfluous to capital in general—as both consumers and workers. The ongoing digitalization of the global economy portends an even sharper reduction in capital's need for living labor, which in turn aggravates the perennial problem of overaccumulation and causes serious crises of legitimacy for national states around the world. This is the backdrop to the present slide into authoritarian political systems and the reorientation of more and more global economic activity around the repression of surplus populations. Robinson (2020, 3) underscores that *militarized accumulation*, or *accumulation by repression*, is both a means of making profit and "contain[ing] the real and the potential rebellion of the global working class and surplus humanity." We are haunted, in his view, by the specter of a global police state principally concerned with the "*coercive exclusion* of surplus humanity" (Robinson 2020, 5).

So where does militarized migration management fit into the picture? Robinson (2020, 94) argues that the repression of migrants is "a source of accumulation in a double sense." On the one hand, the business of detaining and deporting redundant migrant workers is a highly profitable enterprise in its own right. On the other hand, immigration raids and other forms of state violence facilitate the superexploitation of those migrant and immigrant workers whose labor is still in demand. Repression may be present in both cases, but it functions differently in what amounts to two *distinct* forms of

160 David B. Feldman

profit-making: accumulation by repression and accumulation by exploitation. In the former, it leads to the commodification of migrants themselves (as detainees for private prisons and raw materials for the immigration industrial complex more generally). In the latter case, repression allows for the extraction of more surplus value from the labor of migrant and immigrant workers. These two activities complement each other up to a certain point, but the forces pushing for detention and deportation may become strong enough to begin eating into capital's necessary labor supply. In other words, repression may eventually turn into a *fetter* on the continued accumulation of capital through exploitation.[5]

The sharpening of this contradiction in recent years is indicative of broader trends in global political economy, and crucially, it announces a crisis of the regime of migrant illegalization and a potential transition to militarized migration management. While it may be considered a component of a nascent global police state, the concept of militarized migration management operates on a lower level of abstraction that is capable of taking into account the *specific political mechanisms* for the regulation of migrant labor through both coercive exclusion and inclusion—as well as the transformation of regulatory systems over time. I find social structure of accumulation theory and the French Regulation school to be useful complements to the world-systems perspective that allow us to think through these questions with greater analytical clarity and precision.[6]

Militarized Migration Management

In the United States, much of Western Europe, and many other countries around the world, illegalization has served as an informal way of regulating and disciplining low-wage migrant and immigrant workers at the bottom end of the labor market during what is often referred to as the post-Fordist, neoliberal era. This informal policy is best understood as an ad hoc but long-lasting and relatively coherent response to historical transformations in global political economy (the expansion of transnational capital and the growth of the services sector in global cities and countries of the traditional core), migration patterns (mass migration and familial settlement from former Second and Third World countries to the former First World), and state regulation (cancellation of guest-worker programs, passage of restrictive immigration legislation in the former First World, retrenchment of the right to claim asylum through the development of remote control policies, and militarization of border zones). The crisis of the informal regime of regulation through illegalization is bound up with the economic dislocations of the Great Recession and the more recent Corona Crash, but it also stems from a heightening of the regime's *internal* contradictions, as undocumented immigrants fall out of favor with employers in the face of heightened and unpredictable government enforcement (Feldman 2020a, 2020b, forthcoming).

If militarized migration management is a potential successor to the illegalization project, it does not represent a total rupture with it. On the surface, the former pushes some of the key components of the latter to their extreme, such as the militarization of borders, the assault on the right to claim asylum, the repression of undocumented workers, and the transnationalization of migrant policing apparatuses. This paves the way for the replacement of undocumented workers with migrants and immigrants holding various forms of precarious legal status that authorize employment but contain innumerable restrictions that ultimately leave intact the disciplinary threat of deportation (Feldman 2020a).

Let us now turn to a schematic presentation of the nascent project of militarized migration management, beginning with its structural preconditions.

Structural Preconditions

A Global But Highly Segmented Market for Labor Power

If it is true that the birth of the capitalist world-system gave rise to a *world* labor market, what does it mean to speak of the creation of a *global* labor market in recent decades? In making this taxonomical distinction, I am building on Robinson's (2004) argument regarding the shift from a *world* economy in which national economies are linked via trade and financial flows to a *global* one in which the production process itself has transnationalized, and technological improvements have greatly facilitated the flows of commodities and labor across the world. To be clear, a global labor market neither signals the removal of all obstacles to the free circulation of workers, nor the creation of a unitary and homogeneous labor market. Migrants' proportion of the world population has increased steadily over the past half-century, but it remains relatively small (see Table 12.1),[7] and freedom of movement is a mere pipe dream for the most exploited and oppressed. The global market for labor power is highly segmented along axes of citizenship, gender, ethnicity, skill, and so on (Castles 2011). For the present argument, it is also helpful to conceive of the fractionation of the global working class along the lines of a "spatial-productive" axis that distinguishes analytically between workers' *physical mobility* relative to individual nation-states, and the geographic scope of the *expenditure of their labor power* relative to the circuits of production in which they are active (Struna 2009). Migration across national borders is not a precondition for participation in the global labor market; an individual may spend her entire life working in her community of birth but still belong to the global working class so long as the products of her laboring activity enter into transnational circuits of accumulation. I am nonetheless most concerned with the regulation of what Struna terms the "diasporic-global" fraction of the global working class: those precarious migrants who cross

162 David B. Feldman

Table 12.1 International migrants, 1970–2019

Year	Number of migrants	Migrants as % of world population
1970	84,460,125	2.3%
1975	90,368,010	2.2%
1980	101,983,149	2.3%
1985	113,206,691	2.3%
1990	153,011,473	2.9%
1995	161,316,895	2.8%
2000	173,588,441	2.8%
2005	191,615,574	2.9%
2010	220,781,909	3.2%
2015	248,861,296	3.4%
2019	271,642,105	3.5%

Source: World Migration Report 2020, International Organization for Migration, 2019: p. 21. Available at: www.un.org/sites/un2.un.org/files/wmr_2020.pdf.

national borders to work, but are subject to an ever-tightening matrix of political control and surveillance.

Unpredictable Migration and Surplus Populations

The migration of the diasporic-global fraction of workers is best understood as various iterations of *forced migration* (Delgado Wise 2009). It may occur in an orderly or disorderly fashion; it may be circular or permanent in nature; it may or may not benefit capital directly; and so on. During the post-war era, migration between highly industrialized core countries and less-developed and often subsistence-based economies in the periphery was largely circular in character and often took place under the auspices of government-sponsored guestworker programs (Meillasoux 1991; Burawoy 1976; Castles 2000). As these programs were canceled and the post-war regime of accumulation entered into crisis during the 1970s, the seasonal migration of predominantly male workers began to give way to the more permanent settlement of entire families. This is the backdrop to the illegalization project of the last quarter of the twentieth century (Feldman 2020a; Castles 2000). These and other large population movements (i.e., refugee flows from the former Second and Third Worlds) were not explicitly orchestrated by the state, but insofar as they produced a pool of politically disempowered workers to fill the new labor demands of the emergent post-Fordist economy—especially in the services and construction sectors—they benefited capital in the core countries as a whole.

We now appear to be entering an era in which extreme social inequality, political conflict, war, and the ongoing ecological catastrophe are leading to increasingly unpredictable and—from the perspective of global capital—potentially undesirable migration flows (Miller 2017). Due to widespread land grabs and the depredations of the transnational model of development, the migrant labor systems of the post-war era are increasingly nonviable, and millions upon millions of migrants cannot be formally absorbed into the global labor market. To be clear, I am not claiming that migrant and immigrant workers have become entirely redundant to capital; in fact, they are over-represented in those sectors deemed "essential" during the COVID-19 pandemic. Militarized migration management is best understood as an effort to thread the needle between simultaneously managing surplus populations and supplying and controlling precarious migrant and immigrant workers.

The Regulatory Project

Capitalist States and Political Institutions Assume a More Direct Role in the Regulation and Disciplining of Migrant and Immigrant Labor

Temporary contract labor programs have begun to proliferate around the globe in recent years. The so-called "guestworker" is the archetype of the disposable and highly exploitable "unfree" worker: Guestworkers enjoy few legal rights, their legal status is conditional on remaining employed, and they are generally unable to switch employers of their own accord. Such programs are not a recent invention, but with new digital and biometric technologies allowing states to achieve unprecedented levels of surveillance over their populations, we are now seeing a concerted push at the global, national, and subnational levels to channel irregular flows into state-regulated institutional channels. In the United States, for example, the H-2A program for agricultural workers has increased in size by more than ten-fold over the past two decades, and there are ongoing efforts to expand its scope to nonseasonal workers and streamline its bureaucratic red tape. The government of Japan, which has historically remained quite closed to foreign workers, launched a new program in December 2018 that permits up to 340,000 skilled blue-collar workers to enter the country. Five months later, it began allowing a slightly higher number of semi-skilled foreign workers to work in fourteen different sectors with renewable five-year work visas.

In addition to bringing in temporary contract laborers, many states are moving toward granting various forms of temporary and precarious legal status to substantial numbers of long-term undocumented immigrants. Some programs, such as Deferred Action for Childhood Arrivals (DACA) in the United States, are explicitly temporary. But even measures touted as "pathways to citizenship" often subject immigrants to various onerous requirements, and in some instances require the federal government to first meet daunting metrics pertaining to border security and the clearing of visa backlogs (Feldman 2020a).[8] In

164 David B. Feldman

Canada and the EU, expansive "regularization" programs over the last several years have likewise contained many restrictive criteria, including but not limited to harsh employment provisions (Chauvin, Garcés-Mascareñas, and Kraler 2013; Goldring and Landolt 2011).

Finally, many states are seeking to change their distribution of permanent immigration visas to better suit the interests of capital. Australia's "hybrid system" for skilled migrants, which includes both a "points system" for individual merit and an employer sponsorship program, serves as a useful point of reference. The government in the UK is currently talking about moving toward a similar system, and in the US both the Obama and Trump administrations sought to undermine the family reunification principle enshrined (albeit with major limitations) in the 1965 amendments to the Immigration and Nationality Act, and to institute a merit-based points system. Universities often serve as useful sorting mechanisms in this regard; as of April 2019, employers in fourteen industries in Japan may offer permanent jobs to foreigners who graduate from Japanese universities.

The Policing and Warehousing of Surplus Populations Becomes a Permanent Fixture of Global Political Economy

The militarization of border zones during the 1980s, 1990s, and early 2000s forced unauthorized migrant crossers into hostile terrain, encouraging them to settle down without papers in "host" countries rather than to risk expensive and dangerous crossings on a regular basis. While the creation of hermetically sealed borders is an impossible task, it seems that the effect of the current round of border fortification is not simply to break the cycle of unauthorized circular migration, but to keep unauthorized migrants from ever successfully crossing. After two decades of steadily increasing funding for the US Border Patrol, the passage of the Secure Fence Act in 2006 mandated the construction of over seven hundred miles of barriers at the US–Mexico border. In 2013, the Democratic-controlled Senate passed a bill that would have allocated $46 billion to further militarize the southern border. Frontex, which was founded in 2004 to increase cooperation between the border patrols of EU member states, was expanded in 2017 to become the European Border and Coast Guard Agency. Its 2020 budget allocated €101.4 million to create a standing corps of ten thousand border guards by 2027. Some have argued that deportation and highly visible acts of exclusion at national borders serve to discipline undocumented immigrants as tractable and highly exploitable workers, rather than to permanently remove them from any particular country (De Genova 2005). This may have been an accurate assessment in the past, but most deportations from the United States now take place via formal orders of removal that impose serious consequences on migrants, and there has been a dramatic decline in the percentage of deportees who plan on trying to recross (Goodman 2020;

Martínez, Slack, and Martínez-Schuldt 2018; Schultheis and Ruiz Soto 2017). Militarized migration management requires pushing unauthorized crossings down to an absolute minimum and progressively expelling a large number of the undocumented who will be ineligible for any future pseudo-regularization program.

The last several decades have also witnessed a retrenchment of the right to claim asylum and an attack on the principle of non-refoulement, as enshrined in the 1951 UN Refugee Convention and its 1967 Protocol. During the 1980s and 1990s, governments in the former First World began applying "remote control" policies to skirt around these rights. These include the following: interceptions in the high seas, the levying of sanctions on airline carriers for transporting migrants deemed inadmissible, the imposition of visa requirements for individuals from countries with a high rate of applying for asylum, the creation of "buffer states" through the designation of "third-party safe countries," the signing of readmission agreements between states, and the use of *barbicans* or offshore processing centers where rights are severely limited (FitzGerald 2019; Miller 2019). The global "architecture of repulsion" has been reinforced in the last few years, often in response to political crises sparked by spikes in refugee outflows from countries such as Syria and the Central American Northern Triangle. In early October 2020, it was revealed that the UK is planning to open offshore asylum processing centers, with the government floating the possibility of using the south Atlantic islands, old ferries, or abandoned North Sea oil platforms. The point is to keep dispossessed migrants from even being able to *apply* for asylum—or at the very least to prevent them from enjoying proper legal and procedural rights when doing so. Meanwhile, some states have also eroded the right to claim asylum by issuing *short-term* legal statuses, such as Temporary Protected Status in the United States, which was written into the Immigration Act of 1990. More recently, the "refugee crisis" of the mid-2010s led Mexico to distribute humanitarian visas to Central American refugees, while Germany began issuing temporary residency permits tied to apprenticeships to Syrian and other refugees.

Concluding Remarks

It is uncertain whether the incipient project of militarized migration management will congeal into a full-fledged and coherent global regime in the foreseeable future. What *is* clear, however, is that militarized migration management is a spatially and temporally uneven process. Regions in the periphery and the semi-periphery often appear as "dumping grounds" and buffers for the core. In the immediate aftermath of the US pullout from Afghanistan in August 2021, the EU began drafting proposals for a €600 million aid package to Afghanistan's neighbors in order to keep large flows of refugees from entering the bloc's territory. The legacy of European colonialism and the actual historical development of world capitalism translate into a strong geographical dimension to the contemporary distribution of wealth and power. Nonetheless, the methodological territorialism inherent to the core/periphery language can also obscure the true fault lines and power relations of global capitalism.[9] Sprawling slum complexes sit in the shadow of incredibly opulent neighborhoods in the global cities of the former Third World, while migrant detention centers and "hot spots" proliferate in Europe and North America. In short, we are witnessing the growth of "a *world* of camps" in which surplus populations are relegated to wherever they can be denied political rights and prevented from challenging the prevailing capitalist order (Le Monde Diplomatique 2017; Babels 2017; Karakayali and Rigo 2010). The legacy of the COVID-19 lockdowns is not yet clear, but it appears to have provided an impetus to the consolidation of a global regime of militarized migration management. On the one hand, governments around the world temporarily closed their borders to varying degrees, with the Organization for Economic Co-operation and Development reporting that inflows to "rich countries" in 2020 fell 30 to 80 percent from their 2019 levels. On the other hand, initial labor shortages in industries reliant on guestworkers prompted capital in those countries to press for—and in some instances win—important regulatory changes in its favor.

Fully grasping the significance of militarized migration management as a unique historical project requires the adoption of an intermediate level of abstraction that has been largely absent from recent analyses of migration from the world-systems perspective and is much more characteristic of midrage Marxist theories of capitalist development such as social structure of accumulation theory and the French regulation school. Like all regulatory systems under capitalism, militarized migration management is riddled with many contradictions that are necessarily absent from the schematic presentation offered earlier. The political disagreement over the regulation of migrant labor alluded to in the introduction is very real, and it is partially—but by no means exclusively—rooted in the divergent material interests of various fractions of capital, as well as the efforts of the global political elite to legitimate a capitalist order that is increasingly unable to meet even the basic needs of the majority of humanity. But such conflict and contradiction does not preclude the existence of an underlying unity. I have deliberately highlighted the mutual interdependence of the various components of militarized migration management here to show that the superficially pro-migrant liberalism on display in the UN Global Compact is not an effective antidote to the rise of explicitly exclusionary anti-migrant politics. Only a radically egalitarian and democratic movement of the global working class, with an eye toward transitioning to a form of democratic socialism, has a chance at achieving true migrant justice.

Notes

1. www.iom.int/global-compact-migration
2. Of course, there are limitations to such a schematic model. For a good illustration of the coexistence of various forms of coercive labor arrangements in the world during this time period, see Rediker, Chakraborty, and Van Rossum 2019.
3. As Potts shows, the available labor supplies in regions, such as the Americas, were not actually sufficient.
4. For her part, Potts speaks of the era of industrial capitalism giving rise to "international labor migration" from Africa, "labor migration" from Asia and Latin America, and Latin American and African "brain drain."
5. For an analysis of the immigration industrial complex and exploration of this contradiction in greater detail, see Feldman (forthcoming).
6. My initial effort at synthesizing social structure of accumulation theory and a world-systems-inspired "stages of capitalism" approach can be found in Feldman (2021).
7. Source: www.un.org/sites/un2.un.org/files/wmr_2020.pdf. Nearly two-thirds are estimated to be labor migrants (p. 2).
8. In this respect, the proposed U.S. Citizenship Act of 2021 was significantly more generous than the legalization provisions included in the Border Security, Economic Opportunity, and Immigration Modernization Act passed by the Democratic-controlled Senate in 2013, but it too failed to pass.
9. Even when applied to earlier epochs these concepts pose important analytical problems. Arrighi and Piselli (1987: 687–8, emphasis added) define "peripheralization" as "a process whereby some *actors or locales*, that participate directly or indirectly in the world division of labor, are progressively deprived of the benefits of such participation, to the advantage of other actors or locales." In practice, however, their analysis privileges geographical territories over social groups that operate within and across them. They state that the Crotonese *latifondisti* transferred surplus out of their region by placing funds in national and international financial markets, which expanded "markets and productive facilities in northern Italy, thereby further widening the developmental gap between core regions and peripheral locales such as the Crotonese." For the Crotonese *latifondisti*, however, these investments did not deprive them of benefits but rather provided them with financial returns. For a critique of this tendency to reify space, see Robinson 2014, chapter 3.

13

DILEMMA OF THE RISING GIANT

China's Food Import Strategy and Its Constraints

Shaohua Zhan and Lingli Huang

Introduction

In a commentary in 1995, Wallerstein postulated that the capitalist world-system was unable or unwilling to meet the demands from labor while also maintaining profitability.[1] This was evidenced by the counterattacks on workers' rights in both Western and Third-World countries since the 1970s (Wallerstein 1995b). Extending Wallerstein's proposition, Arrighi and Silver (2001) noted that the capitalist world-system under the hegemony of the Netherlands, the United Kingdom (UK), and the United States (US) had progressively internalized the costs of protection, production, and transaction but none had internalized reproduction costs. The externalization of reproduction costs constitutes a quintessential feature of the capitalist world-system and of capitalist economies. It has also been a source of tension and conflict between capital and labor as the latter demands a living wage to cover reproduction costs. Arrighi and Silver thus contend that the underlying contradiction of the capitalist world-system is that it "promotes the formation of a world proletariat but cannot accommodate a generalized living wage (that is, the most basic of reproduction costs)" (2001, 276–77).

There have been multiple strands of research on the externalization of reproduction costs. One strand examines how powerful nations, particularly core states in the world-system, externalize reproduction costs beyond national borders through colonial expansion and unequal trade relations (Amin 1979; Arrighi 1994). This strand of research is concerned about the unequal and exploitative relations between core and peripheral countries. As China rises, it is argued that the country will reproduce such relations and that its development can only be achieved at the expense of countries in the periphery. As

DOI: 10.4324/9781003325109-16

far as food is concerned, China has been accused of extracting food resources overseas and thus increasing the risk of global food shortages, particularly in the developing countries (GRAIN 2008; Hofman and Ho 2012).

Our chapter engages this literature and examines the externalization of food costs by China. We regard food as an essential cost of labor reproduction. The costs of food in a society are associated with food demand and the resources devoted to food production and food imports. In China, due to rapid urbanization and the spread of the middle-class diet, the demand for food has soared, while the resources for food production such as labor and land have become limited and expensive. The Marxist literature regards this phenomenon as "the underproduction crisis of food." That is, with capitalist expansion, there is a tendency toward a situation where food production cannot catch up with increasing demand, thus pushing up food prices and causing food shortages (Moore 2015, 91–110; Zhan and Huang 2017). Increasing food prices lead workers to demand higher wages and push up the prices of other commodities, which heightens the costs of labor reproduction. In a situation of underproduction crisis of food, a country would develop a strong motivation to import food.

The externalization of food costs occurs when a country imports food and food materials (e.g., animal feed) for domestic consumption, which would have been more costly to produce domestically. Large volumes of food imports to China in the past two decades apparently lend support to the thesis that China has been following in the footsteps of other powerful capitalist countries by externalizing reproduction costs. For example, the country has become the largest soybean importer in the world, importing nearly two-thirds of all soybeans traded in the global market. It has also imported large quantities of meat, dairy, edible oil, fruits, and cereals.

This chapter contends, however, that China's strategy to feed its population through food import is subjected to both internal and external constraints. The economic compulsion to import more food and the constraints that force China back to domestic production constitute a fundamental contradiction in China's rise. How China tackles this contradiction has implications not only for the country's food supply but also for the global food system.

This contradiction also sets China apart from world hegemons such as the UK and the US. The UK was able to rely on food imports from its colonies to feed a growing working class in the nineteenth century. The United States has been a large food exporter due to its vast agricultural resources and the intensification of food production (Silver and Arrighi 2003; Friedmann and McMichael 1989; McMichael 2009). During the consolidation of its hegemony after the Second World War, the US wielded food aid as a powerful weapon to support anti-communist regimes and to depress world grain prices to its advantage (Friedmann 1982). If measured by the population to land ratio, food conditions in China appear closer to those in the UK. But unlike the latter, until very recently, overseas agricultural resources played a marginal role

170 Shaohua Zhan and Lingli Huang

in the country's food system. In other words, the cost of food production has been absorbed within its national borders. The rapid economic growth in the past three decades has elevated the cost of food in China, while the end of the Cold War and the transition to a neoliberal corporate global food regime have provided conditions for China to tap overseas food resources. Nevertheless, unlike the UK, China faces constraints that mean it may not be able to rely on external food resources to cover a large part of food supply in the foreseeable future.

The rest of this chapter will first provide an overview of China's food conditions and how the country managed to feed itself before it was integrated into the capitalist world-economy in the 1990s. This is followed by the section on China's pursuit of overseas agricultural resources in recent two decades. The subsequent section will examine the constraints that force the country back to domestic production. The last section concludes.

How China Has Fed Itself and the Limits

During the Mao period (1949–1976), the Chinese population had grown rapidly from 542 million to nearly one billion, adding tremendous pressure on food provision. The US-led international trade embargo in this period blocked China from importing food, while a lack of foreign exchange also prevented the country from purchasing food from the global market. The growing food demand had to be met with domestic production. In the 1950s, the country promoted agricultural production through land reclamation and irrigation development, and partly as a result, grain production grew from 132 million tons in 1950 to 198 million tons in 1958 (NBS 2009, chapter 1–32). However, the Great Leap Forward diverted human and financial resources away from agriculture while the radical push to establish the People's Communes undermined the coordination of agricultural production at the grassroots level (Lin 1990). Grain production plummeted to 144 million tons in 1960 (NBS 2009, chapter 1–32), resulting in a tragic famine with millions of deaths.

The famine taught a hard lesson to Chinese communists and forced them to import food. Nevertheless, food imports only accounted for a tiny portion of total consumption, less than two percent for most years in the 1960s and 1970s. The year of 1961 saw the highest share of grain imports due to emergency measures to lessen the impact of the famine, but it still amounted to only 3.2 percent of total consumption (MOA 1989, 520–25).

In the 1960s and 1970s, China's agricultural policy was centered on promoting grain crops, known as "take grains as the key line" (*yiliang weigang*). As potential land for reclamation was nearly exhausted, the focus was shifted to introducing agricultural technologies such as high-yield seeds, new methods of cultivation, and chemical fertilizers (Perkins 1969; Schmalzer 2016). Grain production experienced steady growth and reached 305 million tons in 1978.

However, due to the growth of the population, which nearly doubled, grain production per capita increased rather modestly. In 1952, grain production per capita was 285 kilograms, and it grew only to 317 kilograms in 1978, up 11.2 percent (NBS 2009). The results are similar if all food products are counted. The peak level of food consumption in the 1950s was 2,300 kcals per capita per day in 1956 and 2,400 kcals in 1978, an increase of only 100 kcals in more than two decades (Bramall 2009, 293).

While the Mao period was the only time that China experienced serious food shortages since 1949, it left a lasting impact on China's food strategy. The trade embargos and the famine revealed how perilous the situation could become if the country was unable to produce enough food for its population. In 1978, China implemented rural reform and replaced collective farming with household farming. The reform was followed by a surge in grain production, which jumped from 305 to 407 million tons between 1978 and 1984 (Figure 13.1). And this allowed the country to become a net grain exporter in 1985 for the first time since 1961. In the 1980s and early 1990s, the source of food in China mainly came from domestic production. As far as grains were concerned, the self-sufficiency rate never fell below 96 percent. It was even more than 100 percent in some years (1985, 1992–93), when grain exports exceeded imports.

In 1994, Lester Brown published a report titled *Who will feed China?* triggering a heated discussion of the country's ability to feed itself. Brown's report was not based on actual food exports and imports. In 1993, China exported six million tons more grain than it imported, and its overall food

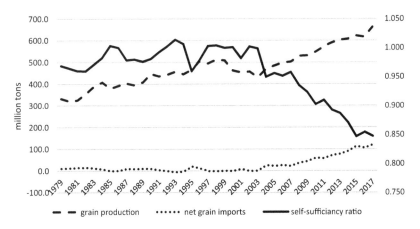

FIGURE 13.1 China's Grain Production, Net Grain Imports, and Grain Self-sufficiency Ratio: 1979–2017

Data source: *China Statistical Yearbooks* (various years).

exports also exceeded its imports (NBS 1999, Tables A55–6). His report was a prediction based on the experience of neighboring East Asian countries and an analysis of China's resource constraints, particularly the shortage of water and land. "Within 30 years or so, each [of the East Asian nations] had gone from being largely self-sufficient in grain to importing most of their supplies. In 1994, Japan imported 72 percent of the grain it consumed, for South Korea, the figure was 66 percent, and for Taiwan, 76 percent" (Brown 1995, 14).

Brown's report failed to consider the effects of the post-war food regime on food imports to Japan, South Korea, and Taiwan (McMichael 2000b). In addition, it underestimated the potential of China's grain production by exaggerating the constraints of water and land, as his critics pointed out (Heilig, Fischer, and Van Valthuizen 2000; Smil 1995). Nevertheless, the report led China to release a white paper in 1996 declaring that the country would produce 95 percent of grains that it consumes. To increase domestic grain production, the Chinese state raised grain prices and increased funding for agricultural infrastructure, along with a policy tying grain security to local officials' performance. Its grain production reached a new height in 1996, exceeding 500 million tons. In the decade from 1994 to 2003, China's grain imports saw little growth, and net imports even declined to only three million tons a year on average. The grain self-sufficiency ratio was maintained above 99 percent on average (Figure 13.1).

Externalizing Food Costs

Food imports started to increase rapidly after 2004. For example, grain imports, including soybeans, increased from 23 million tons in 2003 to 121 million tons in 2017, up 426 percent (Figure 13.1). The trade war since 2018 has led to a decrease in the volume of grain imports by China, but only to a limited extent. In 2019, China imported 106 million tons of grains, only 12 percent less than the peak level in 2017 (NBS 2020, Ch.11–07). This reflects the strong demand for food imports in China. This section examines how the underproduction of food and the incorporation of China into the global food system have led to the rapid rise of food imports to China.

Underproduction of Food

The underproduction of food is serious in China because the country must support with limited resources a huge population whose demand for resource-intensive food products such as meat and dairy has grown rapidly as a result of diet "modernization" and nutrition transition (McMichael 2020; Schneider 2014). China's resource constraints were the key factor leading Brown to question whether the country can feed itself. An often-cited fact in the literature is that China's land per capita is less than half of the world average while available water per person is about one-third (World Bank 2020). The acceleration of urbanization and industrialization since the 1980s has added further stress on the resources available for grain production. Despite efforts to preserve farmland in China, arable land per capita had declined from 0.114 hectare per person to 0.077 hectare per person between 1985 and 2014, down 32 percent, while the total area of arable land had shrunk by 15 million hectares. This figure may underestimate the actual scale of farmland contraction. Our research finds that the newly reclaimed farmland is often of poorer quality than the farmland lost to industrial or urban expansion. Insofar as water is concerned, cities and industrial activities have taken away a significant proportion of agricultural water while an even larger proportion of water resources are polluted. Furthermore, the shortage of agricultural water resources is most serious in main grain-producing regions, such as arid northern provinces (Zhan and Huang 2017).

The other aspect of the underproduction of food is growing demand for food, particularly resource-intensive food, due to rising living standards and dietary shifts (Christiansen 2009; Huang 2016; Schneider 2014; Tilman, Balzer, Hill, and Befort 2011). For example, China's meat consumption per capita, including pork, beef, lamb, and poultry meat, tripled from 12.8 kg in 1980 to 38.5 kg in 2018 (NBS 1991, 273; NBS 2019). The growing demand for meat increased grain consumption in China because a significant proportion of grains has been used for animal feed. Thus, although grain production has exceeded 600 million tons in recent years (significantly higher than 500 million tons in the 1990s and 400 million tons in the 1980s), China still imported 122 million tons of grains (including soybeans) in 2017.

The underproduction of food has reduced the incentive of local actors to use resources such as land and water for grain production while amplifying voices for more food imports. Local governments, particularly those in industrializing regions or areas near large cities, tend to divert agricultural resources such as land and water to industrial and urban sectors. Our field research in Hunan and Sichuan, two major grain-producing provinces, found that the area for grain production there had been shrinking as the local governments expropriated both land and water for industrial and urban usages (Zhan 2017; Zhan and Huang 2017).

The resource and environmental pressures have also shifted the balance toward the groups advocating for more imports at the central level. For instance, a 2014 research report by the State Council Development Research Center, the top government-sponsored think tank, criticized the grain self-sufficiency policy while calling for a further increase in grain imports and overseas agricultural investment (Han 2014, 20). The editor of the book, Jun Han, who is now the Deputy Minister of Agriculture and Rural Affairs, has played a key role in changing China's grain policy toward more imports.

Incorporation Into the Global Food System

China was accepted into the World Trade Organization (WTO) in 2001 with significant concessions made on agriculture, including easing restrictions on the entry of foreign agribusiness and lowering tariffs on agricultural imports (Bhala 1999; Huang and Rozelle 2002). The accession to the WTO facilitated the incorporation of China into the global food system, contributing to the increase in food imports. For example, under the agreement for accession to the WTO, China set a low three-percent tariff on soybean imports and removed the import quota (Gale, Valdes, and Ash 2019). This has led to a steady growth of soybean imports since 2004. Without tariff protection, the area for soybean production in China shrunk significantly, which further fueled imports to meet growing domestic demand. Also, under the WTO agreements China lifted restrictions on the entry of transnational agribusinesses. The leading global agribusiness corporations, such as ADM, Bunge, Cargill, Louis Dreyfus, and Monsanto (now Bayer), increased their presence in the country and exerted an growing degree of control over agricultural inputs, processing facilities, and food trade networks (Wang 2011; Yan, Chen, and Ku 2016).

The incorporation into the global food system also facilitated the growth of Chinese agribusiness companies. They either entered into alliances with global agribusiness corporations or competed with the latter for extending and controlling agricultural commodity chains. This is evidenced by their increasing overseas agricultural investment. Although agriculture accounted for a tiny share of China's overall outward direct investment (ODI) (1.3 percent in 2016 according to official statistics), it grew rapidly at an annual rate of 36 percent from 2005 to 2016. The country's accumulated ODI in agriculture reached 27.9 billion dollars by the end of 2016 (Zhan, Zhang, and He 2018).

Internal and External Constraints

The domestic underproduction of food motivated China to increase imports, while its incorporation into the global food system opened a space for it to do so. However, the food import strategy, although it appears economically rational, is subjected to both internal and external constraints.

Internal Constraints

A nation's food policy is not only determined by profitability but also shaped by concerns over regime legitimacy. Scholars have noted the acute contradiction between accumulation and regime legitimacy in China (Lee 2007), and that the Chinese Communist Party may suppress capitalist interests to accommodate popular demands (Arrighi 2007). Food provision is a good example to show the contradiction. This section investigates the internal constraints on China's food import policy deriving from concerns over regime legitimacy.

The most significant internal constraint is the ingrained belief in grain self-sufficiency among policy makers and in the society. "Grains" in the Chinese context are broadly defined to include cereals, oilseeds, and root tubers. The belief has much to do with the anxiety deriving from the experience of food shortages and the trade embargo in the Mao period, as noted earlier. Whenever domestic grain production declined or stagnated, criticism would arise and compel the party-state to take action. For example, grain production stagnated in the second half of the 1980s, and the criticism pushed the central government to improve the irrigation system and set higher grain prices in the early 1990s. Between 1999 and 2003, grain production experienced a five-year decline, which again gave rise to the criticism of the rural policy from scholars, news media, and even officials within the government.

To stabilize grain production and counter the trend of underproduction, the Chinese state implemented strict measures to protect farmland. In 2006, the central government drew a red line on the conversion of farmland into non-agricultural land and stipulated that it must retain at least 120 million hectares of farmland by 2020. In 2016, the Ministry of Land Resources set a new target of retaining 124 million hectares of farmland and demarcated 103 million hectares for "permanent basic farmland," which cannot be used for non-agricultural purposes (Xinhua 2017). To further protect farmland, the government set a quota for each province on how much farmland can be converted for non-agricultural uses. Under these quotas, local governments must submit their land use plans for approval, and they must reclaim the same amount of farmland to compensate for the land lost to industrial and urban expansion.

Another internal constraint is the pressure to support peasant livelihoods. Agricultural production provides sources of food and livelihood for hundreds of millions of people in China. While China has been pushing to accelerate urbanization, it would take decades to move this enormous population to the city, if it can be achieved at all (Zhan 2020). In a press conference in February 2019, the Ministry of Agriculture and Rural Affairs of China highlighted that there were 230 million households in rural areas, of which 210 million cultivated a farm of less than 0.65 hectare (MOARA 2019). The impoverishment and displacement of this population due to the impact of large food imports would jeopardize communist party rule in the countryside.

The decline in grain production in 1999–2003 is a good example. The decline was associated with a general rural crisis that triggered intense social unrest: peasants protested excessive taxation, land expropriation, and officials' abuse of power (Bernstein and Lü 2003; O'Brien and Li 2006). These protests alarmed the party-state and contributed to the policy of "building a new socialist countryside," which abolished nearly all agricultural taxes and fees while providing subsidies and development funds to support agriculture (Ahlers 2014; Day 2013). It was estimated that governments at both the central and local levels allocated at least 20 trillion yuan (3.1 trillion US dollars) over the decade from

176 Shaohua Zhan and Lingli Huang

2008 to 2017 to rural areas to support agriculture and increase rural household income (Zhan 2019b, 88). In 2017, China launched a *National Strategic Plan for Rural Revitalization (2018–2022)*. The plan provides further evidence that the Chinese Communist Party feels compelled to provide support for rural households to engage in agricultural and food production, even though it may run against the capitalist logic of profit maximization.

External Constraints

The strategy to externalize food costs also faces external constraints. The first constraint is the backlash against Chinese overseas agricultural investment. Starting in the early 2000s, China encouraged agribusiness companies to go out and invest overseas. Although the scale of its overseas agricultural investment remained relatively small as compared with the US and European countries, it was quickly singled out as "a land grabber" practicing neocolonialism in media and geopolitical discourses since the mid-2000s. For example, China was accused of taking large swathes of land in Africa and thus it would threaten already precarious food security there (Brautigam and Zhang 2013; Hofman and Ho 2012). This later proved untrue, but the fear and backlash against Chinese agricultural investment have persisted and spread to other regions and countries. The backlash also compelled the Chinese government to clarify that overseas agricultural and land investments were not intended to grow food crops for export to China.

Partly as a result of the backlash, many countries have enacted laws to restrict land concessions and crop exports to foreign powers, targeting particularly China, and large land deals with China were either cancelled or never materialized (Brautigam 2015; Oliveira 2018). In host countries, local authorities, opposition political parties, civil society organizations, and villagers often invoked discourses such as "Chinese takeover," "neocolonialism," and "neoimperialism" to push back land deals or negotiate for better terms with Chinese investors (Lu and Schönweger 2019). This not only restricts the scale of Chinese investment but also renders the investment much more costly. For this reason, Chinese overseas agricultural investment has focused much less on grain crops than on non-grain cash crops such as rubber and palm oil or food processing and manufacturing activities (Chen, Li, Wang, and Wang 2017). Thus, the attempt to directly control overseas agricultural resources such as land on a large scale to externalize food costs appears neither politically nor economically viable.

The US–China trade dispute and the signs of a new "Cold War" since 2018 are likely to create a more difficult situation for Chinese overseas agricultural investment (Westad 2019; Zhao 2019). Australia is a case in point. As a strong ally of the US, Australia has been pushing back Chinese agricultural investment in recent years. It was reported that Chinese investment in Australia including agricultural investment fell by 58.4 percent, that is, from 8.2 billion US dollars in 2018 to 3.4 billion in 2019 (Rowley 2020). It is expected that Chinese investment will further decline in the country as the ongoing hostility between the two countries intensifies.

Another constraint is the instability of the global food system. Since the 2007–08 food crisis, the global food market has reversed the trend of declining food prices and oversupply that had characterized previous decades. The global food supply entered an era of price fluctuations and short-term shortages of certain food commodities (Clapp and Moseley 2020; van der Ploeg 2020). The overall supply of food has remained sufficient, and this gave China an advantageous position as a major food importer, so much so that it could use food imports as a bargaining chip in the US–China trade negotiations. However, the instability of the global food system, which may deteriorate further due to climate change and financialization of food, has been a concern to Chinese policy makers. The COVID-19 pandemic is a case in point. The pandemic led to temporary export embargos, the shutdown of food processing facilities, and the disruption of trade networks, which destabilized food imports to China. Against this background, Chinese wheat farms suffered a modest harvest reduction in the summer 2020 and calls to reduce food waste quickly gave rise to fears that China may face a food shortage (CBN 2020). This prompted the Chinese authorities to repeatedly clarify that the country had enough food.

These external and internal constraints on China's food import strategy forced the Chinese authorities to stress the importance of domestic production. Since 2004, while food imports to China have grown, China has also produced more food for itself. China's grain production achieved a 12-year consecutive growth between 2003 and 2015, up to 621 million tons from 431 million tons. The growth slowed down the decline in the country's grain sufficiency rate, which was still around 85 percent in 2017 (Figure 13.1). In a key policy document released in March 2021, the Chinese government set a long-term goal to maintain 650 million tons of annual domestic grain production through the year of 2035. Thus, it can be inferred that promoting domestic production will remain a key focus in China's food policy in the foreseeable future (Zhan 2022).

Conclusion

The constraints on China's food import strategy reveal the dilemma that the country confronts in a context of rapid economic growth driven by capitalist expansion. On the one hand, the underproduction crisis of food has given China a strong incentive to import food to feed its huge population. And the neoliberal corporate food regime, which promotes food trade across borders, has provided a space for China to do so. On the other hand, the instability of the global food system and the backlash against Chinese overseas agricultural investment have forced the country to maintain domestic production.

Furthermore, the fear of food shortages and the pressure to provide livelihood for hundreds of millions of peasants compelled the party-state to promote domestic production.

The dilemma reveals that China, as a rising economic power, has failed to replicate the experiences of the UK and the US. The UK in the nineteenth century, with vast resources in its colonies, could import nearly unlimited food to feed its swelling working class. The US, faced with much less population pressure than China, was able to export surplus grain and employ food aid as a weapon to increase its geopolitical influence after the Second World War. China's experience has been very different from these. Up until the 1990s, China had very limited economic power in the world, and its food supply had been mainly derived from domestic production. Since the 1990s, rapid economic growth and integration into the capitalist world-economy have lifted China to the second largest economy. China imported a growing volume of food and became a major food importer in the world. Nevertheless, China must still produce the bulk of food that it consumes due to its enormous population size and its inability to control the global food system. The pressure to internalize food costs will be a counterforce to Chinese capitalism as it compels the country to allocate resources to maintain unprofitable grain production and support small farmers' livelihoods.

Note

1. The writing of this chapter is supported by a Singapore MOE AcRF Tier 1 Grant (2020-T1–001–142). The manuscript was presented at the 44th PEWS Annual Conference in September–November 2020. We are enormously grateful to Beverly Silver and other participants of the conference for helpful comments.

REFERENCES

Abu-Lughod, Janet. 1994. *From Urban Village to East Village: The Battle for New York's Lower East Side*. Oxford: Blackwell.

Ackerman, Spencer. 2021. *Reign of Terror: How the 9/11 Era Destabilized America and Produced Trump*. New York: Viking.

Adaş, Emin B. 2006. "The Making of Entrepreneurial Islam and the Islamic Spirit of Capitalism." *Journal for Cultural Research* 10(2): 113–37.

Adas, Michael. 1989. *Machines as the Measure of Men: Science, Technology, and Ideologies of Western Dominance*. Ithaca: Cornell University Press.

Adeboye, Olufunke. 2004. "Pentecostal Challenges in Africa and Latin America: A Comparative Focus on Nigeria and Brazil." *Afrika Zamani* 11&12: 136–59.

Aglietta, Michel. 1979. *A Theory of Capitalist Regulation: The U.S. Experience*. London: New Left Books.

Agnew, John. 1994. "The Territorial Trap: The Geographical Assumptions of International Relations Theory." *Review of International Political Economy* 1(1): 53–80.

Ahlers, Anna. 2014. *Rural Policy Implementation in Contemporary China: New Socialist Countryside*. Abingdon, UK: Routledge.

Aksakal, Mustafa. 2008. *The Ottoman Road to War in 1914: The Ottoman Empire and the First World War*. Cambridge: Cambridge University Press.

Alimahomed-Wilson, Jake. 2016. *Solidarity Forever? Race, Gender, and Unionism in the Ports of Southern California*. Lanham, MD: Rowman & Littlefield.

Alimahomed-Wilson, Jake. 2020. "Racialized Masculinities and Global Logistics Labor." *Into the Black Box: A Collective Research on Logistics, Spaces, and Labour*, July 7. http://www.intotheblackbox.com/articoli/racialized-masculinities-and-global-logistics-labor/

Allen, Terry J. 2011. "Global Land Grab: Fear of Unrest and Hunger for Profit Are Sparking Massive Acquisitions of Farmland." *In These Times*, August 22.

Amin, Samir. 1975. *La acumulación en escala mundial*. Buenos Aires: Siglo Veintiuno Editores.

Amin, Samir. 1979. *Imperialism and Unequal Development*. New York: Monthly Review Press.

180 References

Amin, Samir. 1997. *Los desafíos de la mundialización*. México D.F.: Sigloveitiuno Editores.

Amin, Samir. 2019. "Forum on Samir Amin's Proposal for a New International of Workers and People." *Journal of World-Systems Research* 25(2): 247–53.

Amin, Shahid, and Marcel van der Linden, eds. 1997. *"Peripheral" Labour? Studies in the History of Partial Proletarianization*. Cambridge: Cambridge University Press.

Amsden, Alice H. 2004. "Import Substitution in High-Tech Industries: Prebisch Lives in Asia!" *CEPAL Review* 82: 75–89.

Anderson, Allan H. 2005. "New African Initiated Pentecostalism and Charismatics in South Africa." *Journal of Religion in Africa* 35(1): 66–92.

Andreas, Joel. 2008. "Changing Colours in China." *New Left Review*: 123–42.

Aneesh, A. 2015. *Neutral Accent: How Language, Labor, and Life Become Global*. Durham, NC: Duke University Press.

Angotti, Thomas, and Sylvia Morse. 2016. *Zoned Out!: Race, Displacement, and City Planning in New York City*. New York: Urban Research.

Angotti, Tom. 2011. *New York For Sale: Community Planning Confronts Global Real Estate*. Cambridge, MA: MIT Press.

Angotti, Tom. 2012. *The New Century of the Metropolis: Urban Enclaves and Orientalism*. New York: Routledge.

Angotti, Tom. 2016. "Land Use and Zoning Matter." Pp. 18–44 in *Zoned Out! Race, Displacement, and City Planning in New York City*, edited by Tom Angotti and Sylvia Morse. New York: Terreform.

Antonopoulos, Paul, Daniel França Ribeiro, and Drew Cottle. 2021. "Liberation Theology to Evangelicalism: The Rise of Bolsonaro and the Conservative Evangelical Advance in Post-Colonial Brazil." *Postcolonial Interventions* 5(2): 240–81.

Arrighi, Giovanni. 1978. *La geometria del imperialismo*. México D.F.: Sigloveintiuno Editores.

Arrighi, Giovanni. 1990. "The Developmentalist Illusion: A Reconceptualization of the Semiperiphery." Pp. 11–42 in *Semiperipheral States in the World-Economy*, edited by W. G. Martin. Westport: Greenwood Press.

Arrighi, Giovanni. 1994 [2010]. *The Long Twentieth Century: Money, Power, and the Origins of Our Time*. London: Verso.

Arrighi, Giovanni. 1998. *A ilusão do desenvolvimento*. Petrópolis: Vozes.

Arrighi, Giovanni. 1999. "Globalization and Historical Macrosociology." Pp. 117–33 in *Sociology for the Twenty-First Century: Continuities and Cutting Edges*, edited by Janet Abu-Lughod. Chicago: University of Chicago Press.

Arrighi, Giovanni. 2004. "Hegemony and Antisystemic Movements." Pp. 79–90 in *The Modern World-System in the Long Duree*, edited by I. Wallerstein. Boulder: Paradigm Publishers.

Arrighi, Giovanni. 2007. *Adam Smith in Beijing: Lineages of the 21st Century*. London: Verso.

Arrighi, Giovanni, Nicole Aschoff, and Ben Scully. 2010. "Accumulation By Dispossession and Its Limits: The Southern Africa Paradigm Revisited." *Studies in Comparative International Development* 45(4): 410–38.

Arrighi, Giovanni, Terence K. Hopkins, and Immanuel Wallerstein. 1989. *Antisystemic Movements*. London and New York: Verso.

Arrighi, Giovanni, Po-keung Hui, Krishnendu Ray, and Thomas Reifer. 1999. "Geopolitics and High Finance." Pp. 37–95 in *Chaos and Governance in the Modern World System*, edited by Giovanni Arrighi and Beverly Silver. Minneapolis: University of Minnesota Press.

References 181

Arrighi, Giovanni, and Fortunata Piselli. 1987. "Capitalist Development in Hostile Environments: Feuds, Class Struggles, and Migrations in a Peripheral Region of Southern Italy." *Review (Fernand Braudel Center)* 10(4): 649–751.

Arrighi, Giovanni, and Beverly J. Silver. 1999. *Chaos and Governance in the Modern World System.* Minneapolis: University of Minnesota Press.

Arrighi, Giovanni, and Beverly J. Silver. 2001. "Capitalism and World (Dis) Order." *Review of International Studies* 27(5): 257.

Arrighi, Giovanni, and Lu Zhang. 2010. "Beyond the Washington Consensus: A New Bandung?" Pp. 25–57 in *Globalization and Beyond: New Examinations of Global Power and its Alternatives*, edited by J. Shefner and P. Fernández-Kelly. University Park, PA: The Pennsylvania State University Press.

Asian Americans for Equality. 2002. *Rebuild Chinatown Initiative: The Community Speaks.* https://www.aafe.org/2002/11/rebuild-chinatown-report.html

Asian Americans for Equality. 2004. *Rebuild Chinatown Initiative. America's Chinatown: A Community Plan.* https://www.aafe.org/2004/04/rebuild-chinatown-initiative-final-report.html

Atasoy, Yıldız. 2009. *Islam's Marriage with Neoliberalism: State Transformation in Turkey.* Basingstoke and New York: Palgrave Macmillan.

Atia, Mona. 2012. "'A Way to Paradise': Pious Neoliberalism, Islam, and Faith-Based Development." *Annals of the Association of American Geographers* 102(4): 808–27.

Austin, Garet, and Gerardo Serra. 2015. "West Africa." Pp. 241–78 in *Routledge Handbook of the History of Economic Thought*, edited by V. Barnett. New York: Routledge.

Babels. 2017. *De Lesbos à Calais—Comment L'Europe Fabrique des Camps.* Calvados: Le Passager Clandestin.

Babones, Salvatore. 2015. "What is World-systems Analysis? Distinguishing Theory from Perspective." *Thesis Eleven* 127(1): 3–20.

Bair, Jennifer. 2005. "Global Capitalism and Commodity Chains: Looking Back, Going Forward." *Competition and Change* 9(2): 153–80.

Bair, Jennifer, ed. 2009. *Frontiers of Commodity Chain Research.* Stanford, CA: Stanford University Press.

Bair, Jennifer, and Marion Werner. 2011. "The Place of Disarticulations: Global Commodity Production in La Laguna, Mexico." *Environment and Planning A* 43: 998–1015.

Baldwin-Edwards, Martin. 2008. "Towards a Theory of Illegal Migration: Historical and Structural, Components." *Third World Quarterly* 29(7): 1449–59.

Balto, Simon. 2019. *Occupied Territory: Policing Black Chicago from Red Summer to Black Power.* Chapel Hill: University of North Carolina Press.

Barkawi, Tarak, and Stuart Schrader. 2020. "Interview with Stuart Schrader." *International Politics Reviews* 8(1): 41–56.

Barker, Isabelle V. 2007. "Charismatic Economies: Pentecostalism, Economic Restructuring, and Social Reproduction." *New Political Science* 29(4): 407–27.

Barkey, Karen. 2008. *Empire of Difference: The Ottomans in Comparative Perspective.* New York: Cambridge University Press.

Baronov, David. 2018. "The Analytical-Holistic Divide within World-Systems Analysis." Pp. 6–16 in *The World-System as Unit of Analysis: Past Contributions and Future Advances*, edited by R. P. Korzeniewicz. New York: Routledge.

Beeson, Mark, and Iyanatul Islam. 2005. "Neo-Liberalism and East Asia: Resisting the Washington Consensus." *Journal of Development Studies* 41(2): 197–219.

Belluzzo, Luiz Gonzaga. 2013. *O capital e suas metamorfoses.* São Paulo: Editora Unesp.

182 References

Bernstein, Thomas P., and Xiaobo Lü. 2003. *Taxation without Representation in Contemporary Rural China*. Vol. 37. Cambridge: Cambridge University Press.

Besson, Mark. 2014. *Regionalism and Globalization in East Asia: Politics, Security and Economic Development*. 2nd ed. New York: Palgrave Macmillan.

Bhala, Raj. 1999. "Enter the Dragon: An Essay on China's WTO Accession Saga." *American University International Law Review* 15: 1469–538.

Bhambra, Gurminder. 2007. *Rethinking Modernity: Postcolonialism and the Sociological Imagination*. New York: Palgrave Macmillan.

Bhattacharyya, Gargi, John Gabriel, and Stephen Small. 2002. *Race and Power: Global Racism in the Twenty-first Century*. London: Routledge.

Bhatty, Kiran, and Nandini Sundar. 2020. "Sliding from Majoritarianism Toward Fascism: Educating India under the Modi Regime." *International Sociology* 35(6): 632–50.

Billings, Dwight B., and Shauna L. Scott. 1994. "Religion and Political Legitimation." *Annual Review of Sociology* 20: 173–201.

Blackledge, Paul. 2013. "Thinking about New Social Movements." Pp. 259–75 in *Marxism and Social Movements*, edited by C. Baker, L. Cox, J. Krinsky, and A. G. Nilsen. Leiden: Brill.

Boatcă, Manuela. 2006. "Semiperipheries in the World-System: Reflecting Eastern European and Latin American Experiences." *Journal of World-Systems Research* 12(2): 321–46. https://doi.org/10.5195/jwsr.2006.362.

Bodley, John H. 2014. *Victims of Progress*. Lanham, MD: Rowman & Littlefield.

Bonacich, Edna, and Jake B. Wilson. 2008. *Getting the Goods: Ports, Labor, and the Logistics Revolution*. Ithaca, NY: Cornell University Press.

Bonefeld, Werner. 2001. "The Permanence of Primitive Accumulation: Commodity Fetishism and Social Constitution." *The Commoner* 2: 1–15.

Bonefeld, Werner, ed. 2008. *Subverting the Present, Imagining the Future*. New York: Autonomedia.

Bornstein, Erica. 2003. *The Spirit of Development: Protestant NGOs, Morality, and Economics in Zimbabwe*. New York: Routledge.

Boyd, Michelle. 2005. "The Downside of Racial Uplift: Meaning of Gentrification in an African American Neighborhood." *City & Society* 17(2): 265–88.

Boyer, Robert. 2016. *La Economía Política de Los Capitalismos. Teoría de La Regulación y de La Crisis*. Moreno: UNM Editora.

Bozkurt, Umut. 2013. "Neoliberalism with a Human Face: Making Sense of the Justice and Development Party's Neoliberal Populism in Turkey." *Science & Society* 77(3): 372–96.

Bramall, Chris. 2009. *Chinese Economic Development*. New York: Routledge.

Brass, Tom. 2011. *Labor Regime Change in the Twenty-First Century: Unfreedom, Capitalism, and Primitive Accumulation*. Chicago: Haymarket Books.

Braudel, Fernand. 1970. *La Historia y las ciencias sociales*. Madrid: Alianza Editorial.

Braudel, Fernand. 1979 [1992]. *Civilization and Capitalism, 15th–18th Century, Vol 3: The Perspective of the World*. Oakland, CA: University of California Press.

Braudel, Fernand. 1992. *Civilization and Capitalism, 15th–18th Century, Volume II: The Wheels of Commerce*. Berkeley: University of California Press.

Braudel, Fernand. 1995. *Civilização Material, economia E Capitalismo: As Estruturas Do Cotidiano*. São Paulo: Martins Fontes.

Braudel, Fernand. 1996a. *Civilização Material, Economia E Capitalismo: O Jogo Das Trocas*. São Paulo: Martins Fontes.

Braudel, Fernand. 1996b. *Civilização Material, Economia E Capitalismo: O Tempo Do Mundo*. São Paulo: Martins Fontes.

References   **183**

Brautigam, Deborah. 2015. *Will Africa Feed China?* Oxford: Oxford University Press.

Brautigam, Deborah, and Haisen Zhang. 2013. "Green Dreams: Myth and Reality in China's Agricultural Investment in Africa." *Third World Quarterly* 34(9): 1676–96.

Brenner, Robert. 2009. *El Desarrollo Desigual y La Larga Fase Descendente: Las Economías Capitalistas Avanzadas Desde El Boom Al Estancamiento.* Madrid: AKAL.

Bridge, Gavin. 2008. "Global Production Networks and the Extractive Sector: Governing Resource-Based Development." *Journal of Economic Geography* 8: 389–419.

Brown, Lester R. 1995. *Who Will Feed China? Wake-up Call for a Small Planet.* New York: WW Norton & Company.

Brown, Wendy. 2019. *In the Ruins of Neoliberalism: The Rise of Antidemocratic Politics in the West.* New York: Columbia University Press.

Brubaker, Rogers. 2002. "Ethnicity Without Groups." *European Journal of Sociology* 43(2): 163–89.

Brubaker, Rogers. 2017. "Between Nationalism and Civilizationism: The European Populist Moment in Comparative Perspective." *Ethnic and Racial Studies* 40(8): 1191–226.

Bunker, Stephen G., and Paul S. Ciccantell. 2005. *Globalization and the Race for Resources.* Baltimore, MD: Johns Hopkins University Press.

Bunker, Stephen G., and Paul S. Ciccantell. 2007. *East Asia and the Global Economy: Japan's Ascent with Implications for China's Future.* Baltimore, MD: Johns Hopkins University Press.

Burawoy, Michael. 1976. "The Functions and Reproduction of Migrant Labor: Comparative Material from Southern Africa and the United States." *American Journal of Sociology* 81(5): 1050–87.

Burbank, Jane. 2006. "An Imperial Rights Regime: Law and Citizenship in the Russian Empire." *Kritika* 7(3): 397–431.

Busà, Alessandro. 2017. *The Creative Destruction of New York City: Engineering the City for the Elite.* Oxford: Oxford University Press.

Bush, Roderick. 1999. *We Are Not What We Seem: Black Nationalism and Class Struggle in the American Century.* New York: New York University Press.

Bush, Roderick. 2009. *The End of White World Supremacy: Black Internationalism and the Problem of the Color Line.* Philadelphia: Temple University Press.

Butko, Thomas J. 2004. "Revelation or Revolution: A Gramscian Approach to the Rise of Political Islam." *British Journal of Middle Eastern Studies* 31(1): 41–62.

Cabral, Amilcar. 1973. *Return to the Source: Selected Speeches of Amilcar Cabral.* New York: Monthly Review Press.

Camarinha, Isis. 2020. "Longa Duração, Sistema Mundo Moderno Capitalista, Tempoespaço Cíclico-Ideológico e a natureza do declínio da Hegemonia Americana: contribuição para uma análise da conjuntura." Tese de Doutorado. UFRJ.

Cardoso, Fernando H., and Enzo Faletto. 1979. *Dependency and Development in Latin America.* Berkeley, CA: University of California Press.

Castles, Stephen. 2000. *Ethnicity and Globalization.* London: Sage Publications.

Castles, Stephen. 2011. "Migration, Crisis, and the Global Labour Market." *Globalizations* 8(3): 311–24.

CBN. 2020. "Liangshi Anquan Wu Jinyou Dan Xumou Yuanlǜ (No Immediate Problems with Grain Security But Long-Term Consideration Is Needed)." *China Business Network*, August 26.

Chang, Gordon. 2019. *Ghosts of Gold Mountain: The Epic Story of the Chinese Who Built the Transcontinental Railroad.* Boston: Houghton Mifflin Harcourt.

184 References

Chase-Dunn, Christopher, and Thomas Hall. 1997. *Rise and Demise: Comparing World-Systems*. Boulder, CO: Westview Press.

Chatterjee, Ipsita. 2010. "Globalization and the Production of Difference: A Case Study of the Neoliberal Production of Hindu Nationalism in India." *Comparative Studies of South Asia, Africa and the Middle East* 30(3): 621–32.

Chauvin, Sébastien, Blanca Garcés-Mascareñas, and Albert Kraler. 2013. "Working for Legality: Employment and Migrant Regularization in Europe." *International Migration* 51(6): 118–31.

Chen, Yangfen, Xiande Li, Lijuan Wang, and Shihai Wang. 2017. "Is China Different from Other Investors in Global Land Acquisition? Some Observations from Existing Deals in China's Going Global Strategy." *Land Use Policy* 60: 362–72.

Chitty, Christopher. 2020. *Sexual Hegemony: Statecraft, Sodomy, and Capital in the Rise of the World-system*. Durham, NC: Duke University Press.

Chodor, Tom. 2015. *Neoliberal Hegemony and the Pink Tide in Latin America: Breaking Up With TINA?* London: Palgrave Macmillan.

Christiansen, Flemming. 2009. "Food Security, Urbanization and Social Stability in China." *Journal of Agrarian Change* 9(4): 548–75.

Ciccantell, Paul S. 2020. "Liquefied Natural Gas: Redefining Nature, Restructuring Geopoltics, Returning to the Periphery?" *American Journal of Economics and Sociology* 79(1): 265–300. http://doi.org/10.1111/ajes.12313.

Ciccantell, Paul S. 2022. "Commodity Chains and Extractive Peripheries: Coal and Development." Pp. 21–44 in *Resource Peripheries in the Global Economy*, edited by Felipe Irrarazavel and Martin Arias. London: Springer.

Ciccantell, Paul S., and Paul K. Gellert. 2022. "Migration, Resource Frontiers, and Extractive Peripheries: Toward a Typology." Pp. 29–44 in *Migration, Racism and Labor Exploitation in the World-System*, edited by D. O'Hearn and P. Ciccantell. New York: Routledge.

Ciccantell, Paul S., and David Smith. 2009. "Rethinking Global Commodity Chains: Integrating Extraction, Transport, and Manufacturing." *International Journal of Comparative Sociology* 50(3–4): 361–84.

Ciscel, David H., Barbara Ellen Smith, and Marcela Mendoza. 2003. "Ghosts in the Global Machine: New Immigrants and the Redefinition of Work." *Journal of Economic Issues* 37(2): 333–41.

Clapp, Jennifer, and William G. Moseley. 2020. "This Food Crisis Is Different: Covid-19 and the Fragility of the Neoliberal Food Security Order." *The Journal of Peasant Studies* 47(7): 1393–417.

Cohen, Robin. 1987. *The New Helots: Migrants in the International Division of Labour*. Aldershot: Gower.

Cohen, Stanley. 1985. *Visions of Social Control*. Cambridge: Polity Press.

Comaroff, Jean. 2012. "Pentecostalism, Populism and the New Politics of Affect." Pp. 41–66 in *Pentecostalism and Development: Churches, NGOs and Social Change in Africa*, edited by D. Freeman. New York: Palgrave Macmillan.

Comaroff, Jean, and John L. Comaroff. 2000. "Privatizing the Millennium: New Protestant Ethics and Spirits of Capitalism in Africa, and Elsewhere." *Afrika Spectrum* 35(3): 293–312.

Coronil, Fernando. 1996. "Beyond Occidentalism: Toward Nonimperial Geohistorical Categories." *Cultural Anthropology* 11: 51–87.

Correia, David, and Tyler Wall. 2018. *Police: A Field Guide*. New York: Verso.

References 185

Corrigan, Philip. 1977. "Feudal Relics or Capitalist Monuments? Notes on the Sociology of Unfree Labour." *Sociology* 11: 435–63.

Costa, Carlos E. L., and Manuel J. F. Gonzalez. 2014. "Infraestrutura e integração regional: a experiência do IIRSA na América do Sul." *Boletim de Economia e Política Internacional—BEPI* 18: 23–40.

Current Population Survey. 2020. "Labor Force Statistics from the Current Population Survey: Household Data Annual Average Employed Persons by Detailed Industry, Race, Sex, and Hispanic and Latino Ethnicity." *United States Census Bureau.* https://www.census.gov/programs-surveys/cps/data.html

Davidoff, Leonore. 1974. "Mastered for Life: Servant and Wife in Victorian and Edwardian England." *Journal of Social History* 7(4), Summer: 406–28.

Day, Alexander F. 2013. *The Peasant in Postsocialist China: History, Politics, and Capitalism.* Cambridge: Cambridge University Press.

Day, Keri. 2015. *Religious Resistance to Neoliberalism: Womanist and Black Feminist Perspectives.* New York: Palgrave Macmillan.

De Angelis, Massimo. 2007. *The Beginning of History: Value Struggles and Global Capital.* London: Pluto Press.

De Angelis, Massimo. 2008. "Marx and Primitive Accumulation: The Continuous Character of Capital's 'Enclosures'." Pp. 27–49 in *Subverting the Present, Imagining the Future,* edited by Werner Bonefeld. New York: Autonomedia.

De Genova, Nicholas. 2005. *Working the Boundaries: Race, Space, and "Illegality" in Mexican Chicago.* Chapel Hill: Duke University Press.

de Graaff, Nana. 2020. "China Inc. Goes Global. Transnational and National Networks of China's Globalizing Business Elite." *Review of International Political Economy* 27(2): 208–33.

Delgado Wise, Raúl. 2009. "Forced Immigration and US Imperialism: The Dialectic of Migration and Development." *Critical Sociology* 35(6): 767–84.

Delgado Wise, Raúl. 2018. "Is There a Space for Counterhegemonic Participation? Civil Society in the Global Governance of Migration." *Globalizations* 15(6): 746–61.

Deringil, Selim. 2003. "'They Live in a State of Nomadism and Savagery': The Late Ottoman Empire and the Post-Colonial Debate." *Comparative Studies in Society and History* 45: 311–42.

Dicken, Peter. 1992. *Global Shift: The Internationalization of Economic Activity.* Berkeley, CA: University of California Press.

DIEESE—Departamento Intersindical de Estatística e Estudos Sócio-econômicos. 2010. "Desindustrialização: Conceito e a situação no Brasil." n°100, junho. https://www.dieese.org.br/notatecnica/2011/notaTec100Desindustrializacao.pdf

Dilger, Hansjörg. 2007. "Healing the Wounds of Modernity: Salvation, Community and Care in a Neo-Pentecostal Church in Dar Es Salaam, Tanzania." *Journal of Religion in Africa* 37(1): 59–83.

Dos Santos, Theotônio. 1993. *A Economia Mundial: Integração & Desenvolvimento Sustentável.* Vozes: Petrópolis.

Dos Santos, Theotônio. 2000. *A teoria da dependência: balanço e perspectivas.* Rio de Janeiro: Civilização Brasileira.

Dos Santos, Theotônio. 2004. *Do Terror à Esperança: auge e declínio do neoliberalismo.* Aparecida: Idéias & Letras.

Dos Santos, Theotônio. 2016. *Desenvolvimento e civilização: homenagem a Celso Furtado.* Rio de Janeiro: EDUERJ & CLACSO.

186 References

Dunaway, Wilma A., and Donald A. Clelland. 2017. "Moving Toward Theory for the 21st Century: The Centrality of Nonwestern Semiperipheries to World Ethnic/ Racial Inequality." *Journal of World-Systems Research* 23(2): 399–464.

Emmanuel, Arghiri. 1972. *Unequal Exchange: A Study of the Imperialism of Trade.* New York: Monthly Review Press.

Evans, Peter. 1979. *Dependent Development: The Alliance of Multinational, State, and Local Capital in Brazil.* Princeton, NJ: Princeton University Press.

Evans, Tony. 2011. "The Limits of Tolerance: Islam as Counter-hegemony?" *Review of International Studies* 37: 1751–73.

Evcimen, Gamze. 2017. "Anti-capitalist Muslims in Turkey: The Gezi Resistance and Beyond." Pp. 67–84 in *Domestic and Regional Uncertainties in the New Turkey,* edited by H. Tabak, O. Tufekci, and A. Chiriatti. Newcastle upon Tyne: Cambridge Scholars Publishing.

Ezenwe, Uka. 1993. "The African Debt Crisis and the Challenge of Development." *Intereconomics* 28(1): 35–43.

Fanon, Frantz. 1967 [1952]. *Black Skin, White Masks.* New York: Grove Press.

Federici, Sylvia. 2004. *Caliban and the Witch: Women, the Body, and Primitive Accumulation.* New York: Autonomedia.

Federici, Sylvia. 2008. "Precarious Labor: A Feminist Viewpoint." *Upping the Anti,* June 7.

Feldman, David B. 2020a. "Beyond the Border Spectacle: Global Capital, Migrant Labor and the Specter of Liminal Legality." *Critical Sociology* 46(4–5): 729–43.

Feldman, David B. 2020b. "The Question of Borders." *Catalyst* 4(1): 146–81.

Feldman, David B. 2021. "Globalization without Neoliberalism? Social Structures of Accumulation and the Latin American Pink Tide." Pp. 117–33 in *Elgar Handbook on Social Structures of Accumulation,* edited by Terrence McDonough, David Kotz, and Cian McMahon. Cheltenham: Edward Elgar Publishing.

Feldman, David B. Forthcoming. "Between Exploitation and Repression: The Immigration Industrial Complex and Militarized Migration Management." In *Marxism and Migration,* edited by Shahrzad Mojab, Sara Carpenter, and Genevieve Ritchie.

Felker-Kantor, Max. 2018. *Policing Los Angeles: Race, Resistance, and the Rise of the LAPD.* Chapel Hill: University of North Carolina Press.

Fenelon, James V. 2016. "Genocide, Race, Capitalism: Synopsis of Formation within the Modern World-system." *Journal of World-Systems Research* 22(1): 23–30. https:// doi.org/10.5195/jwsr.2016.607.

Fenelon, James V. 2022. "Immigration as Racial Dominance since 1492: Migration and the Modern World-System of the Americas." Pp. 11–28 in *Migration, Racism and Labor Exploitation in the World-System,* edited by Denis O'Hearn and Paul S. Ciccantell. New York: Routledge.

Fenelon, James V., and Jennifer Alford. 2020. "Envisioning Indigenous Models for Social and Ecological Change in the Anthropocene." *Journal of World-Systems Research* 26(2): 372–99. https://doi.org/10.5195/jwsr.2020.996.

Ferguson, James G. 1999. *Expectations of Modernity: Myths and Meanings of Urban Life on the Zambian Copperbelt.* Berkeley: University of California Press.

Fernandes, Leela, and Patrick Heller. 2006. "Hegemonic Aspirations: New Middle Class Politics and India's Democracy in Comparative Perspective." *Critical Asian Studies* 38(4): 495–522.

Fernández, Víctor Ramiro. 2014. "Global Value Chains in Global Political Networks: Tool for Development or Neoliberal Device?" *Review of Radical Political Economics* 47(2).

References **187**

Fernández, Víctor Ramiro, and Luciano Moretti. 2020. "Un Nuevo Sistema Mundo Desde El Sur Global : Gran Convergencia y Desplazamiento Geográfico Acelerado." *Geopolitica(s) Revista de Estudios Sobre Espacio y Poder* 11(2): 313–44.

Fernández, Víctor Ramiro, and Emilia Ormaechea. 2019. "The State in the Capitalist Periphery: From the Structuralist Vacuum to the Neo-Structuralist Deviations and Beyond." Pp. 123–55 in *Development in Latin America*, edited by V. R. Fernández and G. Brondino. Cham: Springer International Publishing.

FIESP-CIESP—Departamento de Pesquisa e Estudos Econômicos. 2015. *Perda de Participação da Industria de Transformação no PIB.* https://www.fiesp.com.br/arquivo-download/? id=191508

FIESP-CIESP—Departamento de Pesquisa e Estudos Econômicos. 2019. *Panorama da Indústria de Transformação Brasileira.* https://www.fiesp.com.br/arquivo-download/? id=252933

Finnland und Russland: Die internationale Londoner Konferenz. 1911. Leipzig: Verlag con Duncker & Humblot.

Fiori, José Luis. 2007. "Nicholas Spykman e a América Latina." *Le Monde Diplomatique,* November 24.

Fitch, Robert. 1993. *The Assassination of New York.* London: Verso.

Fitch, Robert. 1994. "Explaining New York City's Aberrant Economy." *New Left Review* 207: 17.

FitzGerald, David. 2019. *Refuge Beyond Reach: How Rich Democracies Repel Asylum Seekers.* New York: Oxford University Press.

Frank, Andre Gunder. 1966. *The Development of Underdevelopment.* New York: Monthly Review Press.

Frank, Andre Gunder. 1977. "On So-Called Primitive Accumulation." *Dialectical Anthropology* 2(1–4): 87–106.

Frank, Andre Gunder. 1978. *World Accumulation, 1492–1789.* New York: Monthly Review Press.

Frank, Andre Gunder, and Marta Fuentes. 1990. "Civil Democracy: Social Movements in Recent World History." Pp. 139–80 in *Transforming the Revolution: Social Movements and the World-System*, edited by S. Amin, G. Arrighi, A. G. Frank, and I. Wallerstein. New York: Monthly Review Press.

Freeman, Dena. 2012. "The Pentecostal Ethic and the Spirit of Development." Pp. 1–38 in *Pentecostalism and Development: Churches, NGOs and Social Change in Africa*, edited by D. Freeman. New York: Palgrave Macmillan.

Freston, Paul. 1995. "Pentecostalism in Brazil: A Brief History." *Religion* 25(2): 119–33.

Friedmann, Harriet. 1982. "The Political Economy of Food: The Rise and Fall of the Postwar International Food Order." *American Journal of Sociology*: S248–S86.

Friedmann, Harriet, and Philip McMichael. 1989. "Agriculture and the State System: The Rise and Decline of National Agricultures, 1870 to the Present." *Sociologia ruralis* 29(2): 93–117.

Frobel, Folker, Jurgen Heinrichs, and Otto Kreye. 1980. *The New International Division of Labour: Structural Unemployment in Industrialised Countries and Industrialisation in Developing Countries.* Cambridge: Cambridge University Press.

Gale, Fred, Constanza Valdes, and Mark Ash. 2019. *Interdependence of China, United States, and Brazil in Soybean Trade.* New York: US Department of Agriculture's Economic Research Service (ERS) Report. Pp. 1–48.

Galtung, Johan. 1971. "A Structural Theory of Imperialism." *Journal of Peace Research* 8(2): 81–117.

188 References

Garcia, Ana Saggioro, Carlos Eduardo Martins, and Roberto Goulart Menezes. 2021. "Editorial." *Reoriente: estudos sobre marxismo, dependência e sistemas-mundo* 1(1): 5–8.

Garland, David. 2001. *The Culture of Control*. Chicago: Chicago University Press.

Gates, Leslie C. 2009. "Theorizing Business Power in the Semiperiphery: Mexico 1970–2000." *Theory and Society* 38(1): 57–95.

Gates, Leslie C. 2018. "Populism: A Puzzle Without (and for) World-systems Analysis." *Journal of World-Systems Research* 24(2): 325–36.

Gates, Leslie C., and Mehmet Deniz. 2019. "Puzzling Politics: A Methodology for Turning World-Systems Analysis Inside-Out." *Journal of World-Systems Research* 25(1): 59–82.

Gedicks, Al. 2001. *Resource Rebels: Native Challenges to Mining and Oil Corporations*. Cambridge, MA: South End Press.

Genell, Aimee. 2013. "Empire by Law: Ottoman Sovereignty and the British Occupation of Egypt, 1882–1923." Doctoral dissertation. Columbia University, New York.

Gereffi, Gary. 1994. 'The Organization of Buyer-Driven Global Commodity Chains: How U.S. Retailers Shape Overseas Production Networks." Pp. 95–122 in *Commodity Chains and Global Capitalism*, edited by G. Gereffi and M. Korzeniewicz. Westport, CT: Praeger.

Gereffi, Gary. 1996. "Global Commodity Chains: New Forms of Coordination and Control Among Nations and Firms in International Industries." *Competition & Change* 4: 427–39.

Gereffi, Gary. 2018. *Global Values Chains and Development: Rethinking the Contours of 21st Century Capitalism*. Cambridge: Cambridge University Press.

Gereffi, Gary, and Miguel Korzeniewicz, eds. 1994. *Commodity Chains and Global Capitalism*. Westport, CT: Praeger.

Gereffi, Gary, and Olga Memdovic. 2003. *The Global Apparel Value Chain: What Prospects for Upgrading by Developing Countries?* Vienna, Austria: United Nations Industrial Development Organization.

Gereffi, Gary, and Donald Wyman, eds. 1990. *Manufacturing Miracles: Paths of Industrialization in Latin America and East Asia*. Princeton, NJ: Princeton University Press.

Gilmore, Ruth Wilson. 2007. *Golden Gulag: Prisons, Surplus, Crisis, and Opposition in Globalizing California*. Berkeley, CA: University of California Press.

Glassman, Jim. 2006. "Primitive Accumulation, Accumulation by Dispossession, Accumulation by 'Extra-economic' Means." *Progress in Human Geography* 30(5): 608–25.

Glassman, Jim. 2018. *Drums of War, Drums of Development: The Formation of a Pacific Ruling Class and Industrial Transformation in East and Southeast Asia, 1945–1980*. Lieden: Brill.

Globalizations. 2018. Special issue on "Migration, Civil Society and Global Governance." 15(6): 733–885.

Go, Julian. 2016. *Postcolonial Thought and Social Theory*. Oxford: Oxford University Press.

Golash-Boza, Tanya Maria. 2015. *Deported: Immigrant Policing, Disposable Labor, and Global Capitalism*. New York: NYU Press.

Goldring, Luin, and Patricia Landolt. 2011. "Caught in the Work-Citizenship Matrix: The Lasting Effects of Precarious Legal status on Work for Toronto Immigrants." *Globalizations* 8(3): 325–41.

Goodman, Adam. 2020. *The Deportation Machine: America's Long History of Expelling Immigrants*. Princeton, NJ: Princeton University Press.

Gopalakrishnan, Shankar. 2006. "Defining, Constructing and Policing a 'New India': Relationship between Neoliberalism and Hindutva." *Economic and Political Weekly*: 2804–13.

Gotham, Kevin Fox, and Miriam Greenberg. 2008. "From 9/11 to 8/29: Post-Disaster Response and Recovery in New York and New Orleans." *Social Forces* 87(2): 1039–62.

Gotham, Kevin Fox, and Miriam Greenberg. 2014. *Crisis Cities: Disaster and Redevelopment in New York and New Orleans*. Oxford: Oxford University Press.

GRAIN. 2008. *Seized: The 2008 Land Grab for Food and Financial Security*. https://grain.org/article/entries/93-seized-the-2008-landgrab-for-food-and-financial-security.

Gramsci, Antonio. 1971. *Selections from the Prison Notebooks of Antonio Gramsci*. Edited by Q. Hoare and G. Smith. New York: International Publishers.

Gregory, Derek, and Alan Pred. 2006. *Violent Geographies: Fear, Terror, and Political Violence*. New York: Routledge.

Grosfoguel, Ramón. 2006. "World-Systems Analysis in the Context of Transmodernity, Border Thinking, and Global Coloniality." *Review (Fernand Braudel Center)* 29(2): 167–87.

Guillén, Arturo. 2019. "USA's Trade Policy in the Context of Global Crisis and the Decline of North American Hegemony." *Brazilian Journal of Political Economy* 39(156): 387–407.

Gutelis, Beth, and Nik Theodore. 2019. *The Future of Warehouse Work: Technological Change in the U.S. Logistics Industry*. UC-Berkeley Labor Center Report, October.

Hackett, Rosalind I. J. 2003. "The Gospel of Prosperity in West Africa." Pp. 199–214 in *Religion and the Transformations of Capitalism: Comparative Approaches*, R. H. Roberts. New York and London: Routledge.

Haeg, Larry. 2013. *Harriman vs, Hill: Wall Street's Great Railroad War*. Minneapolis: University of Minnesota Press.

Hall, Thomas D., and James V. Fenelon. 2009. *Indigenous Peoples and Globalization: Resistance and Revitalization*. Boulder, CO: Paradigm.

Han, Jun. 2014. *Zhongguo Liangshi Anquan Yu Nongye Zouchuqu Zhanlue Yanjiu (China: Food Security and Agricultural Going out Strategy Research)*. Beijing: China Development Press.

Harris, Jerry, Carl Davidson, Bill Fletcher, and Paul Harris. 2017. "Trump and American Fascism." *International Critical Thought* 7(4): 476–92.

Harvey, David. 1998. *La Condición de La Posmodernidad. Investigación Sobre Los Orígenes Del Cambio Cultural*. Buenos Aires: Amorrortu Editores.

Harvey, David. 2003a. *The New Imperialism*. New York: Oxford University Press.

Harvey, David. 2003b. *El "nuevo" imperialismo: acumulación por desposesión*. Buenos Aires: CLACSO.

Hasu, Päivi. 2012. "Prosperity Gospels and Enchanted Worldviews: Two Responses to Socio-economic Transformation in Tanzanian Pentecostal Christianity." Pp. 67–86 in *Pentecostalism and Development: Churches, NGOs and Social Change in Africa*, edited by D. Freeman. Palgrave Macmillan.

Heilig, Gerhard K., Gunther Fischer, and Harrij Van Velthuizen. 2000. "Can China Feed Itself? An Analysis of China's Food Prospects with Special Reference to Water Resources." *The International Journal of Sustainable Development & World Ecology* 7: 153–72.

190 References

Herod, Andrew. 2000. "Implications of Just-in-Time Production for Union Strategy: Lessons from the 1998 General Motors-United Auto Workers Dispute." *Annals of the Association of American Geographers* 90(3): 521–47.

Hever, Shir. 2013. "Israel's Land Injustice Perpetuated by Racist Discourse." *The Real News Network*, April 9.

Hirschman, Albert. 1968. "The Political Economy of Import-Substituting Industrialization in Latin America." *The Quarterly Journal of Economics* 82(1): 1–32.

Hofman, Irna, and Peter Ho. 2012. "China's 'Developmental Outsourcing': A Critical Examination of Chinese Global 'Land Grabs' Discourse." *Journal of Peasant Studies* 39(1): 1–48.

Holt, Thomas C. 2000. *The Problem of Race in the 21st Century*. Cambridge, MA: Harvard University Press.

Hopkins, Terence K. 1978a. "World-System Analysis." Pp. 199–218 in *Social Change in the Capitalist World Economy*, edited by Barbara Hockey Kaplan. Beverly Hills: Sage.

Hopkins, Terence K. 1978b. "World-Systems Analysis: Methodological Issues." Pp. 233–62 in *Social Change in the Capitalist World Economy*, edited by Barbara Hockey Kaplan. Beverly Hills: Sage.

Hopkins, Terence K. 1982a. "The Study of the Capitalist World-Economy: Some Introductory Considerations." Pp. 9–38 in *World-Systems Analysis: Theory and Methodology*, edited by Terence K. Hopkins and Immanuel Wallerstein. Beverly Hills: Sage.

Hopkins, Terence K. 1982b. "World-Systems Analysis: Methodological Issues." Pp. 145–58 in *World-Systems Analysis: Theory and Methodology*, edited by Terence K. Hopkins and Immanuel Wallerstein. Beverly Hills: Sage.

Hopkins, Terence K., and Immanuel Wallerstein. 1977. "Patterns of Development of the Modern World-System." *Review (Fernand Braudel Center)* 1(2): 111–45.

Hopkins, Terence K., and Immanuel Wallerstein. 1982. *World-Systems Analysis: Theory and Methodology*. Beverly Hills, CA: Sage.

Hopkins, Terence K., and Immanuel Wallerstein. 1986. "Commodity Chains in the World-Economy Prior to 1800." *Review (Fernand Braudel Center)* 10(1): 157–70.

Hopkins, Terence K., Immanuel Wallerstein, Resat Kasaba, William G. Martin, and Peter D. Phillips. 1987. "Incorporation into the World-Economy: How the World-System Expands." *Review* 10 (5): 761–902.

Horner, Rory, and Khalid Nadvi. 2017. "The Rise of South-South Trade: Polycentric Patterns." *Global Development Institute Blog*. http://blog.gdi.manchester.ac.uk/polycentric-trade/

Horowitz, Richard. 2004. "International Law and State Transformation in China, Siam, and the Ottoman Empire during the Nineteenth Century." *Journal of World History* 15(4): 445–86.

Hosono, Akio. 2017. *Asia-Pacific and Latin America: Dynamics of Regional Integration and International Cooperation*. Santiago: Economic Commission for Latin America and the Caribbean.

Huang, Jikun, and Scott Rozelle. 2002. *China's Accession to WTO and Shifts in the Agriculture Policy*. Working Paper, University of California at Davis, Department of Agricultural & Resource Economics.

Huang, Philip C. C. 2016. "China's Hidden Agricultural Revolution, 1980–2010, in Historical and Comparative Perspective." *Modern China* 42(4): 339–76.

Hum, Tarry. 2021. "'Flushing—The Bigger, Better and Downright Sexier Chinatown of New York': Transnational Growth Coalitions and Immigrant Economies." Pp. 215–42 in *Immigrant Entrepreneurship in Cities*. Cham: Springer.

Hum, Tarry, and Sam Stein. 2017. "Gentrification and the Future of Work in New York City's 'Chinatowns'." Pp. 207–16 in *Asian American Matters: A New York Anthology*. New York: Asian American and Asian Research Institute.

International Labour Conference (ILO). 2017. *Report: Global Estimates of Modern Slavery: Forced Labour and Forced Marriage*. Geneva: United Nations Organization.

International Monetary Fund. 2009. *Balance of Payments and International Investment Position Manual*. 6th ed. (BPM 6). Washington, DC: International Monetary Fund.

Jalee, Pierre. 1968. *The Pillage of the Third World*. New York: Monthly Review Press.

Jefferson, Brian. 2020. *Digitize and Punish: Racial Criminalization in the Digital Age*. Minneapolis: University of Minnesota Press.

Jeffreys, Sheila. 2008. *The Industrial Vagina: The Political Economy of the Global Sex Trade*. New York: Routledge.

Jessop, Bob. 2009. "Avoiding Traps, Rescaling States, Governing Europe." In *The New Political Economy of Scale*, edited by Roger Keil and Rianne Mahon. Vancouver, BC: University of British Columbia Press.

Jessop, Bob, Neil Brenner, and Martin Jones. 2008. "Theorizing Sociospatial Relations." *Environment and Planning D: Society and Space* 26(3): 389–401.

Jian, Chen, Martin Klimke, Masha Kirasirova, et al. 2018. *The Routledge Handbook of the Global Sixties*. New York: Routledge.

Johansen, Bruce. 2000. "Burma (Myanmar): Forced Labor in the World's Last Teak Forest." *Ratical*.

Jones, Terry-Ann, and Eric Mielants. 2010. *Mass Migration in the World-System: Past, Present, and Future*. Boulder, CO: Paradigm Publishers.

Jules-Rosette, Bennetta. 1985. "The Sacred and Third World Societies." Pp. 215–33 in *The Sacred in a Secular Age*, edited by P. E. Hammond. Berkeley, CA: University of California Press.

Kapadia, Karin. 1995. "The Profitability of Bonded Labour: The Gem-Cutting Industry in Rural South India." *Journal of Peasant Studies* 22(3), April: 446–83.

Karakayali, Serhat, and Enrica Rigo. 2010. "Mapping the European Space of Circulation." Pp. 123–44 in *The Deportation Regime: Sovereignty, Space, and the Freedom of Movement*, edited by Nicholas De Genova and Nathalie Peutz. Durham: Duke University Press.

Karataşlı, Şahan Savas. 2017. "The Capitalist World-Economy in the Longue Durée." *Sociology of Development* 3(2): 163–96.

Karataşlı, Şahan Savas. 2019. "The Twenty-First Century Revolutions and Internationalism: A World Historical Perspective." *Globalizations* 16(7): 985–97.

Karatasil, Sahan Savas, and Sefika Kumral. 2019. "Capitalist Development in Hostile Conjunctures: War, Dispossession, and Class Formation in Turkey." *Journal of Agrarian Change* 19: 528–49.

Karataşlı, Şahan Savas, Sefika Kumral, Daniel Pasciuti, and Beverly J. Silver. 2017. "World Hegemonies and Global Inequalities." Pp. 23–37 in *Mapping a New World Order: The Rest Beyond the West*, edited by V. Popov and P. Dutkiewicz. Cheltenham: Edward Elgar Publishing.

Kaya, Ayhan. 2015. "Islamisation of Turkey under the AKP Rule: Empowering Family, Faith and Charity." *South European Society and Politics* 20(1): 47–69.

Khalili, Laleh. 2020. *Sinews of War and Trade: Shipping and Capitalism in the Arabian Peninsula*. London: Verso.

Khoury, D. R., and S. Glebov. 2017. "Citizenship, Subjecthood, and Difference in the Late Ottoman and Russian Empires." *Ab Imperio* 1: 45–58.

192 References

King, Anthony D. 1990. *Global Cities: Post-Imperialism and the Internationalization of London*. London: Routledge.

Kolluoğlu, Biray. 2013. "Excesses of Nationalism: Greco-Turkish Population Exchange." *Nations and Nationalism* 19(3): 532–50.

Komlosy, A., M. Boatca, and H.-H. Nolte. 2016. "Special Issue Introduction: Coloniality of Power and Hegemonic Shifts in the World-System." *Journal of World-Systems Research* 22(2): 309–14. https://doi.org/10.5195/jwsr.2016.670.

Kopf, Dan, and Tripti Lahiri. 2018. "The Charts That Show How Deng Xiaoping Unleashed China's Pent-up Capitalist Energy in 1978." *Quartz*, December 17.

Korhonen, Juho. 2019. "Empire, Democracy, State, and Nation: Sociological Occlusions of the Russian and German Empires." PhD thesis. Brown University, Providence.

Korzeniewicz, Roberto Patricio, and Corey R. Payne. 2020. "Rethinking Core and Periphery in Historical Capitalism: 'World-Magnates' and the Shifting Centers of Wealth Accumulation." Pp. 155–67 in *Economic Cycles and Social Movements: Past, Present and Future*, edited by E. Mielants and K. S. Bardos. London: Routledge.

Koskenniemi, Martti. 2005. "International Law in Europe: Between Tradition and Renewal." *The European Journal of International Law* 16(1): 113–24.

Krippner, Greta R. 2005. "The Financialization of the American Economy." *Socio-Economic Review* 3: 173–208.

Kwong, Peter. 1979. *Chinatown, Ny: Labor And Politics, 1930–1950*. New York: Monthly Review Press.

Kwong, Peter. 1996. *The New Chinatown*. New York: Macmillan.

Kwong, Peter. 1999. *Forbidden Workers: Illegal Chinese Immigrants and American Labor*. New York: New Press.

Kwong, Peter. 2001. "The Politics of Labour Migration: Chinese Workers in New York." Pp. 293–313 in *Socialist Register-2001*. New York: Monthly Review Press.

Kwong, Peter. 2009. "The Politics of Labour Migration: Chinese Workers in New York." *Socialist Register* 37: 293–313.

Lachmann, Richard. 2020. *First-Class Passengers on a Sinking Ship: Elite Politics and the Decline of Great Powers*. London: Verso.

Lapavitsas, Costas. 2013. "The Financialization of Capitalism: 'Profiting without Producing'." *City* 17(6): 792–805.

LeBrón, Marisol. 2019. *Policing Life and Death: Race, Violence, and Resistance in Puerto Rico*. Oakland: University of California Press.

Lee, Ching Kwan. 2007. *Against the Law: Labor Protests in China's Rustbelt and Sunbelt*. Oakland, CA: University of California Press.

Le Monde Diplomatique. 2017. "Un monde de camps." May, p. 13.

Li, Siyao. 2016. "The New Silk Road: Assessing Prospects for 'Win-Win' Cooperation in Central Asia." *Cornell International Affairs Review* 9(1).

Lieven, Dominic. 2001. *Empire: The Russian Empire and Its Rivals*. New Haven: Yale University Press.

Lin, Jan. 1995. "Polarized Development and Urban Change in New York's Chinatown." *Urban Affairs Quarterly* 30(3): 332–54.

Lin, Jan. 2008. "Los Angeles Chinatown: Tourism, Gentrification, and the Rise of an Ethnic Growth Machine." *Amerasia Journal* 34(3): 110–25.

Lin, Justin Yifu. 1990. "Collectivization and China's Agricultural Crisis in 1959–1961." *Journal of Political Economy* 98(6): 1228–52.

Lin, Ken Hou, and Donald Tomaskovic-Devey. 2013. "Financialization and U.S. Income Inequality." *American Journal of Sociology* 118(5): 1284–329.

Linebaugh, Peter, and Marcus Rediker. 2000. *The Many-Headed Hydra: Sailors, Slaves, Commoners, and the Hidden History of the Revolutionary Atlantic.* Boston: Beacon Press.

Linneman, Travis. 2016. *Meth Wars: Police, Media, Power.* New York: New York University Press.

Lo, Dic. 2020. "Towards a Conception of the Systemic Impact of China on Late Development." *Third World Quarterly* 41(5): 860–80.

Lu, Juliet, and Oliver Schönweger. 2019. "Great Expectations: Chinese Investment in Laos and the Myth of Empty Land." *Territory, Politics, Governance* 7(1): 61–78.

Luce, Mathias S. 2007. "O subimperialismo brasileiro revisitado: a política de integração regional do governo Lula (2003–2007)." MS. dissertation. UFRGS, Porto Alegre, Brasil.

Luce, Mathias Seibel. 2018. *Teoria Marxista da Dependência: problemas e categorias—uma visão histórica.* São Paulo: Expressão Popular.

Mann, Charles C. 2006. *1491: New Revelations of the Americas Before Columbus.* New York: Vintage Books.

Manning, F. T. C. 2015. "Closing the Conceptual Gap: A Response to Cinzia Arruza's 'Remarks on Gender'." *Viewpoint Magazine,* May 4.

Marcuse, Peter. 2009. "Urban Planning in New York City After 9/11." Pp. 75–86 in *The Impact of 9/11 on Politics and War,* edited by M. J. Morgan. New York: Palgrave Macmillan.

Marini, Ruy Mauro. 1996. "Procesos y tendencias de la globalización capitalista." Pp. 49–68 in *La teoria social latino-americana: cuestiones contemporâneas,* edited by R. M. E. Marini and M. Millan. México: UNAM, 1994 t 4.

Marini, Ruy Mauro. 2011a. "Sobre a Dialética da Dependência." In *Ruy Mauro Marini: vida e obra,* edited by Roberta Traspadini and João Pedro Stedile. São Paulo: Expressão Popular.

Marini, Ruy Mauro. 2011b. "Dialética da Dependência." In *Ruy Mauro Marini: vida e obra,* edited by Roberta Traspadini and João Pedro Stedile. São Paulo: Expressão Popular.

Marini, Ruy Mauro. 2012. "Acumulação capitalista mundial e o subimperialismo." *Revista Outubro,* n° 20, Janeiro: 27–70.

Marini, Ruy Mauro. 2013. *Subdesenvolvimento e Revolução.* Florianópolis: Editora Insular.

Martin, Bernice. 1995. "New Mutations of the Protestant Ethic among Latin American Pentecostals." *Religion* 25(2): 101–17.

Martin, David. 1990. *Tongues of Fire: The Explosion of Protestantism in Latin America.* Oxford: Blackwell.

Martínez, Daniel E., Jeremy Slack, and Ricardo Martínez-Schuldt. 2018. "The Rise of Mass Deportation in the United States." Pp. 173–201 in *The Handbook of Race, Ethnicity, Crime, and Justice,* edited by Ramiro Martínez Jr., Meghan E. Hollis, and Jacob I. Stowell. Hoboken, NJ: John Wiley & Sons, Inc.

Martins, Carlos Eduardo. 2018. "A teoria marxista da dependência à luz de Marx e do capitalismo contemporâneo." *Caderno CRH.* Salvador 84: 463–80.

Martins, Carlos Eduardo. 2020. *Dependency, Neoliberalism and Globalization in Latin America.* Brill: Leiden & Boston.

Marx, Karl. 1963. *Poverty of Philosophy.* New York: International Publishers.

Marx, Karl. 1977. *Capital.* Vol. I. New York: Vintage Books.

Marx, Karl. 1978. "On the Jewish Question." In *The Marx-Engels Reader,* edited by Robert Tucker. New York: WW Norton & Co.

194 References

Marx, Karl. 1981. *Capital.* Vol. III. London: Penguin Books.

Marx, Karl. 1990 [1867]. *Capital: A Critique of Political Economy.* Vol. 1. London: Penguin.

Marx, Karl. 2008 [1859]. *Contribuição à crítica da economia política.* São Paulo: Expressão Popular.

Maxwell, David. 1998. "Delivered from the Spirit of Poverty?: Pentecostalism, Prosperity and Modernity in Zimbabwe." *Journal of Religion in Africa* 28(3): 350–73.

McMichael, Philip. 1990. "Incorporating Comparison within a World-Historical Perspective: An Alternative Comparative Method." *American Sociological Review* 55(3): 385–97.

McMichael, Philip. 2000a. "World-Systems Analysis, Globalization and Incorporated Comparison." *Journal of World-System Research* VI(3): 68–99.

McMichael, Philip. 2000b. "A Global Interpretation of the Rise of the East Asian Food Import Complex." *World Development* 28(3): 409–24.

McMichael, Philip. 2009. "A Food Regime Genealogy." *The Journal of Peasant Studies* 36(1): 139–69.

McMichael, Philip. 2012. *Development and Social Change: A Global Perspective.* 5th ed. Los Angeles: Pine Forge Press.

McMichael, Philip. 2020. "Does China's 'Going Out' Strategy Prefigure a New Food Regime?" *The Journal of Peasant Studies* 47(1): 116–54.

McQuade, Brendan. 2019. *Pacifying the Homeland: Intelligence Fusion and Mass Supervision.* Oakland: University of California Press.

Medeiros, Carlos A., and Franklin Serrano. 1999. "Padrões Monetários Internacionais e Crescimento." Pp. 119–51 in *Estados e moedas no desenvolvimento das nações.* Petrópolis: Vozes.

Medeiros, Carlos Aguiar de. 2006. "A China Como Um Duplo Pólo Na Economia Mundial e a Recentralização Da Economia Asiática." *Revista de Economia Política* 26(3): 381–400.

Meillasoux, Claude. 1991 [1975]. *Femmes, Greniers et Capitaux.* Paris: L'Harmattan.

Mele, Christopher. 2000. *Selling the Lower East Side: Culture, Real Estate, and Resistance in New York City.* Minneapolis, MN: University Of Minnesota Press.

Merton, Robert K. 1949. "On Sociological Theory of Middle Range." Pp. 448–59 in *Social Theory and Social Structure*, edited by R. K. Merton. New York: Simon & Schuster/The Free Press.

Meyer, Birgit. 1998. "Commodities and the Power of Prayer: Pentecostalist Attitudes Towards Consumption in Contemporary Ghana." *Development and Change* 29: 751–76.

Mezzadra, Sandro. 2011. "The Topicality of Prehistory: A New Reading of Marx's Analysis of 'So-Called Primitive Accumulation'." *Rethinking Marxism* 23(2): 302–21.

Midnight Notes Collective. 1990. "Introduction to the New Enclosure." *Midnight Notes* 10: 1–9.

Mies, Maria. 1986. *Patriarchy and Accumulation on a World Scale.* London: Zed Press.

Mies, Maria, Veronika Bennholdt-Thomsen, and Claudia von Werlhof. 1988. *Women: The Last Colony.* London: Zed Books.

Mikhail, A., and C. M. Philliou. 2012. "The Ottoman Empire and the Imperial Turn." *Comparative Studies in Society and History* 54(4): 721–45.

Miller, Todd. 2017. *Storming the Wall: Climate Change, Migration, and Homeland Security.* San Francisco, CA: City Lights Books.

Miller, Todd. 2019. *Empire of Borders: The Expansion of the U.S. Border Around the World.* London: Verso.

References **195**

Ministério da Economia, Indústria, Comércio Exterior e Serviços—*Comércio Exterior: Estatísticas de Comércio Exterior*, Séries Históricas. Accessed: 22/01/2020. http://mdic.gov.br/index.php/comercio-exterior/estatisticas-de-comercio-exterior

Mitchell, Timothy. 1999. "Society, Economy, and the State Effect." Pp. 76–97 in *State/Culture: State-Formation after the Cultural Turn*, edited by George Steinmetz. Ithaca: Cornell University Press.

Mkandawire, Thandika. 1988. "The Road to Crisis, Adjustment and De-Industrialisation: The African Case." *Africa Development/Afrique et Développement* 13(1): 5–31.

MOA (Ministry of Agriculture of China). 1989. *Zhongguo Nongcun Jingji Tongji Daquan 1949–1986 (Complete Statistics on China's Rural Economy 1949–1986)*. Beijing: Nongye Chubanshe.

MOARA (Ministry of Agriculture and Rural Affairs). 2019. *Press Conference on Promoting Organic Connections between Small Farming Households and Modern Agriculture*. www.moa.gov.cn/hd/zbft_news/xnhxdnyfz/.

Moore, Jason W. 2015. *Capitalism in the Web of Life: Ecology and the Accumulation of Capital*. London: Verso.

Moore, Jason W., and Raj Patel. 2017. *A History of the World in Seven Cheap Things: A Guide to Capitalism, Nature, and the Future of the Planet*. Berkeley, CA: University of California Press.

Mutluer, Nil. 2019. "The Intersectionality of Gender, Sexuality, and Religion: Novelties and Continuities in Turkey during the AKP Era." *Southeast European and Black Sea Studies* 19(1): 99–118.

Nanda, Meera. 2012. *The God Market: How Globalization is Making India More Hindu*. New York: Monthly Review Press.

Nandy, Ashis. 1989. *The Intimate Enemy: Loss and Recovery of Self under Colonialism*. Delhi: Oxford University Press.

NBS (National Bureau of Statistics of China). 1991. *Chinese Rural Yearbook 1991*. Beijing: China Statistics Press.

NBS (National Bureau of Statistics of China). 1999. *Comprehensive Statistical Data and Materials on 50 Years of New China*. Beijing: China Statistics Press.

NBS (National Bureau of Statistics of China). 2009. *China Compendium of Statistics: 1949–2008*. Beijing: China Statistics Press.

NBS (National Bureau of Statistics of China). 2019. *Statistical Report of the People's Republic of China on the 2018 National Economic and Social Development*. Beijing: National Bureau of Statistics of China.

NBS (National Bureau of Statistics of China). 2020. *China Statistical Yearbook 2020*. Beijing: China Statistics Press.

Negi, Rohit, Marc Auerbach, Bram Büscher, et al. 2009. "The Contemporary Significance of Primitive Accumulation[: An Exchange and Debate]." *Historical Materialism* 2(3): 89–107.

Negri, Antonio. 1984. *Marx Beyond Marx: Lessons on the Grundrisse*. South Hadley, MA: Bergin & Harvey Publishers, Inc.

Neocleous, Mark. 2008. *Critique of Security*. Edinburgh: Edinburgh University Press.

Neocleous, Mark. 2011. "Security as Pacification." In *Anti-Security*, edited by Mark Neocleous and George Rigakos. Ottawa: Red Quill Books.

Neocleous, Mark. 2014. *War, Power, Police Power*. Edinburgh: Edinburgh University Press.

Nepstad, Sharon E. 1996. "Popular Religion, Protest, and Revolt." Pp. 105–24 in *Disruptive Religion: The Force of Faith in Social Movement Activism*, edited by C. Smith. New York: Routledge.

196 References

Newsome, Kirsty, Phil Taylor, Jennifer Biar, and Al Rainnie, eds. 2015. *Putting Labour in Its Place: Labour Process Analysis and Global Value Chains*. London: Palgrave MacMillan.

Nolte, Detlef. 2018. "China Is Challenging But (Still) Not Displacing Europe in Latin America." *GIGA Focus* 1(1): 1–13.

O'Brien, Kevin J., and Lianjiang Li. 2006. *Rightful Resistance in Rural China*. Cambridge: Cambridge University Press.

O'Connor, James. 1973. *The Fiscal Crisis of the State*. New York: St. Martin's Press.

O'Donnel, Guillermo. 1996. *El Estado Burocrático Autoritario: Triunfos, Derrotas y Crisis*. Buenos Aires: Editorial de Belgrano.

Offe, Claus. 1984. *Contradictions of the Welfare State*. London: Hutchinson.

O'Hearn, Denis, and Paul S. Ciccantell. 2022. *Migration, Racism and Labor Exploitation in the World-System*. New York: Routledge.

Oliveira, Gustavo de L. T. 2018. "Chinese Land Grabs in Brazil? Sinophobia and Foreign Investments in Brazilian Soybean Agribusiness." *Globalizations* 15(1): 114–33.

Omahe, Kenichi. 1985. *Triad Power. The Coming Shape of Global Competition*. New York: McGraw-Hill.

Omi, Michael, and Howard Winant. 1994. *Racial Formation in the United States: From the 1960s to the 1990s*. New York: Routledge.

O'Riain, Sean. 2004. "The Politics of Mobility in Technology-Driven Commodity Chains: Developmental Coalitions in the Irish Software Industry." *International Journal of Urban and Regional Research* 28(3): 1203–12.

Oureiro, José L., and Carmela A. Feijó. 2010. "Desindustrialização: Conceituação, causas, efeitos e o caso brasileiro." *Revista de Economia Política* 30(2) (118): 219–32, abril–junho.

Özsu, Umut. 2012. "Ottoman Empire." Pp. 429–48 in *The Oxford Handbook of the History of International Law*, edited by B. Fassbender and A. Peters. Oxford: Oxford University Press.

Paik, A. Naomi. 2020. *Bans, Wall, Raids, Sanctuary: Understanding U.S. Immigration for the Twenty-First Century*. Oakland: University of California Press.

Palabiyik, Mustafa Serdar. 2014. "International Law for Survival: Teaching International Law in the Late Ottoman Empire (1859–1922)." *Bulleting of the School of Oriental and African Studies*: 1–22.

Parnreiter, Christof. 2018. "America First! Donald Trump, the Demise of the U.S. Hegemony and Chaos in the Capitalist World-System." *Zeitschrift Fur Wirtschaftsgeographie* 62(1): 1–13.

Patnaik, Utsa, and Sam Moyo. 2011. *The Agrarian Question in the Neoliberal Era: Primitive Accumulation and the Peasantry*. Cape Town: Pambazuka Press

Patterson, Clayton. 2006. *Resistance: A Radical Social and Political History of the Lower East Side*. New York City: Seven Stories Press.

Peck, Jamie. 2017. *Offshore: Exploring the Worlds of Global Outsourcing*. Oxford: Oxford University Press.

Perelman, Michael. 2000. *The Invention of Capitalism: Classical Political Economy and the Secret History of Primitive Accumulation*. Durham: Duke University Press.

Perkins, Dwight H. 1969. *Agricultural Development in China, 1368–1968*. Chicago: Aldine Publishing Company.

Petry, Johannes. 2020. "Financialization with Chinese Characteristics? Exchanges, Control and Capital Markets in Authoritarian Capitalism." *Economy and Society* 49(2): 213–38.

Piqueras, José A., ed. 2009. *Trabajo libre y coactivo en sociedades de plantación*. Madrid: Siglo XXI Editores.

Plys, Kristin. 2021. "Theorizing Capitalist Imperialism for an Anti-Imperialist Praxis: Towards a Rodneyan World-Systems Analysis." *Journal of World-Systems Research* 27(1): 288–313.

Portes, Alejandro, and John Walton. 1981. *Labor, Class, and the International System*. New York: Academic Press, Inc.

Postone, Moishe. 1996. *Labor, Time and Social Domination: a Reinterpretation of Marx's Critical Theory*. New York: Oxford University Press.

Potts, Lydia. 1990. *The World Labour Market: A History of Migration*. Translated by Terry Bond. London: Zed.

Quijano, Aníbal. 2000. "Coloniality of Power and Eurocentrism in Latin America." *Nepantla* 1(3): 533–80.

Rajagopal, Arvind. 2001. *Politics after Television: Hindu Nationalism and the Reshaping of the Public in India*. Cambridge: Cambridge University Press.

Ransby, Barbara. 2018. *Making All Black Lives Matter: Re-Imagining Freedom in the Twenty-First Century*. Berkeley, CA: University of California Press.

Rediker, Marcus, Titas Chakraborty, and Matthias Van Rossum, eds. 2019. *A Global History of Runaways: Workers, Mobility, and Capitalism, 1600–1850*. Oakland, CA: University of California Press.

Reifer, Thomas E. 2004. "Labor, Race, and Empire: Transport Workers and Transnational Empires of Trade, Production, and Finance." Pp. 17–35 in *Labor vs. Empire: Race, Gender, and Migration*, edited by G. G. Gonzalez, R. A. Fernandez, V. Price, D. Smith, and L. T. Vo. New York: Routledge.

Reinsberg, Bernhard, Thomas Stubbs, Alexander Kentikelenis, and Lawrence King. 2019. "The World System and the Hollowing out of State Capacity: How Structural Adjustment Programs Affect Bureaucratic Quality in Developing Countries." *American Journal of Sociology* 124(4): 1222–57. https://doi.org/10.1086/701703.

Richta, Radovan. 1971 [1969]. *La civilización en la encrucijada*. México D.F.: Sigloveintiuno Editores.

Riley, Denise. 1988. *"Am I that Name?" Feminism and the Category of 'Women' in History*. Minneapolis: University of Minnesota Press.

Robbins, Joel. 2004. "The Globalization of Pentecostal and Charismatic Christianity." *Annual Review of Anthropology* 55: 117–45.

Robbins, William G. 1994. *Colony and Empire: The Capitalist Transformation of the American West*. Lawrence, KS: University of Kansas Press.

Robertson, Roland. 1985. "The Sacred and the World System." Pp. 347–58 in *The Sacred in a Secular Age*, edited by P. E. Hammond. Berkeley, CA: University of California Press.

Robinson, William I. 2004. *A Theory of Global Capitalism: Production, Class, and State in a Transnational World*. Baltimore: Johns Hopkins University Press.

Robinson, William I. 2006. "Aquí Estamos y No Nos Vamos! Global Capital and Immigrant Rights." *Race and Class* 48(2): 77–91.

Robinson, William I. 2014. *Global Capitalism and the Crisis of Humanity*. New York: Oxford University Press.

Robinson, William I. 2020. *The Global Police State*. London: Pluto Press.

Rodney, Walter. 1982. *How Europe Underdeveloped Africa*. London: Bogle-L'Ouverture Publications.

198 References

Rodrik, Dani. 2016. "Premature Deindustrialization." *Journal of Economic Growth* 21(1): 1–33.

Ross, Robert, and Kent Trachte. 1990. *Global Capitalism: The New Leviathan*. Albany, NY: SUNY Press.

Ross, Sherwood. 2011. "Pentagon Allows 'Near Slavery' Conditions Among Foreign Workers in Iraq and Afghanistan." *GlobalResearch*, September 1.

Rowley, Linda. 2020. "Boom and Bust: Is China Bowing Out of Australian Agriculture?" *Beef Central*. www.beefcentral.com/property/boom-and-bust-is-china-bowing-out-of-australian-agriculture/.

Rowthorn, R., and R. Ramaswany. 1999. "Growth, Trade and Deindustrialization." *IMF Staff Papers* 46(1).

Rudnyckyj, Daromir. 2009. "Spiritual Economies: Islam and Neoliberalism in Contemporary Indonesia." *Cultural Anthropology* 24(1): 104–41.

Ruiz, José B., and Alejandro Simonoff, eds. 2015. *Integración y Cooperación Regional en América Latina: Una relectura a partir de la teoría de la autonomía*. Buenos Aires: Editorial Biblos.

Said, Edward. 1979. *Orientalism*. New York: Vintage.

Santiago-Valles, Kelvin. 2005. "World-Historical Ties Among 'Spontaneous' Slave Rebellions in the Atlantic during the 18th and 19th Centuries." *Review* XXVIII(1): 51–83.

Santiago-Valles, Kelvin. 2012. "The Fin-de-Siècles of Great Britain and the United States: Comparing Two Declining Phases of Global Capitalist Hegemony." Pp. 182–90, 413–18 in *Endless Empire: Spain's Retreat, Europe's Eclipse, and America's Decline*, edited by A. W. McCoy, J. M. Fradera, and S. Jacobson. Madison: University of Wisconsin Press.

Sanyal, Kalyan. 2013. *Rethinking Capitalist Development: Primitive Accumulation, Governmentality, and Postcolonial Capitalism*. New Delhi: Routledge India.

Sassen, Saskia. 1988. *The Mobility of Labor and Capital: A Study in International Investment and Labor Flow*. Cambridge: Cambridge University Press.

Sassen, Saskia. 2014. *Expulsions: Brutality and Complexity in the World Economy*. Cambridge, MA: The Belknap Press of Harvard University Press.

Sbragia, Chad. 2020. "China's Military Power Projection and U.S. National Interests." *Testimony before the U.S.-China Economic and Security Review Commission*. Office of the Secretary of Defense Office of the Assistant Secretary of Defense for Indo-Pacific Security Affairs: 1–6.

Schierup, Carl-Ulrik, Branka Likić-Brborić, Raúl Delgado Wise, and Gülay Toksöz. 2018. "Migration, Civil Society, and Global Governance: An Introduction to the Special Issue." *Globalizations* 15(6): 733–45.

Schmalzer, Sigrid. 2016. *Red Revolution, Green Revolution: Scientific Farming in Socialist China*. Chicago: University of Chicago Press.

Schneider, Mindi. 2014. "Developing the Meat Grab." *Journal of Peasant Studies* 41(4): 613–33.

Schrader, Stuart. 2019. *Badges Without Borders: How Global Counterinsurgency Transformed American Policing*. Oakland: University of California Press.

Schrank, Andrew. 2004. "Ready-to-wear Development: Foreign Investment, Technology Transfer, and Learning-by-Watching in the Apparel Trade." *Social Forces* 83(1): 123–56.

Schultheis, Ryan, and Ariel G. Ruiz Soto. 2017. *A Revolving Door No More? A Statistical Profile of Mexican Adults Repatriated from the United States*. Washington, DC: Migration Policy Institute, May.

Scott, James C. 2009. *The Art of Not Being Governed: An Anarchist History of Upland Southeast Asia*. New Haven, CT: Yale University Press.

Scott, Joan W. 1989. "Gender: A Useful Category for Historical Analysis." Pp. 81–100 in *Coming to Terms: Feminism, Theory, Politics*, edited by Elizabeth Weed. New York: Routledge.

Seigel, Micol. 2018. *Violence Work: State Power and the Limits of Police*. Durham, NC: Duke University Press.

Semyonov, Alexander. 2020. "Imperial Parliament for a Hybrid Empire: Representative Experiments in the Early 20th-century Russian Empire." *Journal of Eurasian Studies* 11(1): 30–39.

Serfati, Claude. 2008. "Financial Dimensions of Transnational Corporations, Global Value Chain and Technological Innovation." *Journal of Innovation Economics & Management* 2(2): 35–61.

Silver, Beverly J., and Giovanni Arrighi. 2003. "Polanyi's 'Double Movement': The Belle Époques of British and Us Hegemony Compared." *Politics & Society* 31(2): 325–55.

Silver, Beverly J., and Corey R. Payne. 2020. "Crises of World Hegemony and the Speeding Up of Social History." In *Hegemony and World Order: Reimagining Power in Global Politics*, edited by Piotr Dutkiewicz, Tom Casier, and Jan Aart Scholte. New York: Routledge.

Silver, Beverly J., and Eric Slater. 1999. "Social Origins of World Hegemonies." Pp. 151–216 in *Chaos and Governance in the Modern World System*, edited by Giovanni Arrighi and Beverly Silver. Minneapolis: University of Minnesota Press.

Sites, William. 2003. *Remaking New York: Primitive Globalization and the Politics of Urban Community*. Minneapolis, MN: University of Minnesota Press.

Slater, Eric. 2004. "The Flickering Global City." *Journal of World-Systems Research* 10(3): 591–608.

Smil, Vaclav. 1995. "Who will Feed China?" *The China Quarterly* 143: 801–13.

Smith, Neil. 2005. *The New Urban Frontier: Gentrification and the Revanchist City*. New York: Routledge.

Snyder, Timothy, and Katherine Younger, eds. 2018. *The Balkans as Europe, 1821–1914*. Rochester: University of Rochester Press.

Sohrabi, Nader. 2018. "Reluctant Nationalists, Imperial Nation-State, and Neo-Ottomanism: Turks, Albanians, and the Antinomies of the End of Empire." *Social Science History*: 1–36.

Sowers, Elizabeth, Paul S. Ciccantell, and David A. Smith. 2014. "Comparing Critical Capitalist Commodity Chains in the Early Twenty-first Century: Opportunities For and Constraints on Labor and Political Movements." *Journal of World-Systems Research* 20(1): 112–39.

Sowers, Elizabeth, Paul S. Ciccantell, and David A. Smith. 2017. "Are Transport and Raw Materials Nodes in Global Commodity Chains Potential Places for Worker/Movement Organization?" *Labor and Society* 20(2): 185–205.

Sowers, Elizabeth, Paul S. Ciccantell, and David A. Smith. 2018. "Labor and Social Movements Strategic Usage of the Global Commodity Chain Structure?" Pp. 19–34 in *Choke Points: Logistics Works and Solidarity Movements Disrupting the Global Capitalist Supply Chain*, edited by J. Alimahomed-Wilson and I. Ness. London: Pluto Press.

Stein, Sam. 2016. "Chinatown: Unprotected and Undone." Pp. 122–41 in *Zoned Out! Race, Displacement, and City Planning in New York City*, edited by Tom Angotti and Sylvia Morse. New York: Urban Research.

200 References

Steinfeld, Robert J. 2001. *Coercion, Contract, and Free Labor in the Nineteenth Century.* Cambridge: Cambridge University Press.

Steinmetz, George. 2008. "The Colonial State as a Social Field: Ethnographic Capital and Native Policy in the German Overseas Empire before 1914." *American Sociological Review* 73: 589–612.

Stephanov, Darin. 2019. "Salvos and Sovereignty: Comparative Notes on Ceremonial Gunfire in the Late Ottoman and Russian Empires." *Journal of the Ottoman and Turkish Studies Association* 6(1): 81–102.

Struna, Jason. 2009. "Toward a Theory of Global Proletarian Fractions." *Perspectives on Global Development and Technology* 8: 230–60.

Stubbs, Richard. 1999. "War and Economic Development: Export-Oriented Industrialization in East and Southeast Asia." *Comparative Politics* 31(3): 337–55.

Sugihara, Kaoru. 2019. "The Asian Path of Economic Development: Intra-Regional Trade, Industrialization and the Developmental State." Pp. 73–100 in *Emerging States and Economies: Their Origins, Drivers, and Challenges Ahead,* edited by T. Shiraishi and S. Tetsushi. Singapore: Springer.

Swartz, David L. 2013. *Symbolic Power, Politics, and Intellectuals: The Political Sociology of Pierre Bourdieu.* Chicago and London: The University of Chicago Press.

Swyngedouw, Erik. 2005. "Dispossessing H20: The Contested Terrain of Water Privatization." *Capitalism, Nature, Socialism* 16(1): 81–98.

Taft, Chloe E. 2016. *From Steel to Slots: Casino Capitalism in the Postindustrial City.* Cambridge, MA: Harvard University Press.

Taki, Victor. 2011. "Orientalism on the Margins: The Ottoman Empire under Russian Eyes." *Kritika* 12(2).

Taylor, Peter. 2003. "Recasting World-Systems Analysis for the 21st Century: City Networks for Nation-States." *Contributions in Economics and Economic History* 2: 130–40.

Taylor, Phil, Kirsty Newsome, Jennifer Bair, and Al Rainnie. 2015. "Putting Labour in Its Place: Labour Process Analysis and Global Value Chains." Pp. 1–28 in *Putting Labour in Its Place: Labour Process Analysis and Global Value Chains,* edited by K. Newsome, P. Taylor, J. Bair, and A. Rainnie. London: Palgrave MacMillan.

Teltumbde, Anand. 2006. "Hindu Fundamentalist Politics in India." Pp. 247–61 in *Empire and Neoliberalism in Asia,* edited by V. Hadiz. London: Routledge.

Terlouw, Kees. 2002. "The Semiperipheral Space in the World-System." *Review* 25(1): 1–22.

Tilly, Charles. 1984. *Big Structures, Large Processes, Huge Comparisons.* New York: The Russel Sage Foundation.

Tilman, David, Christian Balzer, Jason Hill, and Belinda L. Befort. 2011. "Global Food Demand and the Sustainable Intensification of Agriculture." *Proceedings of the National Academy of Sciences* 108(50): 20260–64.

Tomich, Dale. 1994. "Small Islands and Huge Comparisons: Caribbean Plantations, Historical Unevenness and Capitalism Modernity." *Social Science History* 18(3): 339–58.

Tomich, Dale. 2003. *Through the Prism of Slavery: Labor, Capital, and World Economy.* Lanham, MD: Roman and Littlefield Publishers.

Torezani, Tomás A. 2019. "Produtividade da indústria brasileira no período 1996–2016: Decomposição do crescimento e padrões de concentração em uma abordagem desagregada." *IV ENEI—Encontro Nacional de Economia Industrial e Inovação—Inovação,* Produtividade e os desafios do crescimento, Campinas, SP. 10–12/9.

References   201

Touraine, Alain. 2000. "A Method for Studying Social Actors." *Journal of World-Systems Research* 6(3): 900–18.

Toye, John. 1991. "Dilemmas of Development: Reflections on the Counter-Revolution in Development Theory and Policy." *Economic Development and Cultural Change* 39(2): 432–35.

Tuğal, Cihan. 2009. *Passive Revolution: Absorbing the Islamic Challenge to Capitalism*. Stanford: Stanford University Press.

Uestebay, Leor. 2019. "Between 'Tradition' and Movement: The Emergence of Turkey's Anti-Capitalist Muslims in the Age of Protest." *Globalizations* 16(4): 472–88.

Ullman, Harlan, and Arnaud De Borchgrave. 2017. "Why Does the U.S. Military Have Such a Staggering Record of Failure?" *UPI*, February 13.

UNCTAD. 2013. *The Asian Developmental State and the Flying Geese Paradigm*. New York: UNCTAD.

Valencia, Adrián, S. 2018. "Subimperialismo y dependencia en la era neoliberal." *Caderno CRH, Salvador, Bahia* 31(84), September/December: 501–17.

Vanaik, Achin. 2001. "The New Indian Right." *New Left Review* 9: 43–67.

van der Ploeg, Jan Douwe. 2020. "From Biomedical to Politico-Economic Crisis: The Food System in Times of Covid-19." *The Journal of Peasant Studies* 47(5): 944–72.

Van Dijk, Rijk. 2012. "Pentecostalism and Post-Development: Exploring Religion as a Developmental Ideology in Ghanaian Migrant Communities." Pp. 87–108 in *Pentecostalism and Development: Churches, NGOs and Social Change in Africa*, edited by D. Freeman. New York: Palgrave Macmillan.

Wacquant, Loic. 2010. "Crafting the Neoliberal State: Workfare, Prisonfare and Social Insecurity." *Sociological Forum* 25(2): 197–220.

Wade, Robert. 2011. "Review of International Political Economy US Hegemony and the World Bank : The Fight over People and Ideas." *Review of International Political Economy* 2290, February: 37–41.

Wallace, Deborah, and Roderick Wallace. 1998. *A Plague on Your Houses: How New York Was Burned Down and National Public Health Crumbled*. New York: Verso.

Wallerstein, Immanuel. 1974a. "Dependence in an Interdependent World: The Limited Possibilities of Transformation within the Capitalist World Economy." *African Studies Review* 17(1): 1–26.

Wallerstein, Immanuel. 1974b. *The Modern World-System I: Capitalist Agriculture and the Origins of the European World-Economy in the Sixteenth Century*. New York: Academic Press.

Wallerstein, Immanuel. 1976. "Semi-Peripheral Countries and the Contemporary World Crisis." *Theory and Society* 3(4): 461–83.

Wallerstein, Immanuel. 1979. *El moderno sistema mundial: la agricultura capitalista y las Orígenes de la economia mundo europea en el siglo XVI. 2.e*. Madrid: Siglo XXI.

Wallerstein, Immanuel. 1983. *Historical Capitalism*. New York: Verso.

Wallerstein, Immanuel. 1988. "The Inventions of Timespace Realities: Towards an Understanding of Four Historical Systems." *Geographical Association* 73(4): 289–97.

Wallerstein, Immanuel. 1990. "Culture as the Ideological Battleground of the Modern World-System." *Theory, Culture & Society* 7: 31–55.

Wallerstein, Immanuel. 1991. "The Ideological Tensions of Capitalism: Universalism versus Racism and Sexism." In *Race, Nation, Class: Ambiguous Identities*, edited by Étienne Balibar and Immanuel Wallerstein. London: Verso.

Wallerstein, Immanuel. 1995a. "The Modern World-System and Evolution." *Journal of World-System Research* 1(19): 629–37.

202 References

Wallerstein, Immanuel. 1995b. "Response: Declining States, Declining Rights?" *International Labor and Working-Class History* 47: 24–27.

Wallerstein, Immanuel. 1995c. "Social Science and Contemporary Society: the Vanishing Guarantees of Rationality." *Inaugural Address, Convegno Internazionali di Studi of Associazione Italiana di Sociologia*, Palermo, October 26–28. [published in *International Sociology*, 1, Mar. 1996]. Papers of Fernand Braudel Center.

Wallerstein, Immanuel. 1996a. "Social Change? Change is eternal. Nothing ever Changes." *Sessão Solene de Abertura of the III Congresso Português de Sociologia*, Lisboa, February 7. Papers of Fernand Braudel Center.

Wallerstein, Immanuel. 1996b. "Time and Duration: The Unexcluded Middle." *Conférence de prestige sur le theme, 'Temps et Durée,* 'Université Libre de Bruxelles, September 25. Papers of the Fernand Braudel Center.

Wallerstein, Immanuel. 1996c. "The Structures of Knowledge, or How Many Ways May We Know?" *Presentation at Which Sciences for Tomorrow? Dialogue on the Gulbenkian Report*, Stanford University, June 2–3. Papers of the Fernand Braudel Center.

Wallerstein, Immanuel. 1996d. "The Rise and Future Demise of World-Systems Analysis." *Paper Delivered at 91st Annual Meeting of the American Sociological Association*, New York, August 16. Papers of the Fernand Braudel Center.

Wallerstein, Immanuel. 1996e. "The Time of Space and the Space of Time: The future of Social Science." *Papers of the Fernand Braudel Center. Tyneside Geographical Society Lecture*, Univ. of Newcastle upon Tyne, co-sponsored by the Institute of British Geographers and the Royal Geographical Society, February 22.

Wallerstein, Immanuel. 1997. "Spacetime as the Bases of Knowledge." *Keynote Address at Convergencia/World Congress of Convergence*, Cartagena, Colombia, May 31–June 5, 1997. Papers of the Fernand Braudel Center.

Wallerstein, Immanuel. 1998. *Utopistics: Or, Historical Choices of the Twenty-first Century.* New York: The New Press.

Wallerstein, Immanuel. 2000. "Peace, Stability and Legitimacy 1990–2025/2050." In *The Essential Wallerstein.* New York. The New Press.

Wallerstein, Immanuel. 2010a. "Structural Crisis." *New Left Review*, London, 62, March–April.

Wallerstein, Immanuel. 2010b. "Free Flows and Real Obstacles: Who Wants Laissez-Faire?" Pp. 13–21 in *Mass Migration in the World-System: Past, Present, and Future*, edited by Terry-Ann Jones and Eric Mielants. Boulder, CO: Paradigm Publishers.

Wallerstein, Immanuel. 2011. *The Modern World-System IV: Centrist Liberalism Triumphant 1789–1914.* Berkeley and Los Angeles: University of California Press.

Wallerstein, Immanuel, and Armand Cleese. 2002. *The World We Are Entering 2000–2050.* Amsterdam: Luxemburg Institute for European and International Studies.

Wallerstein, Immanuel, Charles Lemert, and Carlos Aguirre Rojas. 2013. *Uncertain Worlds: World-Systems Analysis in Changing Times.* Boulder, CO and London: Paradigm Publishers.

Wallerstein, Immanuel, and Mohammad H. Tamdgidi, eds. 2017. *Mentoring, Methods, and Movements: Colloquium in Honor of Terence K. Hopkins.* 2nd ed. Belmont, MA: Ahead Publishing.

Wang, Jinping. 2011. *Chinese Food Security Problems after the Entry of Transnational Capital.* Shenyang: Liaoning University.

West, Michael O., William G. Martin, and Fanon Che Wilkins. 2009. *From Toussaint to Tupac The Black International Since the Age of Revolution.* Chapel Hill: University of North Carolina Press.

References **203**

Westad, Odd Arne. 2019. "The Sources of Chinese Conduct: Are Washington and Beijing Fighting a New Cold War." *Foreign Affairs* 98: 86–95.

White, Richard. 2011. *Railroaded: The Transcontinentals and the Making of Modern America*. New York: W.W. Norton & Co.

Williams, Eric. 1944. *Capitalism and Slavery*. London: Andre Deutsch.

Wong, Diane. 2019. "Shop Talk and Everyday Sites of Resistance to Gentrification in Manhattan's Chinatown." *Women's Studies Quarterly* 47(1/2): 132–48.

World Bank. 2020. *World Bank Open Data*. https://data.worldbank.org/

World Inequality Report. 2018. *World Inequality Report*. https://wir2018.wid.world/

World Migration Report 2020. 2019. *International Organization for Migration*. www.un.org/sites/un2.un.org/files/wmr_2020.pdf

Wynter, Sylvia. 1990. "Afterword: Beyond Miranda's Meanings: Un/silencing the 'Demonic Ground' of Caliban's 'Woman'." Pp. 355–72 in *Out of the Kumbla: Caribbean Women and Literature*, edited by Carole Boyce Davies and Elaine Savory Fido. Trenton, NJ: Africa World Press.

Xinhua. 2017. "China Puts 103 Mln Hectares of Farmland under Permanent Protection." *China Daily*, September 20.

Yalman, Galip. 2012. "Politics and Discourse under the AKP's Rule: The Marginalization of Class-Based Politics, Erdoganisation, and Post-Secularism." Pp. 21–41 in *Silent Violence: Neoliberalism, Islamist Politics, and the AKP Years in Turkey*, edited by S. Coşar and G. Yücesan-Özdemir. Ottawa: Red Quill Books.

Yan, Hairong, Yiyuan Chen, and Hok Bun Ku. 2016. "China's Soybean Crisis: The Logic of Modernization and Its Discontents." *The Journal of Peasant Studies* 43(2): 373–95.

Zhan, Shaohua. 2017. "Hukou Reform and Land Politics in China: Rise of a Tripartite Alliance." *The China Journal* 78: 25–49.

Zhan, Shaohua. 2019a. "Accumulation by and Without Dispossession: Rural Land Use, Land Expropriation, and Livelihood Implications in China." *Journal of Agrarian Change* 19: 447–64.

Zhan, Shaohua. 2019b. *The Land Question in China: Agrarian Capitalism, Industrious Revolution, and East Asian Development*. Abingdon: Routledge.

Zhan, Shaohua. 2020. "The Land Question in 21st Century China: Four Camps and Five Scenarios." *New Left Review* 122: 115–33.

Zhan, Shaohua. 2022. *China and Global Food Security*. Cambridge: Cambridge University Press.

Zhan, Shaohua, and Lingli Huang. 2017. "Internal Spatial Fix: China's Geographical Solution to Food Supply and Its Limits." *Geoforum* 85: 140–52.

Zhan, Shaohua, Hongzhou Zhang, and Dongying He. 2018. "China's Flexible Overseas Food Strategy: Food Trade and Agricultural Investment between Southeast Asia and China in 1990–2015." *Globalizations* 15(5): 702–21.

Zhao, Minghao. 2019. "Is a New Cold War Inevitable? Chinese Perspectives on Us—China Strategic Competition." *The Chinese Journal of International Politics* 12(3): 371–94.

Żuk, Piotr, and Pawel Żuk. 2020. "'Murderers of the Unborn' and 'Sexual Degenerates': Analysis of the 'Anti-Gender' Discourse of the Catholic Church and the Nationalist Right in Poland." *Critical Discourse Studies* 17(5): 566–88.

"20 anos de IIRSA na América do Sul: quem está comemorando agora?" *Le Monde Diplomatique*, September 4. https://diplomatique.org.br/20-anos-da-iirsa-na-america-do-sul-quem-esta-comemorando-agora/

INDEX

accumulation 75, 79, 131, 140
accumulation by repression 159–160
Afghanistan 86, 121, 134, 165, 198
AKP 35–36, 39–40
Amin, S. 12, 81, 87, 90, 123
anti-systemic: movements 32–33;
tendencies 10, 28; alternatives 3, 34,
37–39; anti-capitalist Muslims 10, 28,
37–38, 40
Arrighi, G. 4–5, 7, 8, 12, 19, 81, 83–91,
108, 111, 117, 157, 167–168
Australia 60, 164, 176

Balkans 45, 48
Bandung, New 69, 79–80, 85
Baronov, D. 6–7
Black freedom movement 23
Black Lives Matter 39
Black feminism 39
Black radical tradition 9, 20, 23; *see also*
racial capitalism
Bourdieu, P. 10, 42–43, 52–53
Braudel, F. 82, 90, 112
Braudelian world-systems analysis 12, 81,
84, 87, 110, 113
Brazil 3, 12, 25, 30, 38–39, 93, 96–109,
156
Britain: industrial revolution 63; and
empire 47–48, 129, 135, 158; and
world hegemony *see also* hegemony
Brown, L. 171–172
Bush, R. 50

carceral state 19, 23–26
China 14, 64, 168–178; and Belt and
Road 78; and anti-Chinese racism
64; and China Boom 70, 76; and
investments 145; and communist party
86; and food underproduction 169,
172–175, 177; and grain production
169–178; and grain imports 170–173
Chinatown 138–154
class formation 29, 131, 157
coercion 2, 4, 13, 47, 127, 132, 137
Cold War 72–74, 170, 176; and police
training 19, 23
colonialism 46, 63, 85, 128, 134, 165;
anti-colonialism 8; neo-colonialism 176
commodities boom 78
commodity chains (GCC) 11, 22, 54–65,
71–72, 76–78
core-periphery relations 2–3, 5–6,
10–13, 22–23, 29–30, 33, 38–39,
42–56, 58, 61, 64, 70–72, 77, 79, 85,
89, 92, 98, 103, 106, 110–113, 115,
117–121, 139–145, 154, 158, 160, 162,
166, 168; *see also* semi-periphery
COVID-19 1, 12, 41, 81, 90, 448, 159,
163, 166, 177

Day, K. 39
debt 62, 74–76, 79, 86, 89–90, 128, 134,
137
deindustrialization 11, 93, 97–99, 101,
120, 143

Index

dependency theory 5–6, 8–9, 22, 31, 63, 88, 93–95, 105–106, 109–116, 120, 122
diseconomies of resistance 58, 60–61
displacement 133, 138–139, 141, 143, 145, 147, 149, 151, 153, 155, 157–158, 175

Egypt 10, 28, 30, 34–36, 48–50
enclave elites 138–139, 142–146, 153–154
encompassing comparison 6–7, 21, 25

finance: financial crisis 2; financial capital 9, 35, 70, 74–75, 77, 79, 83–86, 88–89, 91, 95–96, 102–105, 109, 113, 116–119, 122–123, 161, 167, 170; financialization 24, 70, 73, 75–76, 79, 90, 133; FIRE sectors 138–141, 144–145, 154
Finland 48–50
First World War 42, 179
Frank, A.G. 9, 26, 85, 93
fusion centers 23–26

Gates, L. 28, 31
gentrification 139, 143, 145
geoculture 10–11, 42–53, 114
Global North 11, 29, 39, 69, 70–71, 73, 75–79
Global South 2, 3, 9–11, 28–31, 34, 41, 69–80, 85, 91, 133
globalization 12, 20, 29, 34, 75, 81, 85, 88, 90, 92, 109, 133–134, 157–159

Haitian Revolution 135
Han, J. 173
hegemony 2–3, 32, 34, 44, 49, 54, 58, 64, 80–84, 108, 113–115, 135, 137; British hegemony 82, 84, 87, 115, 136–137, 140; and challenges 32–33, 38, 40; and crisis 2, 71, 85, 88; neoliberal hegemony 31, 36, 38–40; US hegemony 19, 24, 70, 73, 82, 86–87, 90, 97, 140, 169
Hindu nationalism 10, 28, 30–31, 34–36
Hopkins, T. 7–8, 10, 13, 19–23, 26–29, 31–33, 40, 54–56, 127–128, 133

incorporating comparison 7
India 3, 10, 28–29, 31, 34–36, 38–39, 122, 134
industrialization 5, 11, 12, 37, 55, 69–70, 72–73, 75–76, 79–80, 93, 95, 97–99, 101, 109, 116, 133, 137, 140, 158; and import substitution 69, 74, 97, 99, 108

international division of labor 12, 56, 74, 94, 96, 110–111, 113–117, 120, 167
international law 43, 45, 47–51
internationalism 5, 19
Islamic Calvinists 10, 28

just-in-time production 59, 62

Kondratieff Cycles 12, 81–82, 87–90, 113, 157

labor time 12, 110–111, 114
Liberation Theology 10, 28, 37–39
Lower East Side (LES) 138, 141, 143, 145, 152–153

Marini, R.M. 9, 12, 81, 89, 91, 93–97, 101–102, 105–106, 109, 111, 114–117, 120
Marx, K. 18, 95, 113–114; and imperialism 109–111; and primitive accumulation 4, 127–133, 136
Marxism 20, 112, 166, 169; and world-systems analysis 12–13, 81–83, 85, 87–89, 91
material expansion 70–71, 76, 78
McMichael, P. 1, 7, 19, 21, 25, 32, 169
migration 3, 133; and militarized migration management 13, 156–166; see also refugees
modernization theory 26–27, 85
Moore, J. 9, 62

nation-state: as actor 5, 18, 43, 51, 75; as unit of analysis 23, 138, 140, 142, 159
neoliberalism 10, 27–41, 88–90, 92, 133, 135, 139, 146, 160, 170, 177; pious neoliberalism 10, 28, 30, 36; neoliberal restructuring 12, 24, 29–30, 75–76, 78–79, 81, 85
neo-Pentecostalism 10, 28, 30, 34–36
New York 13, 25–26, 61, 134, 138, 146, 155–156

oil 59, 61–62, 74, 85, 134, 165, 176
Ottoman Empire 11, 42–53

policing 2, 4, 18, 22–23, 25–26, 134, 161, 164
political Islam 10, 28, 30, 34–35, 37
right wing populism 3, 38–39
Portes, A. 157–158
Potts, L. 158, 167

206 Index

primitive accumulation 4, 13, 114–115,
127–140, 144–145, 153–154, 159;
see also Marx

racial capitalism 40; *see also* Black radical
tradition
racism 9, 11, 19, 55, 61–65, 156
raw materialist lengthened commodity
chains 11, 54–55, 58–59, 64–65
Rebuild Chinatown Initiative (RCI)
138, 145–146, 148, 151, 155, 146, 148
refugees 1, 3, 51, 133–134, 162, 165;
see also migration
regulation: French regulation school 160,
166; moral regulation 31–32; social
regulation 75, 127, 130, 133–135, 137,
144
Robinson, C. 19
Robinson, W. 159, 161
Rodney, W. 9, 14, 55–57, 62–64
Russian Empire 42–53

dos Santos, T. 9, 12, 81, 87–89, 91, 94
Sassen, S. 158
Second World War 71, 87, 95, 97,
157–158, 169
security: effect 18, 23, 26; trap 10, 17–21,
23, 25–27
semi-periphery 5, 13, 29–33, 38–41, 47,
89, 111, 113, 117, 119–120, 138–146,
149, 151, 153–154, 165; *see also*
core-periphery relations
Silver, B. 19, 81, 83–85, 89, 91, 168
slavery 55, 115, 129, 133–137, 158
social conflict 72, 83, 85; Gezi protests
38, 40; social protest 38–40, 153,
175; social unrest 2, 73, 133, 136,
175; struggle 9, 21, 24, 33, 52–53,

85, 87, 89, 91, 136, 157; *see also* social
movements
social movements 3, 5, 55, 59–60, 65, 83,
85, 89–90; *see also* social conflict
social reproduction 4, 13–14, 130–131,
134
sub-imperialism 12, 93–94, 96–97,
99–109, 120
superexploitation 89, 91–92, 111, 113,
115–117, 120, 159
surplus population 12, 159, 162–164, 166
symbolic power 10, 11, 42–53; *see also*
Bourdieu, P.
systemic chaos 1, 3–4, 12, 81–86, 88, 90

Tilly, C. 6, 25
timespace 12, 52, 110–115, 120
Tomich, D. 19, 21, 31–32, 136
Trump, D. 39, 64, 141, 156, 164
Turkey 3, 10, 28–30, 34–40, 48, 109, 140

United Nations 74, 156, 165
United States 3, 14, 25, 27, 29–30,
38–39, 41, 83–86, 88–92, 103, 109,
129, 135, 156, 158, 160, 163–165,
168–169; and dollar 3, 69, 74, 85, 86,
90; and empire 19, 24, 24; *see also*
hegemony

value transfer 110–113, 116, 120
Vietnam 25; US defeat in 73, 74, 85, 91

Wallerstein, I. 8, 10–12, 19, 26, 42–44,
46, 48, 50–53, 55–56, 82–84, 87–88,
90–91, 108, 110, 112, 114, 157, 168
War on Terror 2, 17, 20, 23–24
World Trade Organization (WTO) 174
Walton, J. 157–158

Milton Keynes UK
Ingram Content Group UK Ltd.
UKHW022149250823
427392UK00027B/412